WOMEN,
WRITING,
THEOLOGY

WOMEN, WRITING, THEOLOGY

Transforming a Tradition
of Exclusion

Emily A. Holmes and *Wendy Farley*
Editors

BAYLOR UNIVERSITY PRESS

Cover Design by Cynthia Dunne, Blue Farm Graphics

Library of Congress Cataloging-in-Publication Data

Women, writing, theology : transforming a tradition of exclusion / Emily A.
Holmes and Wendy Farley, editors.
p. cm.
Includes bibliographical references and index.
ISBN 978-1-60258-376-4 (pbk. : alk. paper)
1. Women theologians--History. 2. Christian literature--Women authors-
-History and criticism. I. Holmes, Emily A., 1974- II. Farley, Wendy, 1958-
BR1713.W63 2011
270.082--dc23
2011021754

Printed in the United States of America on acid-free paper with a minimum
of 30% PCW recycled content..

In memory of Marguerite Porete
on the 700th anniversary of her execution by fire
for her writing, June 1, 1310, Place de Grève, Paris.

*Hee, dame Amour, dit ceste Ame, vous m'avez donné la cognoissance,
or l'entendez. Nyent est de l'oeuvre, quant il convient que elle soit nyent; par quoy il
convient, dit ceste Ame, que je soie certaine que ce que j'ay dit est moins que nyent.
Mais ce qui est en moy ou par moy, qui est de divine cognoissance, vous mesmes,
dame Amour, l'avez dit en moy et par moy de vostre bonté, pour mon prouffit et cel-
luy des aultres; et pource a vous en est la gloire et a nous le prouffit, se es auditeurs ne
demoure, qui ce livre liront.*

Ah, Lady Love, says this Soul, you have given me the knowledge, now
listen to it. This work is nothing, for it is fitting that it be nothing; and thus
it is fitting, says this Soul, that I be certain that what I have said is less
than nothing. But whatever is in me or through me, that is of divine knowledge, you yourself, Lady Love, have said it in me and through me out of
your goodness, for my benefit and that of others; and therefore to you is
the glory of it and to us the benefit, if these hearers who will read this book
do not demure.

—Marguerite Porete, *The Mirror of Simple Souls* (chapter 37)

CONTENTS

ACKNOWLEDGMENTS

The seeds of this project originated a decade ago, when many of the contributors were graduate students at Emory University. Inspired by the Italian feminist practice of entrustment (*affidamento*), in which women mentor and assist one another "in full recognition of the disparity that may exist between them in class or social position, age, level of education, professional status, [and] income,"[1] women graduate students and professors at various stages in their careers gathered to support one another's theological work. Across differences of national origin and language, ethnicity and race, denominational affiliation, age, sexual orientation, and partner or parenting status, we met to talk, eat, and present works in progress. The particularity of our lives shaped our theological perspectives and our writing. Our differences in power and experience allowed us to mentor one another in navigating the hurdles of graduate school and in finding a theological voice as a woman in the academy.

This mutual writing support continued after graduation from Emory and our scattering to various other institutions. We convened a panel on "Women, Writing, Theology" at the annual meeting of the Southeastern Commission for the Study of Religion in 2008, where the idea for a published volume first emerged, and we would like to thank the organizers, participants, and audience of that session for the lively and moving discussion of women's theological writing that took place that day.

The Louisville Institute generously sponsored a three-day consultation of the contributors in 2009 as additional authors joined the project. We are grateful to the Louisville Institute for their generosity, foresight, and support of women's theological writing.

We extend gratitude to our editor at Baylor University Press, Nicole Smith Murphy, for her skill and advocacy for this collection.

The Graduate Division of Religion at Emory University provided the intellectual home and theological formation for much of the work that appears in this volume. We would like to thank friends and colleagues from Emory whose intellectual spirit informs this work, especially Melissa Johnston, Kent Brintnall, Ian Curran, Nevell Owens, Dirk Lange, Joy McDougall, Dianne Diakité, Walt Lowe, and Don Saliers, among many others. We are especially grateful to Mark D. Jordan for gently but persistently raising the question of writing, its form and function, in the history of theology and in our own theological efforts. Wesley Barker and Mari Kim deserve special mention as fellow women writing theology. Their friendship, insight, and contributions were essential to this book's development. Without the collegiality of Emory's Theological Studies program, evidenced in endless *Stammtisch* conversations, this volume would not be possible.

Because all the contributors to this volume have been affiliated with the Graduate Division of Religion at Emory University, the question naturally arises: is there an Emory school of theology, a common approach that is reflected in the work of the women and men who emerge from its programs? Many theological schools share a common methodology, but that is not true of Emory. Nor does Emory have a common set of answers. Rather, if anything, it has a set of questions, one of which, for each of us in different ways, was the question of writing—critical reflection on how we write theology. Writing, naturally, emerges from reading, and we are especially grateful to our mentors for teaching us to read from a very wide canon, including texts not always recognizable as theological, both within the Christian tradition (such as the mystics) and outside the tradition (such as literary theory or other sacred texts) through interdisciplinary, transdisciplinary, and comparative work. We were encouraged to engage the Christian tradition with a generosity of spirit, to forego facile criticism in favor of retrieval and construction. Embodiment, religious practices, and beliefs, the various ways personal religious commitment informs academic theology, were all taken seriously. And a feminist and womanist sensibility was well integrated into the theological curriculum at every level. These qualities—the effects of theological formation at Emory—are reflected in the essays that follow.

Much of the editorial work on this volume was done with my (Emily's) newborn, Jacob, on my lap and at my breast. I am grateful for the support of Paul, Dominic, and Jacob, who remind me that women's theological writing is but one embodied piece of the larger texture of life.

1

INTRODUCTION
Mending a Broken Lineage

Emily A. Holmes

Writing and the Theological Tradition

In this collection, twelve constructive theologians investigate the conditions under which women enter a written theological tradition. How have women historically justified their writing practices? What constraints, both internal and external, shape their capacity to write theology? While much work has been done by feminists in recovering the lives and voices of women from the history of Christianity—and even more constructive and creative progress has been made in the areas of feminist, womanist, *mujerista*, Asian, and postcolonial theologies—these essays take a step back to ask about the conditions of our writing. What allows and what inhibits women's writing practices? And, moreover, what does it mean for women to enter a written theological tradition that has been based in part on their exclusion? Through historical accounts, theoretical analyses, and contemporary constructions, the essays in this volume take up these questions.

Writing has been a topic of special interest in philosophical and literary studies since the 1960s.[1] Jacques Derrida in particular has analyzed how speech is privileged over writing in the great books of the Western tradition, paradoxically in the form of written texts.[2] As Derrida explains, metaphysical pairs that structure Western thought—presence and absence, good and evil, spirit and matter, mind and body—form oppositions in which the first term is valued over and above the second. Speech and writing is one such pair, as is male and female.[3] Speech is valued for its purported ability to convey directly the intentions of the speaker through one's immediate presence to the listener. Writing, in contrast, has been seen as secondary, derivative, and merely technical, only necessary because of the writer's absence from the reader.[4] Speech is thought to be more reliable in conveying truth (a speaker can always be asked for immediate clarification); writing operates at a distance and risks misinterpretation. Furthermore, speech can be restricted to an elite circle of listeners, whereas writing can potentially be read by anyone.

Yet what makes writing seemingly derivative and secondary to speech is also what makes it liberating. Writing cannot restrict its own readership: it *can* be read by anyone, and it *can* be "misread." It is open to unending interpretation by generations of readers, and so, in a sense, writing is never finished. A reader does not know what a text "means" until it is read in its entirety; but final meaning is always deferred as texts are read and reread in the context of other writings.

In the Christian tradition, both logocentrism (the privileging of speech) and writing (the subversion of logocentrism through text) are evident in the complex signification of the central category "Word." The Word or Logos at once refers to a person, the revelation of God in Jesus Christ (who is present to Christians in experience, sacrament, and word), *and* the written text of Scripture (which witnesses to the Word through writing) *and* the proclamation of the Word through preaching. David Tracy notes how Christian emphasis on "God's self-presencing in Word as it is rendered in writing" has contributed to hierarchically paired categories of Western metaphysics: "spirit and letter, ideality and materiality, soul and body, reason and feeling, male and female."[5] Because the Word is primarily a person, witnessed in writing (Scripture), the same "Word" suggests "both close proximity and distance, presence and absence, similarity and difference, participation and interruption."[6] These pairs are united in the Christian genre of gospel, where Word is both disclosed and proclaimed in writing.

While much of the Christian tradition participates in the logocentrism described by Derrida—privileging the immediacy of the presence of God (in revelation, proclaimed word, and sacrament) over the distance and *différance* of writing—it does so in complex fashion. The role of Scripture, and therefore writing, in mediating revelation means that, in Tracy's words, "presence is never full, simple, or whole."[7] Writing introduces narrative, distance, difference, alterity, and materiality into the interpretation of the Word, and it opens up the Word to the history of interpretation by readers from multiple perspectives. According to Tracy, "Understood as writing, Scripture exposes all pretensions to full self-presence and corrects the fatal repressions and hierarchizations that have plagued much of Western thought and existence."[8]

The complete story of writing in Christianity, and its complex hermeneutical relation to the multivalent categories of both Word and Scripture, has yet to be fully explored.[9] It is up for debate whether Christian thought ultimately supports Western logocentrism and its violent hierarchies or subverts it. But beginning from the Hebrew and Christian Scriptures, Christianity has been thoroughly shaped by a written theological tradition. Like Judaism and Islam, it is a religion of the book. All theology, which claims to "clarify" truths revealed in Scripture, is "writing after" Scripture, with the same characteristics of absence, distance, difference, and deferral in texts that remain open for unending interpretation.

For most of Christian history, theological writing was restricted to male elites. Both education and ordination have been necessary prerequisites for claiming the authority to write theology—and, with few exceptions, women have largely been excluded from both of these until quite recently. (Where women have left their mark in Christianity, we can only assume that it has been primarily through "women's religion": the material and embodied religious practices of the home and the festivals of the community for which women often provide material support.) Because the written tradition of Christian theology has been constituted by the exclusion of women (and all laity and the illiterate), writing theology is problematic for women. As many of our contributors note, finding a writing voice is especially difficult when entering a tradition that expects women, if they are to write at all, to mask the particularities of their lives and to write like traditional theologians, that is, as educated, ordained men.

But the centrality of writing to Christianity is also promising for women. Writing communicates across distances, through materiality and difference. These features place writing on the side of matter, the body, and the feminine in the hierarchical oppositions noted above. Writing is generative and gestational: it is productive of other writings. In the hands of the oppressed, these features make writing dangerous and subversive. As Barbara Johnson argues, "If, as Derrida claims, the importance of writing has been 'repressed' by the dominant culture of the Western tradition [in favor of speech/presence], it is because writing can always pass into the hands of the 'other.' The 'other' can always learn to read the mechanism of his or her own oppression."[10] In response, writing, and the traces of exclusions and alternate readings that it registers, can be deployed to overturn these violent and hierarchical repressions.

Because writing is available to reading and interpretation, even by those who have previously been excluded by it, writing can forge a path of liberation. Johnson points to the passage in *The Narrative of the Life of Frederick Douglass, an American Slave, Written by Himself* in which Douglass learns how to read. When a slave owner claims that teaching a man to read and write will make him unfit to be a slave, it prompts an awakening in Douglass. "From that moment," he writes, "I understood the pathway from slavery into freedom."[11] The French Algerian writer Hélène Cixous likewise sees writing as the path to liberation for women. Because writing is allied with the feminine, it has subversive, even revolutionary, potential in patriarchal society, language, and tradition. In the words of Cixous' famous manifesto,

> Woman must write her self: must write about women and bring women to writing, from which they have been driven away as violently as from their bodies—for the same reasons, by the same law, with the same fatal goal. Woman must put herself into the text—as into the world and into history—by her own movement.[12]

When women and other "others" begin to read and write, they transform the written tradition, themselves, and the world.

Theological writing is no exception to these observations of the problems, power, and potential of writing. If anything, theological writing is the privileged example of the association of writing with hierarchical power, authority, and presence, on the one hand, and subversion, the "feminine," and difference on the other. Theological writing is at once both logocentric and scriptural, as Tracy argues. And because writing is open to endless rereadings and multiple interpretations, writing is eternal. "Reading, I discovered that writing is endless," Cixous writes. "Everlasting. Eternal. Writing or God. God the writing. The writing God."[13] But God is also the ultimate signifier of authority and power, and as Johnson notes, "What is at stake in writing is the very structure of authority itself."[14] The power to write conveys authority. But writing can also subvert the authority of those who would rule through the repression and exclusion of others.

Given these complex and contradictory features of writing, what does it mean for women to write theology? To enter a tradition in which the authority granted by writing stems in part from its exclusion of women? To enter a tradition in which writing can also subvert that authority and offer a path of liberation? When women and others begin to write, they do so in complicated fashion, reading the tradition against the grain, using the interpretation of written texts to combat their exclusion, and establishing their own authority to write. The way particular women, both historical and contemporary, have undertaken this dance of negotiation through reading, writing, and interpretation is examined in the essays that follow.

Historically, women have written on the margins of the Christian tradition, in works classified as "spirituality" or "mysticism" rather than theology proper. Women's theology-making has often been oral, recorded in traces of sayings or hagiographies by men, or it has appeared as "stealth theology" in the form of poems or hymns. In the past forty years, with the rise of contextual and liberation theologies, women have claimed theology "proper" for themselves and others as womanist, feminist, *mujerista*, Asian, Third World, disabled, and queer women. These theologians are the giants upon whose shoulders our authors stand, and yet within the larger field of academic and ecclesial theology, women theologians are still often found at the margins. Taking a step back from the critical and constructive work of these feminist theologies, it should be asked how women enter the written theological tradition at all. What are the conditions under which women begin to write? What makes writing (im)possible? What forms of writing count as theology, and who qualifies as a theologian?

IDENTIFYING "WOMEN'S WRITING"

Is there any such thing that is identifiable as "women's writing"? None of the contributors to this volume is prepared to make such an essentialist claim, and the history of Christian writings would belie it, since many of the greatest texts written by women have been at some point in their history attributed to men![15] But if there is no such thing as "women's writing" that characterizes all women who write, there are certain themes that recur.[16] It is difficult to say whether these themes emerge from a common experience; what experience could women of such historical, geographical, racial, and other differences possibly share? And yet the women written about and the women doing the writing in this book are all positioned as women by their church and society. This particular positionality is subject to constraint and even as it intersects with other qualities and differences may give rise to certain recurrent features and themes.

How do women negotiate the constraints placed on their religious lives and claim the authority to write theology? What obstacles, both external and internal, lie in the way? The *question of authority* is intrinsic to writing, and establishing authority is a common problem for women writers. Michelle Voss Roberts examines the fear of being the other within patriarchal religious traditions that inhibits the textual authority of two medieval women, one Christian and one Hindu (Kashmir Śaiva). Different strategies of facing fear and claiming a tenuous authority emerge from her comparison. Often, women gain the authority to write through extraordinary spiritual experiences that are recognized by a larger community of women and men. Michele Jacques Early describes how Mother Elizabeth Dabney found authority attributed to her through her traditional women's ministry of prayer in the Church of God in Christ. For Mo. Dabney, writing her theological reflections in the form of a spiritual autobiography was the natural extension of her prayers and epistles for "everybody, everywhere." Likewise, Angela of Foligno, discussed in my own essay, became an authoritative spiritual leader to a group of Franciscan disciples through the production of her book, which details her extraordinary spiritual life. The humility and silence of the contemplative life can play a paradoxical role in establishing the authority to speak and write. Leigh Pittenger examines the way in which these spiritual virtues, so often associated with medieval women mystics, are invoked by the contemporary writer Sara Maitland.

A second common feature is *the dialogical character of women's theological writings.*[17] Women writers are in dialogue with the theological tradition, with male collaborators, and with communities of other women as they reread and combine multiple sources and translate oral teaching into written form. This dialogical feature emerges in Kendra G. Hotz' chapter on the desert ammas, whose sayings are preserved thanks to male admirers, as well as in my chapter on Angela of Foligno, whose book was produced out of her theological dialogue with her confessor. (The preservation of women's words often happens thanks to the men who initially viewed them with suspicion.) Meghan T. Sweeney argues that Edith Stein wrote her own life story through her encounter with women such as Saint Teresa of Avila and in the form of dialogical hagiographical dramas. Dialogue is also a feature of the Latvian women poets and hymnists examined by Kristine Suna-Koro. These women draw on existing sources within indigenous and foreign liturgical traditions and rewrite them in forms that register a multiplicity of voices. The creative combination of multiple sources provides inspiration for writing theology in a postcolonial and diasporic context.

Another recurrent theme: *the particularity of individual lives, bodies, and practices and their intersection with a wider community.* Each writer examined in these chapters, as well as each author, comes from particular social location and historical moment, so that their differences are as

significant as their similarities. But each one's life and writing also intersect with and reflect the discourse of wider communities. Theresa Hak
Kyung Cha's dislocation as an immigrant subject, discussed by Min-
Ah Cho, becomes the occasion for interweaving the particularity of
her own life with other women and with the larger body of Christ in
her writing on the Eucharist. Elizabeth A. Webb notes how Simone
Weil writes hunger on her own body out of compassion for the hunger
of oppressed others; Weil's eucharistic theology shapes the way her
practices of writing and hunger intersect with the community of all
who suffer. Shelly Rambo compares two nineteenth-century American
women, Phoebe Palmer and Emily Dickinson, who wrote in a context
that made either self-sacrifice or loss of community the price of their
writing. In her constructive theological essay, Marcia W. Mount Shoop
calls the intersection of particularity with the discourse of a wider community the idiosyncrasy, ambiguity, and interdependence of women's
lives. Such features are heightened in motherhood, making motherhood
an apt metaphor and model for theological writing. In all, when women
write theology, they do so out of a particular life history and social location marked by multiple and idiosyncratic differences, but they write for
a larger community, both within and outside the church.

The final common feature that emerges from the writings of women
examined in these essays is more formal than thematic: *women's writings
trouble the recognizable forms and categories of the theological tradition.* Women's
theological writings draw on and rewrite earlier genres of Christianity
and often appear in genres and styles not typically considered theology.
They do their theological work through nontraditional categories such
as "Funk" and "the Thing" (Hotz). Because women have historically
been excluded from the work of theology, they negotiated these constraints by turning to alternative genres and rewriting older genres in
creative new ways. For instance, Mo. Dabney's theological reflections
appear in the form of a semiautobiographical guide to prayer, but she
called her own writings both "gospel" and "epistle" (Jacques Early).
The Latvian women poets and hymnists write a stealth theology directly
into the heart of the Christian liturgy (Suna-Koro). Mechthild of Magdeburg (Voss Roberts) and Theresa Hak Kyung Cha (Cho) combine

and juxtapose multiple genres in their books, from poetry, vision, and prophecy to catechesis, dialogue, and film stills. Edith Stein writes both phenomenological treatises and hagiographical dramas and poetry (Sweeney). Simone Weil writes essays and aphorisms, a "hungry" genre (Webb). Sara Maitland rejects writing novels in favor of contemplative silence, paradoxically written in her autobiographical *A Book of Silence* (Pittenger). And Marcia Mount Shoop takes what could be considered one of the defining "genres" of women's lives — motherhood — as an apt metaphor for writing theology.

It is not surprising that many of these genres are implicitly if not explicitly autobiographical: bereft of other forms of authority, women have often appealed to their own experience of God in justifying their entrance into the theological tradition. Excluded from traditional academic institutions and forms of theology, they improvised. But they expand the theological tradition by rewriting older genres and inventing new categories, new forms of writing to convey what needs to be said. By reading these varied genres as theological, the authors of this book are making a claim that implicitly contests received notions of what counts as theology and who counts as a theologian. Reading women who are not always recognized as theologians, we discover how their writings widen the theological canon and open up new avenues for writing theology today. As the rich engagement with the critical questions of life, theology begins in life as it is lived:

> I don't "begin" by "writing": I don't write. Life becomes text starting out from my body. I am already text. History, love, violence, time, work, desire inscribe it in my body, I go where the "fundamental language" is spoken, the body language into which all the tongues of things, acts, and beings translate themselves, in my own breast, the whole of reality worked upon in my flesh, intercepted by my nerves, by my senses, by the labor of all my cells, projected, analyzed, recomposed into a book. Vision: my breast as the Tabernacle. Open. My lungs like the scrolls of the Torah.[18]

To some, "women, writing, theology" might recall Samuel Johnson's quip comparing a woman preaching to a dog walking on its hind legs:

"It is not done well; but you are surprised to find it done at all." But women have been writing theology for a long time—and well—so surprise is unwarranted. There is a lineage of women writing theology, the foremothers of contemporary feminists and womanists, but it is broken and obscured. Much recovery has been done, and much work remains to be done. Much theology has been written by contemporary women, both within and outside of the Christian tradition, and even more remains to be written. This volume hopes to contribute, in some small fashion, to this dual work of restoring a broken lineage of writers and participating in its continuation.

2

FEAR AND WOMEN'S WRITING
Choosing the Better Part

Michelle Voss Roberts

Mary sat at the Lord's feet and listened to what he was saying. But Martha was distracted by her many tasks; so she came to him and asked, "Lord, do you not care that my sister has left me to do all the work for myself? Tell her to help me." But the Lord answered her, "Martha, Martha, you are worried and distracted by many things; there is need of only one thing. Mary has chosen the better part, which will not be taken away from her."

—*Luke 10:39-42, NRSV*

During childhood holiday dinners, I, like Mary of Bethany, chose the better part: I eavesdropped on two generations of pastors while they discussed theology and the women served dessert. When my father, grandfather, and uncles debated women's ordination and the rule barring women delegates from attending the annual meetings of the Synod of the Christian Reformed Church, I admired their mastery of the subject matter and memorized arguments on both sides of the issue. Oddly enough, I had little sense that this debate had anything to do with me. Decades later, when the debate had everything to do with me, I assured my grandfather that I would pursue "only" academics at seminary. In a tradition that values the life of the mind, no one could object to my pursuit of a theological education; but I would not risk controversy by pursuing ordination without that mysterious, unambiguous (as well as gendered and socially constructed) certainty of a "call to the ministry" that had been fostered in the men in my religious community.

Mary chose the better part: she listened and learned from what Jesus said. The gospel does not tell us whether she spoke or questioned. It is unlikely that she took up a pen to write. Graduate school trained me to write, but it was years after seminary that I finally enrolled in a preaching course to attempt to speak my theological voice. The act of proclamation differed from my scholarly writing, and the process of preparation to speak subtly altered what I allowed myself to write elsewhere. I began catching more and more frequent glimpses of the internal censor that, with subtle but vicious efficacy, warned me as a writer when I got too close to the boundary from which my original religious tradition would not allow me to return: "If they knew I'd written that, they'd say I'm no longer a Reformed Christian. If I ever stand up to speak from the pulpit, I'll put myself once and for all on the 'wrong' side of the debates over women's authority." The obstacle that stood between my theological education and any aspiration to a position of religious authority was a peculiar kind of fear that women experience as subjects within patriarchal religious traditions.

Lynn Japinga's survey of fear in the Reformed tradition offers the beginnings of an explanation for my terror. She identifies *fear of the other* as a particularly potent barrier to growth for my home tradition. The original motto of the Christian Reformed Church was "In isolation is our strength,"[1] and the denomination has exhibited schismatic tendencies over issues ranging from Freemason membership to women's ordination. Japinga notes that "fear of women's bodies, women's minds, and women's power . . . has at times led the church to limit and control women's lives."[2] The Reformed fear of the other, so potently directed at religious others, has been directed at women within its fold as well.

Religious traditions take shape amid wider cultural forces. Women are the ultimate other of patriarchal culture, which has been crafted by and for men. Indeed, as Simone de Beauvoir eloquently states in *The Second Sex*, the association of women with the body, coupled with

Christianity's association of sin with "the flesh," ensures that "the flesh that is for the Christian the hostile *Other* is precisely woman."[3] The confluence of these facets of women's otherness within patriarchal religious traditions, I suggest, creates a dynamic in which our fear of the other manifests as fear of *being* the other.

Religious identity is a subtle and complex thing. In the Reformed and Christian Reformed churches there are many ways of determining who belongs and who does not, including ethnic markers such as Dutch ancestry and speaking Dutch, or religious markers such as being baptized as an infant, having "professed" one's faith, or being under church discipline for failure of morals or doctrine. A person might have a sense of insider identity on some criteria but not others. Patricia Hill Collins uses the term "outsider within" to describe African-Americans in the United States who "appear to belong" and have "formal citizenship rights" but do not always enjoy "substantive citizenship rights": theirs is a subject position "riddled with contradictions."[4] Although women may possess the requisite identity markers for membership in religious traditions, they are outsiders to the extent that doctrine, polity, and worship have historically been determined by men.

Because women already dwell on this boundary, they may slip all the more easily into outsider status, especially when communities deny women access to professional theological and pastoral training and therefore to the official language of religious discourse. The witch hunts and heresy trials of independent women in the past stand as a reminder of how women as well as sexual, racial, and ethnic others can serve as scapegoats when opposing religious groups threaten a community's possession of the truth.[5] Today, to embattled minority traditions, women who push for equal status can be painted as the demons of secular humanism battering the gates of faith. It is all too easy for women to become outsiders within their own religious communities.

The paradoxical fear of being the other within someone who is already marked as other might be described as the fear—or even hatred—of oneself. The identity of outsider within solidifies when I realize that the other is inside me, *is* me. Already marked as other, women and other marginalized subjects become especially attuned to the voice of the dominant tradition. Emmanuel Levinas describes this attunement in terms of fear:

> [O]bedience ceases to be obedient consciousness and becomes an inclination. The supreme violence is in that supreme gentleness. . . . Fear fills the soul to such an extent that one no longer sees it, but sees from its perspective.[6]

Aware that "anyone who looks, thinks, or behaves differently"[7] can be a threat to religious identity, subordinate subjects monitor themselves for difference and keep themselves in line. The tradition's fear of the other becomes the lens with which one views oneself and the filter for speech and action. Fear silences women's writing ever so gently from within; but for all its gentleness, the fear does not cease to be supremely violent.[8]

This fear is nothing new to those who "choose the better part" despite being outsiders within their own religious traditions. The dynamics of fear and women's writing can be studied comparatively. Two medieval women from vastly different contexts—Mechthild of Magdeburg, a Christian, and Lalleśwarī of Kashmir, a Hindu—grappled with such fears in differing ways.[9] They represent just two of many possible case studies in writing and speaking despite the fear of being the other. In thirteenth-century Christian Europe, Mechthild of Magdeburg's ambiguous status as a beguine created difficulties that may have impelled her to forsake the apostolic ideal of the mendicant orders for the cloister. Though hailed by Kashmir Śaivism today, the fourteenth-century *yoginī* Lalleśwarī of Kashmir's devotion to the tradition's path of liberation resulted in her exclusion from the ideals of liberated relation in her community. Both women are also outsiders to contemporary Reformed Christianity: Lalleśwarī as a Hindu, and Mechthild as part of a medieval Catholic tradition of spirituality. A comparative approach to fear and writing (or speaking) points to the silencing effect of patriarchy across diverse contexts. As windows into particular forms of the gentle violence that works through fear, the lives and texts of these two women encourage contemporary outsiders within as they write and speak from the margins.

LALLEŚWARĪ OF KASHMIR

Donning the robes of *jnana* [knowledge,] stamp on the tablet of
your heart the words that Lalla spoke.
By means of the mystic syllable OM Lalla attained
oneness with the light of consciousness,
and thus overcame the fear of death. (K102)[10]

Today Lalleśwarī is hailed as a saint by Kashmir Śaivas, members of the
Hindu community, based in the Indian region of Kashmir, that names
ultimate reality as Śiva. Lalleśwarī does not write: she speaks. She relies
upon her experiences of yogic meditation and encapsulates her wisdom
in memorable utterances (*vaakh*s) that subsequently pass through generations of oral transmission to be written down later by those who take
them to heart.

Many of her *vaakh*s evince a quiet confidence in their truth as
well as the hardship she endured to forge them. In the verse above,
Lalleśwarī's mastery of yoga helps her to overcome her "fear of death,"
the fear of being denied access to liberation from the cycle of rebirth in
her lifetime. Her fears recur, but she learns to rely on the wisdom she
has come to know:

I did not pause a moment nor did I trust anything even a while.
For the wine I drank my own *vaakh*;
that enabled me to seize the darkness lurking within me.
I rolled it up and tore it to pieces. (K92)

The "fear of death" (K102) and the "darkness lurking within" (K92)
are, at least in part, fear of being the other. Lalleśwarī cannot trust those
around her. She must take courage from her own words so she will not
be swallowed by the darkness that creeps inside. Her life story suggests
connections between these interior obstacles and the external markers
that make her an outsider within her tradition.

Lalleśwarī's hagiographies document gendered opposition to her
religious aspirations.[11] She was married at a young age, and her husband's family was unsympathetic to her spiritual life. According to one
legend, her mother-in-law secretly starved her by giving her only a stone

covered with a thin layer of rice. After each meal Lalleśwarī would wash the stone and put it back in the kitchen.[12] Another legend reports that the older woman spread rumors of infidelity to account for Lalleśwarī's lengthy absences spent in meditation. Her husband reacted violently to this lie. As Nil Kanth Kotru reports,

> One day, as she was returning with a pitcher of water on her head, he struck the pitcher with a stick. The pitcher broke into pieces, but the water remained frozen on her head. With this she filled all the pots in the house, and threw the rest outside, which formed into a pool still identified as *Lalla Trāg* or Lalla's pond.[13]

Kotru views this event as the turning point that impelled Lalleśwarī to break social ties and conventions and to roam about dispensing her *vaakh*s to anyone who would listen. When people slandered her, she enacted a parable to demonstrate her equanimity in the face of abuse: she cut a piece of cloth neatly in two, and for an entire day she tied a knot in one half for every kind word and a knot in the other half for every insult. At the end of the day she weighed the two ropes: they weighed the same.[14]

Such tales serve a pedagogical function, but they also indicate several ways in which—despite her mastery of yoga and the best insights of Kashmir Śaivism—Lalleśwarī was an "other" to her contemporaries. Lalleśwarī's teachings in the Kashmiri vernacular put her at odds with Kashmir Śaiva initiates who possessed the strictly delineated competence and right (*adhikāra*) to practice the techniques outlined in the tradition's Sanskrit texts. The religious elites "would certainly not approve [that] she spoke of the secret doctrine and its disciplines to all and sundry, disregarding the strict injunctions in behalf of *adhikarabheda* [sic], in the vulgar tongue of the unlettered masses."[15] By translating Śaiva teaching from its esoteric textual casings into the vernacular, she offered its liberating insights to the formal tradition's others: women, multiple castes, and religious outsiders. Jaishree Kak Odin views these teachings as "a subversive act to resist the written discourse to which she and other people did not have access."[16] Although Lalleśwarī's teachings and practices of meditation reside solidly within the boundaries of

Kashmir Śaivism, she transgressed the boundaries when she troubled the privileged status of the Brahmin male elite. Her instruction of the uninitiated (other outsiders) marks her as an outsider within the tradition.

Most Kashmiri exegetes insist that no "restrictions of any caste, creed, sex, status, age, etc. have been recognized with regard to initiation of a disciple into the fold of Śaivism."[17] Lalleśwarī's gender does nevertheless contribute to her outsider status. Kashmir Śaiva religious ideals take shape within male-dominated structures of family and religious authority. The authoritative Sanskrit texts of this tradition are all male-authored, and there are very few exceptions to the de facto restriction of full initiation and teaching status to men. Odin notes that "her location as a woman practitioner . . . placed her spiritual attainment in a contradictory position to the traditional role of a woman and a wife in which self-effacement and subservience rather than self-mastery were promoted."[18] Practices that would not have been transgressive for a man thrust Lalleśwarī outside the threshold of the patriarchal household. These dynamics are best viewed through Lalleśwarī's renunciation of her home, her relationship with her guru, and the problem of her naked body.[19]

First, her renunciation of her home marks a gendered boundary within the Kashmir Śaiva tradition of her time. Kashmir Śaivism distinguishes itself from other Hindu groups in its relationship to the traditional stages of life. In the Vedic tradition of duties of caste and stage of life (*varnāshramadharma*), upper-caste males progress through the four stages of student, married householder, retiree, and renouncer. In the final stage, which anyone at any age may undertake, one leaves behind all familial and social ties to seek liberation. By contrast, Kashmir Śaivism, which accepts the Tantras rather than the Vedas as ultimate textual authority, had by the fourteenth century become the practice of householders rather than wandering ascetic renouncers: "the sect's broad base in society [was] the community of married Śaiva householders."[20] Kashmir Śaivas see no inherent contradiction in carrying out social, familial, and even Vedic ritual duties in public while following a tantric devotional path in private. Formal renunciation is unnecessary. In keeping with this tradition, Lalleśwarī refers to herself as a *jīvanmukta*, one who is liberated while alive (K118),[21] and affirms that "even if attending worldly affairs night and day" or engaging in the "householders' active life" (K110, K111), one can remain awake to one's true identity. Theoretically, she should have been able to maintain her everyday roles in the household, as with the male householders in her tradition, viewing her worldly situation through the lens of liberated knowledge. Despite the orthodox norm followed by her male counterparts, however, Lalleśwarī was not permitted to flourish in the householder life. Renunciation remained one of the only courses of action open to her as a woman.

Second, Lalleśwarī fails to fit the Kashmir Śaiva mold because of the difficulty of placing her within the guru-disciple lineage that authorizes the male teachers in her tradition.[22] Her contemporary translators have attempted to work around this problem by simply claiming a direct line to the founder of Kashmir Śaivism (although Lalleśwarī nowhere names a guru in this lineage)[23] and by positing a branch of disciples stemming from her (although scholars cannot agree who belongs to this community).[24] The nature of her initiation (*dīkṣā*) poses further problems. The qualifications (*adhikāra*) for Kashmir Śaiva initiation assume a male subject, with women's qualifications appearing only in discussions of partners (*dūtīs* or "messengers") for male practitioners of the esoteric sexual rites that Lalleśwarī explicitly rejects (K60–K61).[25] Most commentators agree that Lalleśwarī's initiation must have been conveyed in the most immediate way possible, "without any instruction, either spontaneously or through some non-verbal stimulus such as the guru's glance,"[26] rather than through extended training with a guru.[27] Rather than sitting at the guru's feet for extended expositions of the sacred Śaiva texts, the Tantras, her contact with her teacher may have been limited to a single meeting in which she gained instant enlightenment and thereby surpassed human institutions. This interpretation obviates the gendered problem of engagement in protracted study in a lineage of (male) teachers and disciples.

Third, Lalleśwarī is a problematic representative for Kashmir Śaivism because she is reputed to have wandered naked after her renunciation. Although her unadorned female body becomes a symbol for the liberated saint's freedom from external attachments, the gender dynamics of Lalleśwarī's othering are covered up — sometimes quite literally — in twentieth-century hagiography and commentary. Women's bodies and sexuality are perennially problematic for religious traditions, and Lalleśwarī's behavior brings this confrontation to a head.

> My guru gave me this one precept:
> "withdraw your gaze from without,
> and concentrate on the self within."
> That became the turning point in Lalla's life,
> and naked I began to dance. (K21)

Her self-attested nakedness in this verse distresses some exegetes. J. L. Kaul interprets the last line creatively: he would translate the word *natsun* ("to dance") as "to wander," and read *nangay* ("naked") as a corruption of the word for "mountain flower."[28] Twentieth-century pictorial depictions of Lalleśwarī also veil her transgression. In one, Lalleśwarī's naked body modestly covers itself: her stomach sags downward to cover her pubic area, and her hair covers her breasts. In another rendition, excerpts from her own text are plastered over her midsection from neck to knees. When her admirers look at her, they see only the wisdom of her *vaakh*s.[29] Her body would thus conceal itself for the sake of the unenlightened who would read her performance of liberation in an overtly sexual way. It is possible that Lalleśwarī intended to challenge the lingering antipathy toward the body in her tradition; the concern to cover up her nakedness suggests that the gendered aspects of her performance remain uncomfortable for the tradition today.

Lalleśwarī was ejected by her religious community during her life, but subsequent tradition has attempted to resolve or downplay each of the above markers of Lalleśwarī's outsider within status. Lalleśwarī's otherness is tamed through incorporation into a patriarchal framework. According to the story, Lalleśwarī's husband angrily shattered the jar of water upon her head, but not a drop of water was lost. The hagiographers highlight the influx of positive, though unwanted, attention she receives after the miracle. Kotru suggests that she left her home because she "did not like to make an exhibition" of her powers,[30] but the hagiographies oddly ignore the threat of domestic violence. Hagiographers effectively incorporate her wisdom within a patriarchal framework by placing the blame on her *marriage* family as opposed to her learned and pious family of origin, which, no doubt, would have been more understanding.[31] In contrast to these interpretations, Odin insists that "the specificity of gender and class" puts Lalleśwarī at odds with a "pervasively male-centered" Kashmir Śaiva tradition.[32] Lalleśwarī was unable to secure relationships as a wife and daughter-in-law that accord with her spiritual insights. In leaving home to seek liberated relationships elsewhere, she uncovered a contradiction in the androcentric householder ideal. Apprehension of the tradition's theology becomes a marker of dissent: in discovering the tradition's most liberating insights, she must make a break with its institutions.[33]

Lalleśwarī struggles with outsider status in a tradition whose wisdom she has mastered. In meditation she intuits "the one inside fellow beings" (K58), but she lives in a world that excludes her. Longing for community seeps through many of her verses: "When You and You are all Narayana [God] / wherefore these diverse roles?" (K127). In her search for liberated relationships, she is homeless and adrift:

> With a rope of untwisted yarn
> am I towing my boat on the ocean.
> Would that God heard my prayer and
> ferry me across safely.
> Like water in unbaked plates of clay
> my efforts are going to waste.
> How I wish I would reach home! (K1)

Lalleśwarī's longing for a home gives voice to her fear of being the other. She deals with her loss by transcending her otherness for a spiritual identity, saying, "Now I shall die while alive; what can the world do unto me?" (K130)

> Let good and bad come to me.
> My ears will not hear nor eyes see.

When the inner call comes up in the mind
my lamp will be lighted even by the storm of adversity. (K42)

Odin notes that this strategy of transcendence accounts for why Lalleśwarī "feels so empowered in her spiritual life, even as she is an outcast in her social life";[34] but the strategy is not without cost. In place of the fully integrated Kashmir Śaiva ideal, Lalleśwarī must take on the persona of the autonomous, detached self: "By focusing on transcendence, [she] follows the patriarchal discourse, casting the world in a conflictual stance, wherein the self must transcend the other."[35] When confronted with the otherness assigned to her by her tradition when she reaches spiritual mastery, Lalleśwarī is tempted to deny the tradition's best insights.

Women's gendered experiences of God and society have the potential to disrupt dominant configurations, especially insofar as their lives expose ruptures between religious ideals of relation and the translation of these ideals into concrete situations. The disjunction between Lalleśwarī's liberating knowledge and her experience of society exposes the otherness with which her tradition defines her. Despite her courage, the supreme violence gently stunts the full relational potential of her ideals for liberation. Similar dynamics are at play in the writing of Mechthild of Magdeburg.

MECHTHILD OF MAGDEBURG

I was warned against writing this book.
People said:
If one did not watch out,
It could be burned.
So I did as I used to do as a child.
When I was sad, I always had to pray. (II.26)[36]

Mechthild of Magdeburg's fear of being the other emerges in the context of writing her book, *The Flowing Light of the Godhead*, a text that combines the conventions of courtly love poetry with the medieval Christian tradition of bridal mysticism in a dazzling array of visions, allegories, instructions, dialogues, prophecies, admonitions, and poems. Despite the support of Heinrich of Halle, her Dominican confessor who edited most of her text, Mechthild is "warned against writing." The threat of violence to her work causes the accomplished contemplative to resort to the comfort of her childhood prayers. She not only fears the loss of her writing, but she also fears her outsider status:

> Ah, Lord, if I were a learned religious man,
> And if you had performed this great miracle using him,
> You would receive everlasting honor for it.
> But how is one supposed to believe
> That you have built a golden house on filthy ooze . . .
> Lord, earthly wisdom will not be able to find you there. (II.26)

Mechthild's self-abnegation highlights her triply marginalized position vis-à-vis contemporary systems of ecclesial authority. She is unlearned, for she has not studied Latin like the scholastic theologians and some privileged nuns of her day. She is not "religious," for she belongs to no recognized religious order. And because she is not a man, she lacks religiously authoritative status. Her anxieties about her writing are tied up with her otherness, and she worries that God should have chosen a more fitting and honorable conduit for the revelations in her book.

The thirteenth century witnessed the rise and decline of the beguine movement that made Mechthild's writing possible in spite of her three-fold otherness as a theologian. She left her courtly upbringing and joined a house of beguines in Magdeburg around 1230, and her written instructions to other beguines suggest that she eventually became a leader of that community. Beguines were laywomen who circumvented the two sanctioned paths open to medieval women as wives and nuns. They devoted themselves to chastity, poverty, contemplation, and service in the cities; but they did not take vows and were free to leave their communities if they wished. In the early years of the movement, Mary d'Oingt and other pious women inspired admiration among the clergy and obtained papal approbation, but because such women were relatively unattached to the patriarchal household and church, they were eventually viewed with suspicion of moral laxity (the only other model for unattached women was, after all, that of the prostitute). A Dominican synod in Magdeburg issued a decree critical of beguines in 1261, demanding that they obey their parish priests. Portions of book VI of Mechthild's *The Flowing Light of the Godhead*, written between 1260 and 1269, reflect increasing sensitivity to criticism in matters of orthodoxy. It is possible that Mechthild's choice to enter the Cistercian convent at Helfta around 1270 was precipitated by this mounting opposition as well as failing health.[37] She continued to feel like an outsider during her tenure at Helfta, where the nuns excelled in their Latin education and "treated her less as a member of their community than as an object of veneration to whom they looked for spiritual instruction."[38] The former beguine thus remained an outsider within until she died.

The learned religious men into whose hands Mechthild's writing fell after her death had to manage the problem of her otherness. The German transmitters of Mechthild's book neutralize the problematic of female authorship by posthumously designating her as an instrument of divine authorship and, later, by simply removing her name from the texts reproduced in devotional anthologies. The Latin translators "toned down Mechthild's criticism of the clergy and some of her erotic imagery."[39] Today, Mechthild rarely receives attention as a theologian, for her work is usually discussed as an example of the feminized and devalued category of mysticism. Mechthild's unique female authorship is rendered invisible or safely subordinated to the masculine even as her texts are appropriated in various ways.[40]

As with Lalleśwarī, Mechthild's otherness emerges at the point of mastery of religious principles espoused by her tradition. Mechthild lived shortly after Dominic and Francis founded their new apostolic orders in response to the decadence of the established houses. The friars renounced property and attempted to live like the apostles by preaching, practicing charity, and supporting themselves with alms. As the orders gained popularity, their ideals quickly pervaded Western Christendom. In the early years of the beguine movement, many beguines received support from mendicant friars who provided the Eucharist and served as spiritual advisers and confessors. For Mechthild, Saint Dominic modeled the kinds of activities beguines embraced as their mission:

teaching wisdom to the simple, helping people bear suffering, teaching discipline to the young, and comforting the sick and frail (V.24). Mechthild clearly views herself in tandem with these Dominican ideals. She frames her renunciation in terms of giving all she possessed and becoming "poor and naked and despised" to enjoy intimacy with God (III.3). Her suffering for the sake of poverty makes her like Dominic and like Christ himself.

The ideals of poverty and itinerant preaching, despite becoming more mainstream with the Dominican and Franciscan movements, smacked of heterodoxy when practiced by women. When women like Mechthild attempted to live by the principles of poverty and chastity in the world, they met resistance from the mendicants and the papal curia. For example, although Clare of Assisi desired to follow in Francis' footsteps, the inclusion of radical poverty in her rule was an uphill battle. She was forced to accept the cloister for the female branch of the order. The charge of heresy that loomed for later beguines runs parallel to the church's original opposition to the apostolic renewal movement on at least two charges. First, according to Herbert Grundmann, the apostolic way of life threatened to circumvent contemporary church practices and sacraments. Second, "the heretics who asserted they were leading the apostolic life in poverty did not recognize the *ordo* of the hierarchical Church, placing the legitimacy of ecclesiastical ordination in question."[41] Papal approval of the new mendicant orders did not make the new ideal acceptable for women, and the scent of these two threats lingered over the women's movement. The gendered construction of religious life came to a head when women presumed to take up paths intended for men. In 1311, the year after the execution of the beguine Marguerite Porete, the Council of Vienne officially banned the beguine way of life.[42]

In her writing, Mechthild handles her otherness with a variety of tactics, not all of which directly evince her fear of it. For example, at some points she *denies* that she is an outsider at all. She associates herself with five new saints, each of whom had a specific mission: Saint Dominic to unbelievers, the ignorant, and the despondent; Saint Elizabeth to vain, arrogant women in castles; Saint Francis to greedy priests and arrogant lay persons; Saint Jutta of Sangerhausen to "heathens"; and Saint Peter, a martyr, to heretics. God tells Mechthild that her book is a "messenger to all religious people" (V.34). Mechthild depicts her mission as essential to the maintenance of the institutional church: "if the pillars fall, the building cannot remain standing" (V.34). She also vigorously defends her orthodoxy to the critics she calls "Pharisees," who twist her words and force her into the heterodox position of the heretical other. For example, they interpret a vision in which John the Baptist serves the Eucharist (II.24) as a challenge to priestly authority, and they attempt to paint Mechthild's claims to intimacy with God as a claim for the inherent divinity of the human person outside of grace (I.44). In both cases, her replies are incisive (VI.31, VI.36).

Another of Mechthild's tactics is to *embrace* her status as an outsider within her religious tradition as the very reason for divine authorization of her writing. God reassures her that her writing "flows continuously / Into your soul from my divine mouth" and explains,

> Wherever I bestowed special favors
> I always sought out the lowest, most insignificant, and most unknown
> place for them.
> The highest mountains on earth cannot receive the revelations of my
> favors
> Because the course of my Holy Spirit flows by nature downhill.
> . . . It very much strengthens Holy Christianity
> That the unlearned mouth, aided by my Holy Spirit, teaches the
> learned tongue. (II.26)

Mechthild justifies her authority with a version of the humility topos one finds frequently in the work of medieval Christian women. She claims her voice not in spite of her outsider status but *because* of it. She can best receive God's flowing love because she dwells at the bottom of the church hierarchy. Empowered by the Spirit, the "unlearned mouth" teaches the insiders—the "learned religious men"—of her day.

In a third strategy, Mechthild interprets her suffering in writing as an opportunity to imitate the innocent suffering of Christ. Christ is the despised and rejected divine other who reveals the way to God; his lovers must expect the same treatment. "God guides his chosen children along strange paths. This is a strange path and a noble path and a holy path that God himself trod: that a human being, though free from sin and guilt, suffer pain" (I.25). The gift of theological writing comes with a cost, and even it stands under God's "curse": "May your words perish" (I.7). When Mechthild encounters the opposition of "religious" people, she reasons that God must will for her to experience the kind of scorn Jesus experienced in his life on earth (I.25). God tells her that she must transcend her desire for approval and for insider status:

> When a person so overcomes himself
> That he considers suffering and consolation of equal value,
> Then I shall raise him up into sweetness,
> And thus he shall have a taste of eternal life. (VII.56)

Secure in nothing but the promise of eternal reward, Mechthild embraces the marginal status of her writing and way of life.

Contemporary feminist and womanist theologians are likely to reject Mechthild's approach to the suffering wrought by her outsider status. Christ's passion demonstrates divine solidarity with human pain, but Mechthild runs the risk of valorizing the suffering imposed on the church's others as spiritually helpful or even redemptive. In Mechthild's religious context, the *imitatio Christi* could encourage Christians to endure suffering they might otherwise criticize or resist, as when her belief that human beings can vicariously do penance for those in purgatory impels her to lift burdens too heavy for her to bear (V.34). Her approach also has the potential to condone mistreatment of Christianity's others if not balanced by a strong emphasis on the prophetic principle of justice in the life and ministry of Christ. Delores S. Williams writes, "As Christians, black women cannot forget the cross, but neither can they glorify it. To do so is to glorify suffering and to render their exploitation sacred. To do so is to glorify the sin of defilement."[43] The otherworldly impulse in Mechthild's deferment of full inclusion in her religious community is similarly problematic insofar as it fails to claim justice for the outcast as imperative for this life.

The otherness of Mechthild and Lalleśwarī emerges at the point where they attempt to tread the path of the insider of their religious traditions. Fear of being the other tends not to be the first thing we notice about these luminaries, for this fear leaves its most significant mark in what is left unsaid. We have read closely, and sometimes between the lines, to identify the dynamics by which women internalize the fear of their own otherness, the supreme violence Emmanuel Levinas calls the supreme gentleness. Viewed comparatively, several patterns and strategies emerge as relevant to contemporary theologians who are outsiders within their traditions.

CHOOSING (TO WRITE) THE BETTER PART

The angel Gabriel . . . came to Mary and said, "Greetings, favored one! The Lord is with you." But she was much perplexed by his words and pondered what sort of greeting this might be. The angel said to her, "Do not be afraid. . . ." (Luke 1:26-30, NRSV)

Lalleśwarī and Mechthild exemplify a distinct fear experienced by marginal persons within religious traditions: the fear of being the other. In both contexts, women are barred from embodying their religion's highest ideals, and their paradoxical attempts to choose the "better part" are fraught with danger. Reading them together has demonstrated that this fear is not isolated within Christianity in either its contemporary or medieval forms. The written legacies of both women bear traces of the otherness that accrues to Lalleśwarī as a female renouncer in a non-renunciant guru-disciple tradition, and to Mechthild as an uneducated woman outside of an established religious order. Awareness of their otherness subtly conditions their speaking and writing: as Levinas puts it, "fear fills the soul to such an extent that one no longer sees it, but sees from its perspective."[44] Lalleśwarī's longing for a true home and Mechthild's acknowledgment of the dangers of writing are two examples of the impact this fear has upon women's theological work.

Deep faithfulness to religious traditions is subversive when performed by nondominant subjects for whom the full program of liberation was never intended. Women's contemplation and writing trouble religious parameters so that the dutiful daughter who pursues the liberation proffered by her religious tradition will eventually come into conflict with its androcentric norms. In my tradition of origin,

> Women have been valued as wives and mothers and unpaid church workers, but for much of its history the Reformed tradition has assumed that they are not fully capable of intellectual work or positions of authority in the church. Various reasons have been given including Scripture, tradition, custom, and comfort. Many refuse to recognize women as fully human and made in the image of God. They will grant women spiritual equality before God but not actual equality in the church.[45]

Religious institutions tend to embrace good girls who are obedient, pious, and above all, chaste. Wives and mothers retain their good girl status when they espouse patriarchal values, pass them to their children, and feed, clean up after, and provide emotional support to male leadership. The eavesdropping eight-year-old who desires theology, the adept who speaks her tradition's deepest wisdom to just anyone, and the beguine who pens her longings for divinity all transgress the gendered boundaries imposed upon the search for religious understanding.

The spiritual equality of men and women appears as a tenet within the Hindu and Christian religions: there is theoretically no bar to Lalleśwarī's enlightenment, and Christian Scripture proclaims that "there is no longer male and female" in Christ (Gal 3:28). Nevertheless, gender bars both women from following certain religious ideals: the integrated freedom of the *jīvanmukta*, liberated even while living as householder; the pursuit of apostolic poverty, chastity, and service; and full intellectual and spiritual authority. Lalleśwarī and Mechthild are outsiders in their respective times and places, but the honor accorded them today also bears the traces of the continuing problem of women's authorship and authority. Their "dangerous memories" are in danger of being incorporated into patriarchal structures,[46] as with the patronizing dismissal of mysticism in Christian theology and hagiographical strategies that cover up women's difference and dissent in Kashmir Śaivism. The belated recognition of these women mirrors ways that women in contemporary religious institutions are often slotted into supportive roles that are essential to the day-to-day functioning of communities but have little actual authority.

Reading the lives and work of Lalleśwarī and Mechthild side by side has revealed divergent options for dealing with one's own otherness and internalized fear. Mechthild and Lalleśwarī disagree on how to confront the opposition of others, but their disagreement may enable contemporary readers to discern fitting strategies of women's authority in writing today. When faced with rejection by their communities of origin, Lalleśwarī takes the transcendent approach of nonattachment, whereas Mechthild embraces her sufferings as part and parcel of the imitation of Christ. Each would find the other's tactic unhelpful, for Lalleśwarī sees suffering as an obstacle to liberation and Mechthild finds liberation only by seeking suffering at its center. Feminist and womanist theologians have problems with each of these approaches as well. The way of transcendence has the potential to downplay models of liberation that integrate spiritual with social and material well-being. The way of redemptive suffering has the potential to glorify victimization and cut off prophetic critique. Both fail to render sufficient judgment upon the original oppression.

Lalleśwarī's transcendence and Mechthild's meditation on suffering may nevertheless prove helpful for contemporary theologians on the margins of their traditions insofar as they model the tactic of *embracing one's outsider status.* Lalleśwarī says, "Like water in a willow basket are name and fame" (K64). Her way of transcendence points to the maturity of the woman who releases her need for approval from her original community ("name and fame") and claims her own voice. To the extent that women are infantilized, devalued as full contributors, and controlled by men who know better than they do, women remain children in relation to their traditions. Lalleśwarī steps into her authority as a woman, leaves home in the face of verbal and physical abuse, and clears the path to liberation for herself. Her path marks the transition from the good daughter of her religious tradition to the outsider within. Mechthild's interest in suffering stands as a reminder of the importance of acknowledging the deep wounds sustained by the outsider within.

Mechthild echoes Mary's *Magnificat* when she identifies the lowly as recipients of divine favor and foreshadows the claim of liberation theologies that persons on the margins are essential to the movement of the Spirit in every age. Today, when threats of burning at the stake or excommunication for heresy are in the past, other options for embracing marginality become possible. Some women find sustenance in communities with other outsiders within, in which they hear the stories of others who have suffered rejection by their home traditions, mourn the loss of original community, and form new ties. Others, like contemporary Goddess feminists, intentionally leave their original traditions behind to construct liberating alternatives.

The dutiful daughter's desire for theology is a border crossing insofar as it marks her as the outsider within, but her writing stakes a claim within the borders of religious truth. The above tactics cut through woman's otherness insofar as they lay hold of the core of a religious tradition: Lalleśwarī to the classic Indian value of nonattachment, and Mechthild to the imitation of Christ. Each attempts to make an insider of the outsider within and thus demonstrates another useful tactic: the *bold refusal of outsider status*. By claiming the center, Lalleśwarī and Mechthild demonstrate their mastery of their religious traditions. Both suffer from not being "learned religious men"; but today, formal theological training is more widely available—some Christian divinity schools have even surpassed 50 percent in women's enrollment.[47] Just as Mechthild's words are called forth by the divine figure she identifies as Lady Love, and Lalleśwarī finds in the "wine" of her own poetry all she needs "to seize the darkness lurking within" (K92), asserting oneself as the subject of theology through writing is a risk that women remain compelled to take.

Women's writing exposes us as other—this is the fear—but the otherness of women's writing can change the boundaries of institutions, whether from inside existing institutions or by erecting alternative structures. The unattached woman threatens male-dominated hierarchies, so it is no coincidence that itinerancy is at issue in both of our test cases. Both Mechthild and Lalleśwarī break with dominant institutions. Lalleśwarī's renunciation exposes gender gaps in the liberative ideals of the householder institution; Mechthild's freedom from marriage and the convent enables her to participate in building a new institution that mirrored current apostolic ideals, the beguine way of life. Today, women gather in all sorts of alternative religious settings to affirm their experiences and their wisdom in ways that official church structures cannot. Yet women's actions, voices, and texts do influence institutions, however glacial or retrograde the pace. Levinas maintains that the subordinate other should demand the best of the structures in which she finds herself: "But what does remain free is the capacity to foresee one's own degradation, and arm oneself against it. Freedom consists in instituting outside of oneself an order of reason, in entrusting the rational to a written text, in resorting to institutions."[48] After decades of such demands, in 1995 the Christian Reformed Church extended the option for regional governing bodies to choose whether to ordain women; and in 2007 the national synod officially removed maleness as a criterion for ecclesiastical office. These momentous changes have divided both families and congregations, and some qualified women still face difficulty finding a congregation willing to appoint a female pastor. Wounds remain, but healing comes as women find a voice from *both* the center and the margins.

The holiday dinner table where the men in my family debated theology and polity is a thing of the past. If I could return to it, would I? Perhaps my home denomination has come far enough that I might have a seat, even if not everyone at the table could agree that I should be there. Perhaps some of the other women would risk leaving the duties of dessert and dishes and claim the better part. Yet it is dubious whether I want a seat at that very same table, the one where women and children are simply unobserved observers and where the price of admission is a certain uniformity of doctrine and submission to patriarchal models of authority. My ordained colleagues in many denominations assure me that the presence of women in church leadership has not always been sufficient to change the conversation around their tables. In becoming "one of the guys," some women even end up mimicking the very exercise of power that once excluded them. The theological companionship of Mechthild, Lalleśwarī, and many other women and men, past and present, has encouraged me to long for a different table, an eschatological banquet where persons can be full participants in (and not in spite of) their many differences. Until that table exists, women's theological writing and speaking will remain risky.

The fears and consequences of writing in relation to our religious communities are real; the supreme violence is that the fear of these consequences can silence us before we ever utter a word. Yet choosing the better part need not be a choice between the patriarchal insider and the rejected outsider. The outsider within maintains the creative tension of the boundary. Like others before us, we may transcend acceptance by patriarchal structures, honor and mourn our wounds, claim the center, and search for divinity at the margins. The angel says, "Do not fear." In the face of our fear, we choose the better part: we write.

3

A "WRETCHED CHOICE"?
Evangelical Women and the Word

Shelly Rambo

INTRODUCTION

I am standing outside the gospel tabernacle, staring through the large back windows where teens are perched to watch the evening revival meeting. Rows of long wooden benches span the interior space, and a bombastic-voiced man is holding a Bible in one hand, moving at a frenetic pace back and forth quoting Scripture passages. The invitation to the altar is the pinnacle moment in which young people respond to the evangelistic message by moving out of their seats, walking down the aisle, and kneeling at the front altar as a public sign of a decision to turn over one's life to God. As a teenager, I knew that those who came to the front were dedicated, serious in the life of faith, bold and coura-geous to make that public act before their peers. I also knew that those who remained in their seats had some serious work ahead of them; they were, as the biblical parable says, like hard and thorny soil, unreceptive to the seed—the word of God. By contrast, visiting the altar meant that they were aiming to be fertile soil, receptive to God's word and work.

Teenagers stream in and out of this building for one week each sum-mer. Summer Bible camps like this one are a central part of American evangelical culture. Teens leave behind short shorts and rock music to "get right with Jesus." They gather for a time of revival, to get away from the pressures of worldly life and to be together with youth of similar faith. It is a time when they can anticipate dedicating or rededicating their lives to God, a time to make things right and to begin again, to carry on in the life of faith amid the pressures of teen culture. Thick armor can be developed here to battle against the cultural enemies of alcohol, sex, and drugs. These are the lures of the devil, and one needs faith to withstand the forces of secularism.

My body remembers this space. It is as if I were nine, or twelve, or sixteen years old. I am standing there, more than a quarter century later, trying to figure out what went on in this building year after year, what went on inside of me, what conspired between me and God in those adolescent years of my life. Standing pen and notebook in hand, I am attempting to be an anthropologist of sorts, scanning the subculture that has deeply shaped me. I understand theology to be more than what a person or community professes, more than a set of beliefs that one espouses. Instead, it is a discursive world filled with symbols, words, and practices that craft human lives in particular ways. Theologian Serene Jones calls the teachings of the church "morphological spaces" into which human persons enter; these teachings, referred to as doctrines, give identity and form to peoples' lives, shaping them into being certain kinds of people in the world.[1]

This essay is an attempt to probe the shaping power of theological discourse on evangelical women's identity. In the testimonial tradition of evangelical Christianity, the word of God—the Bible—was speaking; it was taking on flesh through our words. What did this mean for young women within this religious tradition? I explore this question through the image of the altar, a symbol of American evangelical experience with particular morphological—shaping—power. Nineteenth-century theologian Phoebe Palmer believed that a person finds and claims a new identity at the altar. There, a woman finds her life—and her power to speak—in surrendering to the word of God. Emily Dickinson, the teenage girl and future poet, witnessed the movements of young girls toward the altar and believed that this moment of surrender was perilous. Clothing themselves in the prescribed identity of Christianity, they were, in Dickinson's opinion, circumventing the struggle to craft a world. They surrendered to Jesus Christ, who crafted them into his image, the image of the Word; vacating self, they were filled by the Word. Dickinson, by contrast, refused to convert. Dickinson's testimonies to the Amherst religious revivals provide a unique lens through which to view the process of sanctification, the theological term for the life of holiness.[2] These nineteenth-century women writers describe the powerful lure of the altar experience and the drama that encircled it in vivid and life-transforming terms. Both understood the movements to the altar as bound up in women's relationship to language, to words, and to *the* Word.[3]

PHOEBE PALMER

The upright piano quietly plays as the revival speaker begins to invite people to move out of their seats. Kneeling down, hands mounted on top of the altar rail, I surrendered my life to Jesus. My old life offered up to God, I claimed a new life. The words of the gospel chorus narrate this drama far better than I: "I have decided to follow Jesus. No turning back. No turning back."[4] Little did I know that my movements to the altar were scripted a century earlier by Phoebe Palmer, one of the leading figures in the American revival movement. During the time of the Second Great Awakening in the mid-nineteenth century, Phoebe Palmer rose to prominence, first as a coleader of the Tuesday Afternoon Meetings in New York and then as a traveling evangelist and missionary.[5] The sudden and consecutive deaths of her three small children inaugurated her entrance into a full-time religious vocation. After the death of her eleven-month-old daughter Eliza, she writes,

> God takes our treasures to heaven, that our heart may be there also. My darling is in heaven doing an angel service. And now I have resolved, that the service, or in other words, the time I would have devoted to her, shall be spent in work for Jesus. And if diligent and self-sacrificing in carrying out my resolve, the death of this child may result in the spiritual life of many.[6]

She came to understand these losses as the means by which God was ushering her into a dedicated and holy life. Earthly loss was, in fact, heavenly gain.

The constant theme of Palmer's message is sacrifice: God requires a person to give up everything in order to faithfully serve, and the primary symbol of sacrifice is the altar. In her writings, Palmer transforms the image of the sacrificial altar in the Hebrew Scriptures into the locus of Christian salvation and holiness.[7] Palmer believed that the altar was a physical place of encounter in which God meets the human person. The penitent sinner comes before God, deciding to leave behind worldly desires and pleasures and to seek a holy life. At the altar, God sanctifies this sacrificed life and makes believers holy. At the altar, a person surrenders her life. At that moment, a new life begins. Palmer narrates her own altar experience: "this solemn act of entire, absolute, irrevocable renunciation of sin and self! Yes, my all is upon Thine altar."[8] The physical movements to the altar represented the leaving behind of a previous world; kneeling at the altar represented the laying down of one's life attachments. The sacrifice of one's life is met, according to Palmer, with the sacrifice of Jesus, whose own life offering becomes the means by which sinful nature is cleansed. The sacrifice must be made holy, and this happens by means of the saving blood of Jesus.

Palmer undoubtedly shaped understandings of conversion within the American context of tent revivals and Bible camps. Thomas Oden claims that Palmer "visualized" salvation by providing an object around which the drama of the self was enacted. The altar became a central part of the architecture of evangelicalism, where the process of conversion was physically instantiated. Describing Charles Finney's Chatham Street revival tabernacle, Jeanne Halgren Kilde notes the way in which the building itself facilitated the conversion experience. All eyes were centered on the figure in the middle, the preacher who, like a shepherd, is angled in such a way to see all in the fold and to bring them home.[9] This nineteenth-century stadium seating called all sinners to walk away from the dangers of the world, toward Christ, their true home.

In her description of the altar experience, Palmer began to preach and teach about the experience of holiness, modifying John Wesley's teachings on sanctification to meet the new American context.[10] Resisting the more gradual process of holiness that a Wesleyan theology of grace offered, Palmer insists, "there is a shorter way."[11] Wesley described sanctification as a process by which a believer received God's gift of holiness. It was a path. Palmer transformed that path into a moment, claiming that the biblical promise is that God instantaneously sanctifies the gift that we bring before God. The moment of surrender is not the beginning of faith but in fact the whole of faith.[12] Sanctification is claimed in the here and now and is symbolized by the actions of kneeling at the altar.

Palmer outlines her altar theology. She writes, "There are distinctive steps in the attainment of the great salvation!"[13] The first step is entire obedience, the second is faith, and the third is testimony. The emphasis of the first step is on the movement of submission, of relinquishment of self, meaning that one's will is renounced and given up to God. God requires total obedience, and the believer, called forward like Abraham to give up Isaac, brings her life as the living sacrifice. Her life is the Isaac to whom she clings so fiercely. But God does not spare her from the sacrifice; instead, faith demands full and continual sacrifice. Once a person offers her life—her *all*—at the altar, she is no longer her own. Palmer writes, "for it was indeed the *Lord's altar* upon which you laid your offering; and it became His property the moment you laid it there."[14] This second step, then, is faith. She writes in the *Guide to Holiness* in June 1875, "The next step is *faith* . . . *Faith* not in ourselves, but in the Word of God. . . . How presumptuous, and strangely inconsistent, not to believe that God *does* receive you, now that you comply with the conditions, and He is now saying, 'I will receive you.'"[15]

She identifies the third movement of the altar as testimony or confession. It is the most distinctive element of her conversion account and one particularly important for thinking about the role of women within the holiness tradition at this time. Palmer insists that a person must testify to the experience at the altar. This testimonial dimension is the ground upon which women were authorized to speak publicly about the life of faith in this tradition. Testimony and witness are associated with the figure of the Spirit, and sanctification is understood to be the work of the Spirit.[16] Palmer believed that the experience of sanctification was not complete until and unless a believer followed it with a public testimony. A believer is required to testify to the inner transformation. If public testimony is not given, the experience is incomplete and invalid. It would not *hold*. According to Palmer, one's life is presented as a burnt offering; if one does not testify to the gift of faith, the offering will be rejected. Witnessing publicly to one's transformation is essential to securing the work of the altar.

In this threefold movement at the altar, a woman comes to know herself in relationship to the Word. Palmer's language is clear throughout; at the altar, a person encounters the Word. While evangelicalism is often cast in terms of a personal relationship with Jesus, Palmer deliberately describes this encounter as one of entering into the Word. This means, literally, a life lived according to the Bible, the Word of God. Palmer's altar covenant emphasizes the primacy of the Bible in the experience of sanctification:

> My body I lay upon Thine altar, O Lord, that it may be a temple for the Holy Spirit to dwell in. . . . I resolve that I will search the Scriptures daily on my knees (unless circumstances of health altogether prevent) as in the more immediate presence of God; and that my faith and my duties shall be regulated by the unadulterated WORD OF GOD, rather than by the opinions of men in regard to that Word; and that no impressions in relation to doctrines or duties shall be regarded as coming from God, unless the said doctrine or duty be plainly taught in the Holy Scriptures.[17]

This particular induction into the Word is distinctive of Palmer's sanctification path in that the experience of faith is immediately linked not to the person and work of Jesus but to a book, the Bible. For Palmer, "holiness" is equated with becoming what she refers to as a "*Bible* Christian."[18] This is why she writes, "I resolve that I will search the Scriptures daily on my knees."[19] The Bible, interpreted literally, provides clear steps to guide the life of faith.

Despite the passion often evoked in gospel revivals, emotion is largely absent from Palmer's altar formula. The movement to the altar is not marked by frenzied and irrational steps but instead by sure and resolute steps. "I have decided to follow Jesus. No turning back."[20] Followers of Wesley criticize Palmer for her perfunctory approach to sanctification, claiming that she replaces the warming heart with the deliberating mind. They asked if Palmer placed sanctification so solidly within the human grasp that one could only decide to be holy and thus *be* holy. This is seen as audacious, especially for women. It provides a believing woman with a clear means of claiming an identity, propelling her into an otherwise foreign role as a key actor in her world. She can take the steps that determine not only her life path but also her path beyond—her eternal destiny. It was not a matter of the heart but a matter of the will, which, for Palmer, is not as fickle and wavering as theologians like Wesley, Augustine, or even Saint Paul had claimed.

The Tuesday Meetings for the Promotion of Holiness, hosted by Palmer and her sister, Sarah Langford, were a primary venue for women's public testimonies.[21] In a full-length account of the Tuesday meetings, Rev. George Hughes notes,

> Testimony follows testimony in quick succession, interspersed with occasional singing and prayer, as the circumstances may seem to demand. . . The testimony of the seeker of salvation, or of the timid, lisping babe in Zion, is listened to with as much interest as that of the most deeply experienced. Whether male or female, all are one in Christ Jesus.[22]

Many of these accounts were written down, and women were urged to keep a daily log of the pilgrimage of faith. The initiation into the Word not only gave them access to the arena of public speech, it also birthed a literature of sanctification. In collaboration with Rev. Timothy Merritt, the journal *The Guide to Christian Perfection* was launched in 1839. Hughes notes that Merritt addressed Langford one evening, saying, "Sister Langford, it seems to me it would be well if these previous testimonies could be published and scattered abroad for the benefit of others."[23] For over sixty years, this journal included accounts and analysis of the day-to-day steps of holy living. Eventually, the Palmers purchased the journal, and Walter Palmer appointed Phoebe as chief editor in

1846. *The Guide to Holiness* published testimonies of women who experienced entire consecration. It was clear that Palmer understood these testimonies as a means of life instruction; she introduces Mrs. Lydia N. Cox's narrative: "Her history . . . is an example of obedience and blessedness, to teach us how to live and how to die." These narratives—holiness stories—became as authoritative as Scripture, for in fact they served as current commentaries on the primitive apostolic experience called for in the book of Acts. These lives were lived Scriptures and walking testimonies to the validity of God's Word. Women's lives conformed to the Word of God; this Word took on their flesh.

But this incarnation of the Word in the lives of evangelical women is a tricky thing. Scholars of American religion often point to these women as feminist forerunners, as women "before their time" who forged paths for women in the public sphere.[24] These evangelical figures, like Palmer, are recovered as examples of the power of religion to provide women with a voice. But these historical recoveries are not *inherently* liberating for women; it is important to look closely at the content of the message.[25] *What* they speak cannot be overshadowed by the fact *that* they speak. While affording them access to spoken and written words, altar faith, as represented by Palmer, calls for a continual relinquishing of a person's self—of her will and desires. In the *Guide*, Mrs. Hannah H. Pickard writes, "O to be divested of everything pertaining to self. I want to be a whole, continual sacrifice to God, to live a life hidden with Christ in God. I now try to give all anew, and rest in the precious blood of Christ."[26] Were these women bearing and delivering a message that erased (and continually erased) any trace of a self? Did the altar experience give women the power to narrate their lives, or did it urge them to conform their lives to a Word that continually divested them of a self?[27]

EMILY DICKINSON

The very few moments in which I loved my Savior I would not now exchange for a thousand worlds like this. It was then my greatest pleasure to commune alone with the great God & to feel that he would listen to my prayers. I determined to devote my whole life to his service & desired that all might taste of the stream of living water from which I cooled my thirst. But the world

allured me & in an unguarded moment I listened to her syren voice. From that moment I seemed to lose my interest in heavenly things by degrees.
—*Letter to Abiah Root, 28 March 1846*[28]

Emily Dickinson never knelt at the revival altar. Yet she witnessed the multiple conversions of friends and family members between 1842 and 1850 as religious revivals swept through New England. Amherst, Massachusetts, and surrounding towns experienced this curious wave of religious conversions. Dickinson, a contemporary of Palmer's, was surrounded by the energy of these revivals, and her adolescence was dominated by sanctification language.[29] She writes, "There is now a revival in College & many hearts have given way to the claims of God."[30] She was fifteen years old when the first revivals made their impact, and her entrance into the world of poetry paralleled the induction of many young women into a relationship with Jesus, the Logos, the Word.[31] Whereas religious conversion was understood to mark a young girl's passage from childhood to adulthood, from home to society, Dickinson's refusal to convert marked her alternative passage into the world of poetry. Withdrawing from Mount Holyoke Female Seminary in 1848, her formal education ended. She began to write poetry.

Dickinson was both attracted to and repelled by the fervor of faith she witnessed taking place around her. Many biographers exploring her adolescent relationship with religion frame it within the context of death in nineteenth-century New England.[32] Religion clearly offered a way to make sense of the premature deaths that Dickinson and her peers experienced at such a young age. Religious teachings provided assurance, comfort, and security. While conversions were certainly motivated by fear of death and desire for eternal security, a young Emily Dickinson was concerned with the impact of these conversions on her personal social world. Dickinson offers particular insights about the effect of conversion on personal identity, especially for young women. Her friends were not only experiencing a profound personal crisis in conversion, the religious revivals were transforming the social world of Amherst and surrounding areas.[33] She writes to her friend Jane Humphrey on April 3, 1850, "Christ is calling everyone here, all my companions have answered, even my darling Vinnie believes she loves, and trusts him, and I am standing alone in rebellion, and growing very careless."[34]

Her response to the revivals and to faith is often misinterpreted. She was not disdainful or condescending about religious belief. Biographer Roger Lundin cites Alfred Habegger: "In her case, resistance was not a sign of unbelief, since she was intellectually convinced she ought to give up."[35] Her response cannot easily be categorized within a binary structure of belief and unbelief, since she was not choosing unbelief above belief. Lundin responds, "By the end of the year, many of Dickinson's classmates at Mt. Holyoke had 'found hope,' but she had not. To the end, she resisted the 'converting influences' of the Spirit and felt guilty about it."[36] Lundin portrays a much more ambivalent Dickinson. He lists a combination of factors, from her distaste for public confession to her complex family relations. But even these do not capture the full sentiment of her letters.

Reading the letters, it is evident that young Dickinson is not ambivalent about the constitutive beliefs of Christianity but, rather, is reckoning with the lure of Christianity and its curious power to *overtake* a person's identity. It transforms persons—literally. On May 7, 1850, she writes to Abiah Root:

> I presume you have heard from Abby, and know what she now believes—she makes a sweet, girl Christian, religion makes her face quite different, calmer, but full of radiance, holy, yet very joyful. She talks of herself quite frequently, seems to love Lord Christ most dearly, and to wonder, and be bewildered, at the life she has always led. It all looks black, and distant, and God, and Heaven are near, she is certainly very much changed.[37]

Not only are her friends' affections completely transferred to Christ; their physical constitutions change. Dickinson is detecting an actual change of countenance. They are there but, peculiarly, *not* there. In her letters, we witness her struggle to come to terms with these transformations. She recognizes that there is delight and enjoyment in surrendering one's life to God; the promise of God's perfect love is almost irresistible. The anxiety, giddiness, and dramatic frenzy of adolescence are replaced with the calm solemnity of religious faith.

Grappling with this new phenomenon of sanctification, she writes to Jane Humphrey on April 3, 1850:

> It *certainly* comes from God—and I think to receive it is blessed—not that I know it from *me*, but from those on whom *change* has passed. They seem so very tranquil, and their voices are kind, and gentle, and the tears fill their eyes so often, I really think I envy them.[38]

Despite mention of envy and sporadic allusions to the possibility of her own conversion, her relationship to revival faith is less a narrative about her own struggle to believe as it is about coming to terms with the decisions of her close friends and family to convert. She experiences these decisions to convert as abandonment. As she interprets it, a person cannot be invested in worldly relations *and* invested in the heavenly kingdom. Her friends must leave her in order to be committed to Christ and his work. She narrates this departure:

> Where are you now Abiah, where are your thoughts, and aspirings, where are your young affections, not with the *boots*, and *whiskers*; any with *me* ungrateful, *any* tho' drooping, dying? I presume you are loving your mother, and loving the stranger, and wanderer, visiting the poor, and afflicted, and reaping whole fields of blessings. Save me a *little* sheaf—only a very little one! Remember, and care for me sometimes, and scatter a fragrant flower in this wilderness life of mine by writing me, and by not forgetting, and by lingering longer in prayer, that the Father may bless one more![39]

Her words suggest she is losing her friends to their newly found faith. The stranger and wanderer now receive their affections, and she, Dickinson, is left in the wilderness. In choosing religion, they are protected from the anxieties and suffering in the world, but only by removing themselves from the world and its attachments. Paraphrasing the Pauline Scriptures, they are dead to the world and alive in Christ.

The transformation of faith was so profound that Dickinson felt that she was losing her friends to religion. Her correspondence during these years is filled with a sense of loss and an awkwardly expressed jealousy. It was as if she found herself competing with Christ for the affections of her friends. She writes to Jane Humphrey, April 3, 1850: "How strange is this sanctification, that works such a marvelous change, that sows in such corruption, and rises in golden glory, that brings Christ down, and shews him, and lets him select his friends?"[40] It became increasingly evident that the adolescent Dickinson understood the altar to mean the loss of her closest friendships. Her narration of the Amherst revivals is shot through with feelings of loss. In multiple letters, she speaks about faith in terms of separation.

However, this separation is not solely interpersonal. Her friends are not only abandoning her. According to Dickinson, they are abandoning themselves or, more precisely, the possibility of developing a self. Dickinson observes that conversion requires persons to yield their identity entirely to God. In return, they will receive the perfect love of God, rest for the soul, and perfect peace. She was suspicious of this self-emptying and equally suspicious that people employed the love of Jesus to discipline and constrain others. In her journal at Mount Holyoke on June 29, 1848, she writes, "At our morning devotions Miss Lyon's theme was the *constraining* love of Jesus, its power to control us in *every thing.*"[41] Dickinson is keenly aware of what this particular form of Christianity requires. She refers to conversion as the "one thing needful," drawing from the gospel story of Mary and Martha and their different forms of service to Jesus.[42] Although the one thing needful seems to be conversion, Dickinson's growing understanding of conversion equates the experience with self-relinquishment and flight from the world. She writes in 1848,

> I have neglected the *one thing needful* when all were obtaining it, and I may never, never again pass through such a season as was granted us last winter. Abiah, you may be surprised to hear me speak as I do, knowing that I express no interest in the all-important subject, but I am not happy, and I regret that last term, when that golden opportunity was mine, that I did not give up and become a Christian. It is not now too late, so my friends tell me, so my offended conscience whispers, but it is hard for me to give up the world.[43]

Christianity confronts young women with an either-or decision, *either* self and the world *or* Christ.[44]

Dickinson feared that this relinquishing of the world would release a person from what she believed to be the necessary task of a human person: to organize one's experiences, values, and emotions into a "self." Each person has a responsibility to integrate one's beliefs into an experience of the world and, to whatever degree they could, to construct a self *in* the world. Cynthia Griffin Wolff writes,

> No quandary in life presented Emily Dickinson with such wrenching choices as the demand for conversion. . . . Yet against faith was the fact that one must yield one's identity entirely to God, for the conversion experience was an obliterating relinquishment of self—a total loss of independence and autonomy wherein an individual's control over the organization of his or her experience was given over to the Lord.[45]

It was not belief itself that Dickinson opposed but the abnegation of this fundamental responsibility. Instead, religion threatens to replace this important self-formation by offering a "uniform, divinely dictated vision of a world renewed in Christ's love."[46]

Dickinson wants to retain what she understands to be the responsibility of each self to integrate the world. For her, integration is stymied in the experience of conversion. One has merely to submit, to give up this task, in order to step into a uniform identity. The damage of religious identity occurs when a person fails to "show up," when the self is vacated and subsumed *for the sake of* and *in the name of* religion. The religious call around her offers a preset vision of the world into which one has only two choices: to submit or to reject. Union with the Word, according to Dickinson, means that the human processes of self-creation must to be sacrificed to the Word—plain and simple. Wolff provides this assessment of Dickinson's position: "Better to keep one's 'I' intact, even if the promise of Paradise must be rejected."[47]

Dickinson writes to Abiah, asking her to explain the appeal of the Christian message: "I ask what this message *means* that they ask for so very eagerly, *you* know of this depth, and fullness, will you *try* to tell me about it."[48] Palmer's altar theology claims to require *everything* of a person—her whole self. Yet for Dickinson, to require *everything* would be to demand that a person assume the hard work of integration, to confront and construct the self rather than to submit oneself to a uniform and static Word. The difficult task, as Dickinson understood it, is to develop a vision of the world and oneself in it; it requires creativity, struggle, and engagement with the world. For Palmer, this struggle to name and to define oneself ends at the altar. Instead, one receives an identity. Leaving the world behind, all desires and affections are dead, ashes in the burnt sacrifice. In exchange, a new believer receives the identity of a "Bible Christian," one who adheres to the Word.

Dickinson identifies a perilous moment, and she puts her finger on a very sensitive and complex issue about religious identity, especially as it relates to women. At the altar, a self must be renounced. There is power there, but no self to authorize it. The power to speak that a woman gains from the altar experience is not the power to speak her own truth but the power to speak *the Truth*, something that comes from outside of her. For Dickinson, it is as if she is witnessing God's word flowing through each individual like a sweet elixir. This word overtakes them, releasing individuals from the task of crafting a self, of becoming a person in the world. Faith not only requires a transfer of affections from worldly attachments to God, it requires a person to become, in Dickinson's observations, detached, affectless, disconnected from her emotions and desires. For Dickinson, the prescriptions of Christianity—while seeming to stir the deepest passions in a person—actually hollow out these passions. An encounter with the Word is equivalent to self-evacuation; a person is, literally, possessed by another identity.

An adolescent at the time of the Second Great Awakening in New England, Dickinson weighed religious conversion seriously, identifying it as the "wretched choice" that faces her as a young student at Amherst Academy and as a teenager at Mount Holyoke Female Seminary. In the end, she cannot convert. Instead of surrendering to the Word, she finds her salvation, so to speak, in taking up words. Instead of the Bible, Dickinson, in Wolff's words, "falls into language."[49] Dickinson cleaves to the book of words, the lexicon. Noah Webster lived in Amherst from 1812 to 1824, and his influence loomed large at Amherst Academy, even during Dickinson's time there. It is not an overstatement to say that

Dickinson was educated under this ultimate wordsmith. Underlying *Webster's Dictionary* was a whole moral and religious vision about the power and function of words.[50] For Webster, the ability to name the world was a gift; naming the world was a spiritual exercise.[51] Employing words correctly, naming correctly, was infused with moral purpose. It is difficult to ascertain the extent of Webster's influence on Dickinson, but her decision against Christian conversion coincides with her immersion into the world of words. She will be a believer of sorts, but her belief in words does not require the self-abnegation that she ascribes to Christianity. To name the world is not a selfish act but, in fact, a moral duty. Dickinson understands that the mediator between her and God is not *the* Word but, rather, words.

Dickinson's image of the poet's life is the biblical image of Jacob wrestling with the angel at Peniel.[52] Jacob struggles with God, demanding a name and a blessing. The struggle is the struggle of the pen—to name oneself and the world. And this process is, for Dickinson, a wounding process. Instead of the calm and protected shores of Christianity, Dickinson chooses to ride the turbulent seas of the world. In this frequently referenced image from the letters, she describes her choice *not* to become a Christian. It is important to note that, just prior to this image, she expresses fears that she is losing Abiah to faith. She writes,

> You are growing wiser than I am, and nipping in the bud fancies which I let blossom—perchance to bear no fruit, or if plucked, I may find it bitter. The shore is safe, Abiah, but I love to buffet the sea—I can count the bitter wrecks here in these pleasant waters, and hear the murmuring winds, but oh, I love the danger![53]

Dickinson hears, in the message of religious conversion, a quelling of the internal storm. She admits, in other places in her letters, that there is a "sting" and an "aching void" to life that is almost unbearable.[54] Relief may be found by cleaving to the Word, but in the end Dickinson chooses restlessness above relief, worldly dangers above the safe shores of Christianity.[55]

PALMER AND DICKINSON: A "WRETCHED CHOICE"?

As I stand in the back of the gospel tabernacle, Palmer and Dickinson stir within me. Like many women growing up within holiness traditions, I came to know myself within the spaces and vocabularies of faith. The theology lives inside of me, and my body remembers these spaces. When the low hum of the familiar tune "Just as I Am" starts playing, I, years later, seek the altar, as if propelled forward by body memory. There is morphological power in these traditions. Traces of them remain, revealing an often puzzling and irreconcilable convergence of past and present. The altar offered young girls the opportunity to narrate our worlds and to become models of holiness for those around us. Within this tradition, I, and many other evangelical girls, first experimented with public speaking. We began to speak words about God—to testify. Yet these words also undid us, calling us to deny a self and to nip our young passions in the bud. It was within this tradition that we learned to mistrust and extinguish our desires.

It is a mixed inheritance, and one that cannot be so simply understood by pitting Dickinson against Palmer. What seems clear in both women is that their choices came at great cost. Although Palmer was given an arena for speech and for constructing a theological voice, she accepted certain theological constraints in doing so. Dickinson intuited these theological constraints and rejected them, but this cut her off from a broader community. Religious history is filled with testimonies of women who navigate the constraints placed upon them. Feminist theologians have sought to name these constraints and to ask the difficult questions underlying what often appears in the form of an either-or: What drives women to make these choices? How have particular theological scripts shaped womens' lives, and how, in turn, have women reshaped these theological scripts?

Dickinson is right. A theology of the altar has often been death dealing for women. To be united with the Word is to be inducted into an identity that continually calls for death; a person finds new life only through the process of dying.[56] At the altar, women meet Jesus, the bloody sacrifice who provides eternal life for all by his act of death. United with him *in his death*, his death requires nothing less than their death in return—death to self, death to the world. The altar is filled with death imagery: Christ crucified, the slain lamb, the blood of Jesus, denial of the self, worldly renunciation. A sinner's connection to God comes through the death of Jesus, through his atoning sacrifice. The dominant logic of evangelical atonement theology is this: your sinfulness meets the act of Jesus on the cross, and it is transformed. This transaction of death is what affords you life. As a sinner headed to death— eternal peril—your only possibility of life is through Jesus and his death.

Theologians such as Rita Nakashima Brock, Rebecca Parker, and Delores Williams criticize a dominant strain in Christian theology that identifies salvation enacted through death.[57] The concept of salvation and identity through *death* is a limited vision of salvation, according to these thinkers. There is no symbol that links a believer to Christ's life. It is not his incarnation that saves them, but his death. The morphological power of this kind of theology of the cross (enacted at the altar) has particularly negative implications for the female body and all marginalized (or nonnormative) bodies. The message is to continually empty oneself out, to renounce bodily desires, to offer one's self up for the sake of another. Beyond this, new life in Christ, according to altar theology, entails a *continual* encounter with death and the spiritual practices of dying to self, of renouncing a relationship to self and world. When Palmer talks about new life in Christ, she describes it as a continual process of dying to self. It is not a one-time event but, for Palmer, a life of revisiting the altar.[58]

Yet amid the logic of "laying down" one's life, the altar experience also gives rise to new ways of women "taking up" their lives. Although the public meetings were essential for women gathering to profess their new experience of faith, holiness journals provided a venue for women to write and read testimonies. Charles E. White writes, "God's gift of sanctification unstopped the springs of Phoebe Palmer's literary creativity."[59] Women were actively engaging each other in theological matters. In the "Correspondence" section of the *Guide to Holiness*, a woman writes a letter to the editor in 1866:

> When I read your book [*Faith and Its Effects*], the subject was new to me. I had never understood the doctrine of holiness as you teach it;

and least of all did I understand the teaching of our Catechism and our Confession of Faith. When I read the book about half through, I laid it down and knelt by a chair, and began the work of consecration . . . But oftimes, when I read the 'Guide,' the Tempter suggests, 'Do you not think that you receive it too easy?'—Yours in love, Rebecca D. Davenport[60]

The editor, Phoebe Palmer, responds: "You rightly say that the Tempter suggests, 'Do you not think you received it too easy?' You obtained it in the good, old-fashioned, Bible way, first consecrating all, and then with childlike faith believing God's word, 'I will receive you.'—See 2 Cor. vi.17,18 and vii.4."[61] This is the core of Palmer's altar theology presented in letter form. This kind of dialogue between women about theological matters was revolutionary and gave women, through words and through appealing to the Word, a way of making sense of their lives in relationship to God. One woman writes, "I have taken the 'Guide' from its beginning, and the 'Beauty' for a number of years. I prize it next to the Bible, *a great help* in keeping me in the 'way of holiness,' which we have been trying to walk about thirty years."[62] Another woman testifies to the influence of these journals:

> It has been indeed a 'guide' to inexperienced travelers like me. I enjoy such kind of reading better than any other. One sentence, breathing the spirit of holiness, I find more profitable, than pages such I should once have considered truly religious. The 'Herald' furnishes, weekly, some delicious crumbs; the 'Guide' brings a rich monthly report; and, more than all, the Bible supplies an unfailing store of, I had almost said, angel's food.[63]

Women were guiding each other in the life of faith through writing. As they were following the call to lay down their lives, they were also experiencing a call to pick up their pens to write theology.

Might the image of the altar be imagined differently—as a more complex site of integration between words and Word, self and world? Dickinson and Palmer press me to search for a compelling interpretation of the experience of faith that does not force allegiances but instead crafts and nurtures a faith that illuminates and deepens human affections, that demands engagement rather than forces detachment. Instead of the altar representing a "parting of ways" between Palmer and Dickinson, could it represent a unique meeting point out of which a new theological discourse emerges—a discourse of testimony?

This discourse is only possible by engaging a more incarnational vision of the Word, in which the living Word comes to life in a new believer without requiring continual self-evacuation. The Word does not become flesh solely to die.[64] Instead, the claim of incarnation states that God takes on flesh and dwells among us as the living and breathing Word. Palmer's altar theology describes our lives as "living sacrifices," but our lives could equally be described as "living words," as testimonies to the Word incarnating persons. This vision of the altar does not entail renouncing the world but, rather, cocreating the world, a partnership of Word and words. What if sanctification—the process of holiness—was interpreted as a risky process of integrating self and world? In turn, what if women's writing was interpreted as a holy practice of testifying to the incarnation of the Word in women's lives? To encounter the Word means that words—our words—have holy power. Women, with words, participate in the process of making the world holy, of sanctifying it.

For women writing theology, the process of writing becomes a way of incarnating words, of bridging words and Word, of refusing the "wretched choices" often presented to us by our religious traditions. It is courageous work, in which the prohibitions and prescriptions about who can speak authoritatively about the Word are always present. As these traditions live within us, we must also claim morphological power, to shape practices and professions just as we are shaped by them. This process entails a refusal to leave our lives behind in the writing of theology. It also entails a refusal to believe that the Word can be collapsed into the "words of men."[65] Refusing such delineations as spiritual and theological writings, written and enacted theology, practice and theory, life and ideas, women theologians have often attempted to write what falls between the cracks of traditional theology. Between the logic of "laying down" and "taking up," I envision the work of women writing theology as the work of testifying to what cannot be contained within this logic, namely the experiences of loss and desire that often do not make it into words. Might the next generation of feminist theologians narrate a more tangled path of holiness for women? If so, what might this discourse look like?

The perennial task of theology is the work of witnessing between Word and words to the deep mystery of God and the deep mysteries of our lives. The practice of writing keeps this witness alive, ensuring that theology—theo-logos (words about God)—does not become a static discourse, suffering from the condition that Elizabeth Johnson identified as *scotosis*, a "hardening of the mind against unwanted wisdom."[66] In a brief biography of Emily Dickinson, her poetic influence is described in this way:

> A poet who took definition as her province, Emily Dickinson challenged the existing definitions of poetry and the poet's work. Like writers such as Ralph Waldo Emerson, Henry David Thoreau, and Walt Whitman, she experimented with expression in order to free it from conventional restraints. Like writers such as Charlotte Brontë and Elizabeth Barrett Browning, she crafted a new type of persona for the first person. The speakers in Dickinson's poetry, like those in Brontë's and Browning's works, are sharp-sighted observers who see the inescapable limitations of their societies as well as their imagined and imaginable escapes. To make the abstract tangible, to define meaning without confining it, to inhabit a house that never became a prison, Dickinson created in her writing a distinctively elliptical language for expressing what was possible but not yet realized.[67]

I imagine the theologian exchanged for the poet in this passage, and theological figures replacing the named literary figures. As women writing theology, we are sharp-sighted observers who see the inescapable limits of our societies as well as our imagined and imaginable escapes. And as we attempt to make the abstract tangible, we inhabit traditional theological houses without being imprisoned by them. We pick up our pens as if to defy the wretched choices, crafting a language for what is possible but not yet realized.

4

"MY GOD BECAME FLESH"
Angela of Foligno Writing the Incarnation

Emily A. Holmes

Writing the Body

What makes a woman think she can write theology? Where does she gain the authority to produce a book? In medieval Christendom, the idea of a woman writing theology was unthinkable. The problem was not so much that a woman might be chosen by God as a prophet or be granted special graces such as visions and raptures. Scripture provided precedent for women in these roles, and medieval Christianity embraced such miraculous evidence of God's action in the world. The problem was that the particularity of women's bodies impeded their access to the prerequisites for writing in the Middle Ages: education and ordination. The medieval church forbade women to teach, preach, or interpret Scripture based on the Pauline injunction to silence in the assembly. A woman speaking in church risked asserting unnatural authority over men as well as distracting them with her body. The medieval church also prohibited ordination of women on account of their female bodies: regardless of the state of the soul, the female sex was seen as incapable of receiving holy orders—precisely because the female body itself signified a state of subjection.[1]

The medieval church consequently reserved authoritative religious writing for male clerics, educated and ordained. Women's bodies were officially excluded from positions of authority within the church, just as their words were officially excluded from the written tradition for the same reason they were barred from ordination: their material—their bodies, their words—was seen as defective. As a result, women who did write of spiritual matters necessarily engaged in a complex dance of negotiation surrounding their work, simultaneously asserting and denying their own authority to write. Some, like Hildegard of Bingen, sought initial approval from male authorities before sharing their writings.[2] Others, like Hadewijch, disseminated their work within close networks of women's religious communities.[3] All medieval women writers wrote from the complex subject position of concurrent humility and audacity: as the weak, uneducated woman who was nevertheless chosen by God to write.[4] When everything in her religious tradition told a woman that writing is reserved for educated men, it is an extraordinary feat to overcome the forces arrayed against her. A woman writing a book of theology?! Who does she think she is?[5]

Because of the historical hurdles placed before women writing theology, the written Christian tradition as we have received it was built in part on women's exclusion and subordination. Women entering that tradition at any time, even today, enter into another complex dance of negotiation of authority. The challenges women face when writing, moreover, are limited neither to the Middle Ages nor to Christianity. In her autobiographical essay, "Coming to Writing," the contemporary French writer Hélène Cixous depicts the gradual process of beginning to write. She describes the movement toward writing in her own life as the struggle of passion overcoming reason and courage overcoming fear. Writing was both deeply attractive and yet ostensibly forbidden to her because of her religious tradition. She asks herself how any woman can justify writing:

> Wouldn't you first have needed the "right reasons" to write? The reasons, mysterious to me, that give you the "right" to write? But I didn't know them. I had only the "wrong" reason; it wasn't a reason, it was

a passion, something shameful—and disturbing; one of those violent characteristics with which I was afflicted. I didn't "want" to write. How could I have "wanted" to? I hadn't strayed to the point of losing all measure of things. A mouse is not a prophet. I wouldn't have had the cheek to go claim my book from God on Mount Sinai, even if, as a mouse, I had found the energy to scamper up the mountain.[6]

Like many women of different religions, Cixous was excluded from the ongoing written conversation that takes place across the centuries—we call it "tradition"—because of the particularity of her female body. She has no right to write.

But write she does, prolifically and elegantly.[7] So how does a mouse find the energy to scamper up the mountain, to meet God and claim her book? And what happens to the canon of writing when she does? Although not a theologian, Cixous offers one way to enter a tradition of writing built in part on the exclusion of women: by bringing women's bodies directly into language. Cixous practices a form of writing she calls *écriture féminine*, "writing as feminine" or "writing the body," as it is often referred to in English.[8] In Cixous' view, bodily phenomena and emotions are symbolically coded "feminine" with respect to the "masculine" order of language, law, religion, and property rights.[9] Bodily phenomena such as laughter, tears, milk, and blood are found at the borders of language: language cannot fully capture them, and yet they convey meaning. Intentionally emphasizing corporeality and emotion in writing can challenge the law that excludes what is different, other, or feminine. Although Cixous calls this form of writing "feminine," it is not limited to women: she finds evidence of it in works by authors such as James Joyce and Jean Genet as well as Clarice Lispector.

Cixous proposes that "writing the body" might bring women's bodies into language as women themselves produce a form of writing contiguous with their bodies, marked by difference, otherness, and corporeality. Because the Christian tradition has historically often tried to exclude differences in the name of orthodoxy and apostolicity, *écriture féminine* also challenges the canon of theological writing. This canon tends to repress bodily phenomena, difference, and otherness in order to function as unified and authoritative. The repression of these "feminine" features, however, is incomplete: the repressed constantly threatens to return and disrupt the law and language that excluded it. Because women's bodies symbolize what partially escapes, and therefore threatens, the "masculine" religious order, the return of the repressed occurs in a particularly forceful way in women's bodies, which appear as either miraculous or demonic.[10] *Écriture féminine* captures that energy—the energy needed to scramble up Mount Sinai—to write women's bodies and voices back into religious traditions. The act of writing and the texts that are produced have the potential to translate women's bodies into language and thereby transform the tradition that once found them so disturbing.

Writing provided the medieval Italian woman Angela of Foligno (c. 1248–1309) a way to translate her own bodily experience of God into words. Her story tells of the potential of writing to bring women's bodies into the written Christian tradition. Angela was born outside Assisi and married at age twenty, and in 1288 her husband, mother, and sons all died quite suddenly. What modern readers would view as tragic, Angela described as a "great consolation" that freed her to pursue a religious vocation to which she had been increasingly drawn. Living in Italy, her spiritual life was greatly influenced by the Franciscans, and in 1291 she became a tertiary by entering the Franciscan Third Order of Penance.[11] After a dramatic pilgrimage to Assisi that same year during which Angela was found screaming on the floor of the Church of Saint Francis, she began to narrate her spiritual journey to her relative and confessor Brother Arnaldo.[12]

The Book of Blessed Angela that resulted from that narration and Arnaldo's subsequent redaction is divided into two parts.[13] The *Memorial* was written by Brother Arnaldo as Angela dictated in her Umbrian dialect and he translated on the spot into Latin. After the *Memorial* was completed, Angela lived for another thirteen years until her death in 1309. Her *Instructions*, the second half of her *Book*, cover this period in her life and reflect her authority as spiritual mother. They include a collection of letters, teachings, and anecdotes transmitted to her "sons and daughters," a group of Franciscan disciples that gathered around her as her fame as a holy woman grew. Many of these were written after the death of Brother Arnaldo and some after Angela's own death.[14]

Angela's *Book* depicts the complex transition in the life of a holy woman from physical object of male suspicion—screaming on the floor of the church—to a subject who exercises authority over her own words and, through her *Book*, her memory as preserved by others. This transition takes place through writing. In what follows, I will focus on Angela's extraordinary experience during her pilgrimage to Assisi as an example of the transformative potential of writing to bring women's bodies and voices into the written Christian tradition. In Assisi, Angela's body disturbed the order of the church, but that event led to the production of her *Book*, since it was Arnaldo's dismay at Angela's behavior that led him to write. Over a series of meetings with Brother Arnaldo, Angela's physical symptoms gradually receded as she learned to interpret and share her experience of God. Her transmission of what she called her "divine secrets" began under obedience to Arnaldo (her confessor) but continued as she gained confidence in her authority, culminating in her *Instructions* in the spiritual life to her disciples. The transition of Angela from disruptive female body to the subject of her own book took place gradually as an encounter between flesh and word. This transition, I argue in what follows, can best be understood theologically as an interpretation of the incarnation: because the Word became flesh, Angela's own flesh issues in words that transform her position as a woman within the Christian tradition. This theological interpretation of Angela's experience has implications for how Christians understand the body of Christ today. For Angela, "writing the body" is, at its heart, writing the body of Christ.

ANGELA IN ASSISI

In 1291 Angela's spiritual life intensified as she focused on the passion of Christ: "What I wanted was to perform even greater penance. So I enclosed myself within the passion of Christ and I was given hope that therein I might find deliverance."[15] We do not know why Angela became consumed with doing penance. Some scholars speculate that she had committed a sexual sin; her evident wealth and life of luxury may have also provoked feelings of guilt in a Franciscan context that valued poverty.[16] Whatever the reason, as her acts of penance led to a deeper experience of Christ, bodily symptoms signified her spiritual experience. She forgot to eat. She stood in prayer and never tired of genuflections. She screamed frequently and suffered from fevers. Receiving a consolation, she fell to the ground and lost her power of speech. Her female companion thought she was "on the verge of death or already dead." Such somatic responses were only symptoms of her increased desire for Christ; she told him, "even if you should offer me the whole universe, I would not be satisfied. I want only you." The response to this prayer took her by surprise: "Hurry, for as soon as you have finished what you have set out to do the whole Trinity will come into you."[17] What she had "set out to do" was to undertake a pilgrimage to Assisi as a sign of her penance.

Angela described her spiritual journey from her initial conversion in the form of thirty steps of increasing conformity to Christ. Arnaldo narrates these to the reader in order and mostly in Angela's own words, but he interrupts his narration at step twenty—the pilgrimage to Assisi—in order to clarify how he "came to know of these things and was compelled to write all about them," producing the book his reader now holds.[18] Arnaldo's narrative aside marks the twentieth step and the road to Assisi as a decisive moment in Angela's itinerary, as well as the episode that brought Angela and Arnaldo together in their collaborative work.[19] Assisi is also the place where Angela's bodily symptoms reached a climax and then began to recede, as her speech was heard and written. Assisi is so important, in fact, that the reader will learn of what happened there twice, from two different perspectives.

First, from Arnaldo's perspective, Angela's behavior in Assisi was the occasion of his writing: "The true reason why I wrote is as follows. One day the aforementioned person, Christ's faithful one, came to the church of St. Francis in Assisi, where I was residing in a friary. She screamed greatly while she was sitting at the entrance to the portals of the church."[20] Arnaldo identifies himself as her confessor, blood relative, and special counselor and acknowledges that he was "greatly ashamed" of her behavior, especially in front of his Franciscan brothers who knew them both. While her companions on the pilgrimage watched her behavior with reverence, Arnaldo admits,

> my pride and shame were so great that out of embarrassment and indignation I did not approach her; instead, I waited for her to finish screaming, and I kept myself at a distance. After she had ceased her screaming and shouting and had risen from the entrance and come over to me, I could hardly speak to her calmly. I told her that, henceforth, she should never again dare to come to Assisi, since this was the place where this evil had seized her.[21]

To Arnaldo, Angela's screams and shouts were too public, too ostentatious. Despite the reverence of her companions, Angela was out of order and out of place. Her shouting disrupted the peace and quiet of the church as her body blocked the door. He was embarrassed for her, and even more for himself. Was she possessed by an evil spirit? Arnaldo wanted to know.

"Wanting to know the cause of her shouts, I began to press her in every way that I could to tell me why she had screamed and shouted so much in Assisi."[22] After swearing him to secrecy, Angela began to tell of her spiritual journey, including the graces and visions of Christ she had received. Arnaldo tried his best to introduce doubt. "Amazed as I was and suspicious that it might come from some evil spirit, I made a strong effort to arouse her suspicions because I myself had so many. I advised her and compelled her to tell me everything." He began to take notes for himself, which he called a "memorial," to remember what she said and to show to another man. "I wished to write absolutely everything," he explains,

> so that I could consult with some wise and spiritual man who would have never heard of her. I told her that I wished to do this so that she could in no way be deceived by an evil spirit. I strove to inspire fear in her by showing her by examples how many persons had been deceived, and consequently how she could be similarly deceived. Because she did not yet have the degree of clarity and perfect certitude which she had later—as will be found in the writings which follow—she began to reveal the divine secrets to me and I wrote these down.[23]

The tableau is striking. Angela screams and shouts incomprehensibly, sitting at the doors. Arnaldo is shocked and embarrassed, and he angrily tries to ban her from the church in Assisi. He then sets out to convince her she is possessed by an evil spirit, in part by writing down her words. But instead, she convinces him of the truth of her "divine secrets." He sets out to write for other men; instead, Angela and Arnaldo together produce a book that records her life, words, and experience of God.

After this lengthy aside explaining the origin of the book, Arnaldo returns to the narrative and describes once again the screaming and shouting episode in Assisi. This time he writes from Angela's perspective and, to the degree possible, in her own words. Angela had asked Saint Francis to feel Christ's presence, to observe his rule well, and for the grace of true poverty. Her visions and consolations had increased, along with her somatic reactions—inedia, screaming, fever, aphasia—and she had been promised an indwelling of Holy Trinity, although she was skeptical of its fulfillment. But on the road to Assisi, Angela received a revelation from the Holy Spirit, who comforted her and promised to accompany her as far as the church of Saint Francis. The Spirit whispered to her all along the way: "My daughter, my dear and sweet daughter, my delight, my temple, my beloved daughter, love me, because you are very much loved by me; much more than you could love me."[24] With an indescribable feeling of joy and sweetness, the Holy Spirit repeated the promise to accompany Angela until the second time she entered the church of Saint Francis, at which point this experience would end.

> After [the Holy Spirit] had withdrawn, I began to shout and to cry out without any shame: "Love still unknown, why do you leave me?" I could not nor did I scream out any other words than these: "Love still unknown, why? why? why?" Furthermore, these screams were so choked up in my throat that the words were unintelligible. . . . As I shouted I wanted to die. It was very painful for me not to die and to go on living. After this experience I felt my joints become dislocated.[25]

The arrival of the Holy Spirit was sweet and marked by his words of endearment. But his withdrawal was painful and provoked her protest.

Angela's symptoms signified the end of her divine encounter as a traumatic experience—a desire for death, dislocation of limbs, incomprehension, and inability to speak. The words got caught in her throat and were unintelligible to those who merely saw a woman screaming and shouting on the floor by the doors to the church. Her utter lack of self-consciousness or shame during the incident contrasts strongly with Arnaldo's professed embarrassment at her behavior.

The shouted words initially caught in Angela's throat were later elaborated and translated into written form with the assistance of Brother Arnaldo. On the way home from Assisi, Angela began to speak about God to her companions. She received an experience of the cross and the love of God within her body and soul.[26] In the days that followed, Angela smelled extraordinary fragrances, her companion saw her body emanating a glowing star, and, after meditating on the flesh driven into the wood by the nails of the cross, Angela received a vision of the beauty of the body of Christ. Her own body stretched out on the ground in response. All of this was told to Arnaldo, who quickly wrote it down with the intent of showing it to those who could determine the authenticity and source of Angela's extraordinary experiences. While Arnaldo initially succeeded in making Angela doubt herself, the tables turned as she soon convinced him of the genuineness of her revelations and their divine source. Angela assuaged both their doubts with the reassurance she received: "'God is present in all those things which you are writing and stands there with you.' My soul understood and felt that God indeed delighted over all that had been written."[27]

Angela began her spiritual journey before meeting Arnaldo. But Assisi was a turning point,[28] and not simply because of the extraordinary consolation she received from the presence of the Trinity. In Assisi, Angela's experience was manifested physically, in inarticulate screams and shouts. Her words caught in her throat. It took Arnaldo's embarrassment, suspicions, and masculine authority as her relative and confessor to help her get those words out. Once her words were set to paper (and Angela told him he would need a lot of paper![29]), she quickly asserted control over what was written, accepting or rejecting Arnaldo's version of her speech. No longer screaming inarticulately, she claimed spiritual authority as she received further and richer divine secrets. She obtained God's approval of the book, and God occasionally even specified what to write.[30] At the end of the *Memorial*, God told Angela, "Everything which has been written is in conformity with my will and comes from me, that is, issues forth from me.' Then he added: 'I will put my seal to it.'" Charmingly, Angela did not understand what God meant by "seal," and so God "clarified these words by saying: 'I will sign it.'"[31] Angela's shouted protest of God's departure in Assisi led to the production of a book in which she found God again—this time in what she and Arnaldo had written together, above God's own signature.

Angela's experience serves as a powerful metaphor for the position of women in the Christian tradition. Like Angela at the doors of Saint Francis, women are too often sitting at the doors, neither inside nor outside, neither heard nor understood on account of the perceived disruptive effect of their bodies. The historical response has been to contain and control women's bodies through cloisters, marriage, or the stake. What happened in Assisi could have ended there, with Angela cloistered like Clare or, demonic influence confirmed, burned like Marguerite Porete. Instead, the doors to the church of Saint Francis in Assisi opened onto a moment of collaboration between a man of authority and a woman who needed to speak. Together they translated the words that were caught in her throat into language the church might hear. This translation took place through the encounter of Angela's body with the written word.

ANGELA IN HER CONTEXT: WOMEN'S BODIES AND WOMEN'S WORDS

The historian Caroline Walker Bynum has shown how medieval women's bodies became the privileged site for miracles attesting to God's presence in the world. Women saints were widely admired for their extreme feats of suffering in imitation of Christ and their food miracles, such as their own inability to eat or their miraculous feeding of others. Medieval women's piety took this particular shape, Bynum argues, because of women's bodily identification with Christ who, by becoming wounded flesh that is broken and eaten, was thought to have identified in a special way with them.[32] The incarnation, the passion, and the Eucharist thus became the focus of women's piety, and their bodies became the locus where God was manifest through extraordinary and miraculous phenomena. The historian Amy Hollywood, however, has noted important differences between the hagiographical texts that are the basis for most of Bynum's claims, which were largely written by men, and medieval women's own theological writings, such as those of Hadewijch, Mechthild of Magdeburg, Beatrice of Nazareth, and Marguerite Porete. In works written by their own hands, women focused less on the bodily miracles and physical suffering that preoccupied male hagiographers of women saints. Instead, these medieval women writers were much more interested in understanding the spiritual and theological significance of their mystical experience.[33]

Angela of Foligno falls somewhere between the two groups of medieval women, call them "saints" and "writers," examined by Bynum and Hollywood, respectively. Because her book includes features of both, Angela's journey indicates how a woman might have moved from one category, as we see it today, to the other. Angela's life repeated many of the themes of medieval women's piety identified by Bynum—focus on the humanity of Christ, and especially his passion; drinking from the wound in Christ's side; a strong eucharistic piety; abjection through the ingestion of a leper's scale; inedia; and so on—and Arnaldo admired her greatly for it. Her body responded to the body of Christ repeatedly in prayer and in visions: she stood or lay down as required, stripped herself naked at the foot of the cross, and even entered into his tomb on Holy Saturday where he pressed her cheek against his. These bodily reactions intensified in the steps immediately prior to the incident in Assisi: when Angela was not screaming and shouting, she was struck with aphasia; she had a fever; she could not eat. They reached their apex when she choked on her own words and her screams made her appear possessed.

Arnaldo's text could have been another hagiography, written by an admiring male confessor who reported (and constructed) the extraordinary phenomena surrounding a woman's body for his own didactic purposes. But something else happened in Assisi that brought Angela much closer to the medieval women *writers* studied by Hollywood. When Angela's screaming provoked Arnaldo's desire to know, she became the origin—and coauthor—of her book. Her body was no longer merely symptomatic of God's miraculous work on her. Through her conversations with Arnaldo, Angela asserted the authority to interpret her experience, and she increased in confidence and certainty until she became a spiritual mother to her Franciscan sons and daughters, as recounted in the second part of her *Book*. The transition from acting as a spectacular, if suspicious, female body on the margins of the church to exercising authority over the spoken and written word began in Assisi and continued with Arnaldo's collaboration. Through this collaboration, Angela's flesh was translated into written word.

How do we make sense of Angela's movement from one category of medieval religious woman to another—from spectacular body to author, from ineffable mystical experience to book, from symptomatic flesh to written word? Both Bynum and Hollywood write as historians, and it is tempting to account for Angela's experience, and the production of her book, through purely empirical means. Because we simply do not have direct access to her experience of God, we must rely on her book for evidence. Her book, however, is heavily mediated by Arnaldo's influence and tells us little directly about her life before their collaboration. Consequently, this approach attributes primary agency to Arnaldo as the author of Angela's book; Angela herself only appears as one of the "saints" admired for her miraculous experience, rather than as a writer of theology in her own right. Alternatively, psychoanalytic categories such as hysteria have been used to describe Angela's experience.[34] Certainly, her physical behavior frequently resembled hysterical symptoms (such as bodily contortions, aphasia, and her inability to eat) which receded as she began to speak to her confessor. This approach places Arnaldo in the role of analyst who cures his patient by listening to her words. But psychoanalytic categories have been widely criticized as both ahistorical and reductive when applied to the complexities of medieval religion. Although these theoretical categories, whether psychoanalytic or historical, may help to highlight different facets of Angela's experience, they simply do not exhaust the meaning of Angela's extraordinary transformation. Because they do not view Angela as a writing subject, they cannot account for her entry into a collaborative writing practice or the authorial control she asserts in cowriting her book.

Angela understood her own experience in theological terms, and consequently a distinctive theological lens is needed for the contemporary interpreter as well. A theological view of Angela's transformation has the advantage of using categories that Angela would understand, and so it arises organically from her own writings. A theological lens takes the body seriously—so important for both the historical and the psychoanalytic approaches—by relating Angela's bodily experience directly to her experience of the body of Christ. A theological lens has the additional advantage of not being reductive: instead of explaining away Angela's strange bodily feats and utterances as either symptomatic or as Arnaldo's construction, a theological lens deepens their mystery.

Angela's intense interest in the body of Christ is a clue to the transformative journey her own life takes. Using a theological lens, we can understand Angela's transformation into a writer as a response to her experience of the incarnation of Christ. The incarnation, in the words of the Fourth Gospel, is the movement by which the divine Word becomes flesh and dwells among us in the person of Jesus Christ, who is both divine and human. This movement has been traditionally understood as both unique and hierarchical: in a top-down movement, the second person of the Trinity descends and becomes human for the sake of human salvation.[35] Human flesh, taken from Jesus' mother Mary, is passive and receptive to the action of the divine Word. Angela's experience, however, points to a much more expansive understanding of the incarnation, which sheds new light on her entry into the written Christian tradition. Her transition from disruptive body to writer/theologian can best be understood through this broadened theological lens of the incarnation, at the intersection of word and flesh.

WRITING THE BODY OF CHRIST

Angela's *Instructions* include theological reflections on the incarnation that take this doctrine in radically new directions. In her letter to her followers known as "Angela's Testament," she offers her view of the incarnation as the "highest mystery" of God—one of her "divine secrets" shared with Arnaldo and, through him, with her readers and disciples. Her letter of instruction takes the form of a prayer:

> O incomprehensible love! There is indeed no greater love than the one by which *my God became flesh in order that he might make me God.* O heartfelt love poured out for me! You gave of yourself in order to make me when you assumed our form; You did not let go of anything in yourself in any way that would lessen you or your divinity, but *the abyss of your conception makes me say these visceral words*: O incomprehensible one, made comprehensible! O uncreated one, made creature! O inconceivable one, made conceivable! O impalpable one, become palpable![36]

For Angela, the incarnation had personal significance: God's enfleshment enabled her own divinization.[37] God became flesh so that Angela might become God. Perhaps even more startling, God's incarnation had a direct effect on her speech: "the abyss of your conception makes me say these visceral words." Angela poured out her own flesh into words in response to the mystery of God's Word made flesh.

The centrality of the incarnation to Angela's self-understanding is reiterated in Angela's final *Instruction*. On her deathbed, she shared the vision she had been granted of heaven's preparation for her death. In the vision, her soul was washed in the blood of Christ and clothed in colorful royal garments. Christ, her divine spouse, compared her to a bride hastening to her wedding. And then she saw "the Word":

> Then God showed me the Word, so that now I would understand what is meant by the Word and what it is to speak the Word. And he said to me: "This is the Word who wished to incarnate himself for you." At that very moment the Word came to me and went all through me, touched all of me, and embraced me.[38]

In this passage, the Word takes flesh in Angela's own dying body. The focus of Angela's spirituality on Christ reached its consummation on her death/bridal bed. For Angela, "to speak the Word" meant not only to preach or teach. When touched and embraced by the divine Word, her own flesh was transformed. This transformation issued in the words shared with her disciples.[39] Much more dramatically than preaching or teaching, for Angela to speak the Word is to incarnate the Word: in her own body and in her book.

These two teachings at the end of her life indicate the significance of the incarnation to Angela's spirituality and self-understanding. For Angela, the incarnation is not a unique event but an ongoing encounter on a two-way street. God's Word became flesh so that her flesh might become divine word(s). Those words pour out in conversation with Arnaldo, in her teachings to her disciples, and take flesh once again in the book disseminated under her name and God's signature. Christ's incarnation was the theological lens through which she understood her own spiritual experience, and, consequently, it is the lens through which we might best understand her transition from disruptive female body to authoritative woman writer.

When Brother Arnaldo first encountered Angela in Assisi, she was shouting incomprehensibly and, to his horror, making a scene. Angela's screaming fit led directly to Brother Arnaldo's desire to know, and then write, about her experience. As their discussions progressed, however, Angela claimed coauthorship of her book (along with Arnaldo and God) and eventually became the teacher and spiritual mother of Franciscan disciples. Whereas at the beginning of her relationship with Arnaldo Angela was viewed as a female bodily disturbance to the church, by the end of her life Angela had written her body into speech, her flesh become words. The union of word and flesh in the body of Christ provided justification for Angela's own writing and teaching authority. This understanding of the incarnation gave her the words to speak and the impetus to translate her experience of God into the written word. It also provides a theological paradigm for the contemporary interpreter. Because Angela's experience was so deeply incarnational, it can be best understood in incarnational language. The encounter between word and flesh enabled Angela to write the body of Christ in her own flesh and words.

CONCLUSION

In Angela's memorable visit to the cathedral in Assisi, her body was the object of male suspicion. The encounter with Arnaldo, however, led to the writing of her book and her entry into the written Christian tradition. Hélène Cixous had a strikingly similar experience while visiting a cathedral, not this time as a pilgrim, but rather as a tourist:

> One summer I get thrown out of the cathedral of Cologne. It's true that I had bare arms; or was it a bare head? A priest kicks me out. Naked. I felt naked for being Jewish, Jewish for being naked, naked for being a woman, Jewish for being flesh and joyful!

Like Angela, her body became the object of male suspicion. Unlike Angela, however, Cixous' identity marks her as doubly if not triply "other" to Christian orthodoxy. She is Jewish and woman and flesh, thrown out for violating the male Christian space of the cathedral. She responds by rejecting the institutional church while, perhaps surprisingly, embracing its written tradition. "So I'll take all your books," she writes. "But the cathedrals I'll leave behind. Their stone is sad and male. The texts I ate, sucked, suckled, kissed. I am the innumerable child of their masses."[40]

No one can prevent Cixous from reading books the way one might banish her from a building. Writing has "innumerable children"—well beyond the initial or perhaps intended audience. Every text written is a product of the texts that came before, their "masses" and their "incarnations." Angela's *Book* is no different; it draws on earlier genres of spiritual itineraries and epistles; it contains a multiplicity of voices (Angela, Arnaldo, and God) that collaborate in its production;[41] and it generates further texts and interpretations by those who read it, including this one.[42] Just as Angela saw the incarnation take place in and through multiple bodies, her text registers multiple voices. These voices speak of those who came before and to those who come after; together they weave the written Christian tradition.

In a Christian theological perspective, writing is both an expression of and a response to the incarnation of God in Christ. When a woman

enters the theological tradition of writing, she brings her bodily difference with her, just as Angela and Cixous brought their bodily differences
with them into the space of the cathedral. While the traditional reaction
has been to exclude these bodies and voices from the theological canon
as heretical, or to subordinate them as "spirituality" rather than the more
serious and authoritative "theology," a more hospitable response wel-
comes such differences. These differences reveal the diversity already
present within the written theological tradition. They further indicate the
diversity within the church as the body of Christ. In Angela's expansive
and inclusive view, this diversity extends all the way to the incarnation.
Because the Word became flesh, all flesh has the potential to become
divine and to issue forth in words, spoken and written. The innumerable
plurality of these incarnate words paved the way for Angela's own writing and for those who follow her.

SPEAKING FUNK
Womanist Insights into the Lives of Syncletica and Macrina

Kendra G. Hotz

Now it is told of Abba Sisoes that when he had grown old "his disciple said to him, 'Father, you are growing old. Let us now go back nearer to inhabited country.' The old man said to him, 'Let us go where there are no women.' His disciple said to him, 'Where is there a place where there are no women except the desert?' So the old man said, 'Take me to the desert.'"[1] Abba Sisoes was one of the hordes of Christians who, beginning in the early fourth century, began to move out into the deserts of Egypt, Syria, and Palestine to seek lives of simplicity and poverty. He had likely spent a long life as a monk, an ascetic, who struggled to overcome his "passions," those distortions of reason that constantly distracted sinful humanity from complete devotion to God. He had disciplined his body with fasting and other renunciations in order to refine his soul so that he might live a life of virtue and grow into the purified image of God through Christ. Now at the end of his life he planned to escape to the desert where he could devote himself completely to contemplation and prayer. In the desert he would not be distracted by younger disciples constantly seeking counsel. In the desert he would not be tempted by a passing glance at a beautiful woman. The desert afforded protection from such temptations.

Those who took up the ascetic life gave up everything they owned and devoted themselves to works of charity and to the disciplines of constant prayer and contemplation. They trained for purity and virtue as athletes train for competition. They left behind friends and families, abandoning all desire for social acceptance, and deliberately took on roles that placed them both geographically and spiritually on the fringes of society and civilization. In a world in which social security depended on familial relationships, they renounced the very marriage and sexual activity that could assure such security. In an age plagued by fear of famine, they lived in the places least likely to provide them with the food they needed and conquered their hunger through long fasts. In an age that feared civilization would be lost to invading barbarians as an empire came unraveled, they chose lives in the wild, untamed places beyond the reach of civilization. And in spite of all of this, they captured the imaginations of Christians of late antiquity and became the model for Christian life in that era. So many sought the solitude that Abba Sisoes yearned for that they "made the desert a city."[2]

Abba Sisoes would have been most distressed, however, to learn that the desert was filled with women who had devoted themselves to the ascetic disciplines, who mentored disciples, and who wrestled with passions of their own. Male ascetics often found themselves frustrated by the presence of women in the desert. Amma Sarah once received as visitors "two old men," abbas of the desert. It is told that "when they arrived one said to the other, 'Let us humiliate this old woman.' So they said to her, 'Be careful not to become conceited thinking to your-self: "Look how anchorites are coming to see me, a mere woman."' But Amma Sarah said to them, 'According to nature I am a woman, but not according to my thoughts.' She also said to the brothers, 'It is I who am a man, you who are women.'"[3] Amma Sarah met the frustrations of male ascetics with plucky resolve, but also with an unsettling self-loathing. She made herself acceptable by denying her sex and seeking to conform herself to an assumed male norm for redeemed humanity. Ascetic training aimed to renew and restore the image of God to sinful and corruptible humanity, and Amma Sarah affirmed emphatically that she bore the image of God—a decidedly male image.

Womanist Theology: Making Sense of Sarah
and Finding Alternatives

Womanist theology emerged in the twentieth century among African-American women who experienced marginalization in multiple ways. They had been excluded from the public construction of theology and from the centers of social power not simply because of their race or gender or class, but even more so because of the ways that these three dimensions of their identities worked together to render them virtually invisible within the dominant culture.[4] Central to the project of womanism, therefore, is the goal of providing theological resources for interpreting marginalization and strategies for building alternative communities in which black women of all social classes may thrive. The project of womanism, therefore, may help us to interpret the marginalization of fourth-century women and to analyze the strategies they employed for building alternative communities.

Womanists employ methods that have profound implications for how theology is done, as well as for its substantive claims. Womanists, for instance, often draw on the narratives of black women's lives, searching them for signs of the theological commitments embedded in their everyday practices.[5] This method results in theology that values the ordinary. Because marginalized women rarely wrote, womanists have learned to draw on the resources of a rich oral culture. Such a method results in theology that is, at its core, modeled on the informal give-and-take of conversation.[6] Womanists have likened this method to "audiation" in jazz, the skill that allows jazz musicians to play off of one another, to improvise.[7] Theological audiation results in a theology that seeks conversation partners, theology with what Delores Williams has called a "dialogical intent."[8]

In this essay, I propose that the insights of womanism may help us to understand Amma Sarah's response to her visitors and her easy assumption that men represent the norm for human life. In both its method and substance, womanism offers a profound critique of that response and an alternative vision of salvation that may shed light on the experiences of other fourth-century women ascetics. Womanism's attention to the multiple, interlocking dimensions of marginalization, its special emphasis upon the importance of social class, its methodological preference for drawing on narratives of women's lives, the high value it places on the ordinary, its incorporation of oral traditions as a source for theology, and its "dialogical intent" make it especially well suited to offer insights into the lives of women ascetics in late antiquity.

In addition to drawing on womanist methods, this essay draws insights from the content of womanist theology, especially its analysis of black women's responses to a culture that insists on their inherent unworthiness. Delores Williams explains that womanist theology draws on the theological resources implicit in black women's experiences, specifically the tendency to internalize a sense of unworthiness as black women and to accept the defilement of their own bodies.[9] A culture that elevates male over female and white over black imposes a double burden on black women, and when those women accept their role in a socially constructed hierarchy as natural, they succumb to sin in its most destructive form. Using the language of Toni Morrison's novels, Dwight N. Hopkins describes the dynamic of naturalizing the denigration of black womanhood as the triumph of the *Thing*. "The Thing," he explains, "is a demonic, sterile, life-denying spirituality. . . . It is a political attack, in the sense that it subverts black women's power to control the space they occupy on earth, and it is a cultural attack in the sense that it negatively defines the identity of African American women."[10]

The Thing attempts to thwart black women's ability to define themselves and to live in God's liberating spirit by reducing them to objects for the use and pleasure of those at the center of the dominant, white culture. But black women find within their own experience resources to resist the Thing and the sense of unworthiness it seeks to create in them. Williams argues that salvation for black women of the nineteenth century brought "liberation from 'unworthiness' . . . to a state of 'somebodiness,' which they felt was granted by their encounter with the sacred in their visions."[11] Becoming a somebody—a person defined by belonging to God, a body worthy of respect and delight—empowered black women to claim religious authority for themselves. They required no permission from ecclesiastical authorities to speak and embody the truth revealed to them in sacred visions.

Somebodiness denaturalizes unworthiness; it resists the Thing's constant whispering to black women that they are by nature inferior and unworthy. Again following Morrison, Hopkins names this refusal to internalize objectification the *Funk*. Funk empowers black women to live in God's liberating spirit, to resist the powers that would define them instrumentally, and to reject the defilement of their own bodies.

> The Funk undermines the Thing culturally and politically. God's spirit of liberation gives women the power to know themselves and be connected to themselves culturally. The ability to know who they are and thus define themselves aids these women in the transformation of the conditions in which they find themselves politically. The ability to determine and alter the space and conditions around them, in turn, provides these women more freedom further to define themselves. In brief, freedom to be themselves (a cultural act of spiritual liberation) stands in a vibrant relationship with freedom to determine their space (a political act of spiritual liberation).[12]

To experience liberation, to live with Funk, is to define oneself, to experience oneself as a somebody. The power of somebodiness flows from the vision of God, but it flows through connectedness to a particular culture and community. Hopkins argues that the spirituality of Funk is rooted in the value of connectedness—connectedness to self, to a particular community, to the broader community, and to nature.

Amma Sarah's response to her visitors clearly demonstrates her acceptance of her own unworthiness as a woman. She thwarted their attempt to humiliate her only by denying her own womanhood and hurled the label "woman" at her visitors as though it were an insult. She disconnected from herself as a woman, accepted a cultural definition of woman as inferior, and managed to thrive only by conforming herself, at least "in thought," to the norms of the dominant culture.[13] What features of late antique culture and religion contributed to the triumph of the Thing in the lives of fourth-century ascetic women? What resources were available for those who had had "an encounter with the sacred in their visions" that affirmed their somebodiness? Were there women of Funk among these ascetics?

Christianity offered women a life option that had not previously been available to them. The celibate life of Christian asceticism offered women a religious vocation that freed them from the obligation to marry and procreate. It gave them space to define their identities apart from their biological capacity to reproduce. But, as we shall see, Christian asceticism offered women that space within certain carefully circumscribed limits. The stories of two women—Syncletica, an amma in the Egyptian desert, and Macrina, the founder of an ascetic community in Asia Minor—can help us to understand how the forces of the Thing affected ascetic women of the fourth century, but also how their Funk, insistent somebodiness, and connectedness to themselves and to their communities forged a place for women to define themselves in diverse ways and to shape their own place in the world of Christian late antiquity. These women spoke, and in speaking gathered around themselves remarkable communities. They did not write, did not fix their theology in a permanent medium, and so what we know of them we know from men who heard their speech and wrote their lives. This dynamic of speaking and having-been-written opens for us intriguing questions about the differing characteristics of conversational and literary theology. Remembering the lives of these two remarkable women—filtered as they are through the memories of the male theologians who recorded them—sheds light on the pervasive and destructive Thinginess of male normativity and on the extraordinary perseverance and redemptive possibilities of women's Funk.

Before recounting their stories, though, it is useful to note two interlocking cultural forces that presented challenges to fourth-century women choosing an ascetic life and obstacles to their experiencing somebodiness: the role that social rank played in restricting choice and the nature of men's legal guardianship over women.[14] First, although the ascetics deliberately stepped outside the bounds of civilized society, for women at least, the capacity to make that choice seems to have depended upon having first received high social status. In a number of essays on Christian women's asceticism in late antiquity, Elizabeth A.

Clark points out the important role that social status played in determining the shape of and possibilities for Christian women's lives.[15] "The women about whom *vitae* are composed," she explains, "are not those who illustrate the social mobility or 'achieved status' of [Peter] Brown's 'holy men'; their status rather derives from their vast inherited wealth and social position, whose prestige they carry into monastic life."[16] These women were born into noble families with vast wealth and land holdings. Their decisions to take up an ascetic life and to use their inherited wealth to support ascetic communities and the work of the church did not nullify the social distinctions between themselves as nobility and those lower on the social scale. To a large degree it was precisely their social status that ensured their ability to live as they chose.

But their capacity to live as they chose depended not only on their inherited status but also on their familial and marital status, on their ability to gain independence from male legal guardianship. Gillian Clark, in a helpful study of legal codes pertinent to the women of late antiquity, explains that "a woman remained in the *potestas* [legal guardianship] of her father, not of her husband, when she married, and became legally independent on her father's death."[17] A Christian woman under her father's *potestas* would not be free simply to choose an ascetic life; she would need his consent not to marry. Only a woman who was both legally independent (i.e., no longer under her father's or guardian's *potestas*) and free from marital obligations would be free to enter the ascetic life, unless she could convince her husband to join her in that life or her father to consent to it. One notable woman, Olympias, for example, became a widow after less than two years of marriage and refused remarriage, even to a relative of the emperor. This pattern holds for Syncletica and Macrina. The most influential Christian women ascetics, then, were those who were born into noble families[18] and who managed to gain financial independence either by managing never to marry or through refusing remarriage after a spouse's death. Christian asceticism offered women a new life option, in other words, but it did so without diverging from the limitations of its cultural context.

Syncletica's Somebodiness: "Let Us Now Rule Over Those Who Once Ruled Over Us"

Syncletica's parents moved from Macedonia to Alexandria when she was young. Prompted by their devotion to the church and by their appreciation of the desert ascetics, they sought to live in closer proximity to the Egyptian desert and to the great church of Alexandria that enjoyed such a close relationship with the desert abbas and ammas. Syncletica had two brothers and one sister. One of her brothers died in childhood and the other at the age of twenty-five, just before his wedding. Since her sister was blind, Syncletica represented her wealthy family's only hope of continuing the family line. She was, moreover, very beautiful. Such a wealthy, beautiful young woman would be highly sought after by families hoping to consolidate their own wealth and power by having their sons marry her and by families hoping to move up the social ladder by marrying into a wealthy family with no male heir of its own. But Syncletica showed no interest in marriage and secretly followed ascetic practices by denying herself food for days at a time. She avoided encounters with men and prayed constantly to be delivered from her passions. When her parents died, Syncletica seized the opportunity to pursue the ascetic life. She gave away all of her wealth, cut her hair, and took her blind sister with her into the desert where she became a great amma and gathered around her a large group of disciples.

Syncletica fits the pattern for female asceticism noted by Elizabeth Clark and Gillian Clark: she hailed from a wealthy family and carried the authority of that wealth and social status into the desert with her even after she distributed her family's treasure to the poor; she also achieved liberation from the *potestas* of a male by delaying marriage during her father's lifetime. At his death she achieved the independence necessary to allow her to pursue her ascetic calling. Following Caroline Walker Bynum, Grace Jantzen argues that pursing ascetic disciplines within the father's household, especially fasting, could effectively render a woman unmarriageable by compromising her beauty and her ability to bear children.[19] Syncletica refused to allow herself to be defined by her relationship to a husband, by the wealth of her family, or even by her own beauty. Instead, she steadfastly defined her own identity and cultural space, and in doing so claimed and celebrated her own somebodiness.

Much of what we know of Syncletica concerns her teachings. She spoke, and others wrote. Her hagiographer reports the general contours of her life and her practices, but by far the majority of the written words of the hagiography are reports of Syncletica's spoken words. Eighty-two of the one hundred three chapters of her hagiography are devoted to her words. We also have a substantial collection of Syncletica's teachings included in the ironically named collection *The Sayings of the Desert Fathers.* Her teachings focused on humility and on the variety of ways in which God works in individual lives. These themes were commonplace among her male peers, the desert fathers. But she spoke much more than the abbas did about recognizing the difficult path that so-called "secular" Christian women trod because of the "great hostility in the world" toward women[20] and often drew on images of women at work washing clothing, cleaning a home, or giving birth. She drew directly on the life experiences most likely to be invisible to her male peers and to be dismissed as insignificant precisely because they come from the domestic realm of women's work. These images also frequently pointed to work relegated to household servants, thereby elevating that work, drawing it out into the visible realm of public discourse.

For instance, Syncletica frequently reminded her disciples not to assume that God would work in the same way in every life. God knows our hearts and accommodates divine grace to our differing gifts and various flaws. To demonstrate this theme, typical among ascetics, she used imagery familiar to and drawn from the experiences of women in a household. She compared human souls to different kinds of cloth that need to be washed in different ways. Some cloth is more delicate and would tear from vigorous wringing. Other cloth is coarse and will come clean in no other way. The disciplines the ascetics adopt must be tailored to the needs of the soul. There can be no one-size-fits-all asceticism.[21] "Just as one diet is not suitable for all animals," she explained, "so the same instruction is not appropriate for all people."[22]

Syncletica also emphasized that deification, being made like God, was a slow process that progressed over the course of a lifetime. Ascetic disciplines refine the soul only with long practice and constant repetition. God chisels away the rough edges of our souls, she taught, and bestows on us the image of Christ even as a sculptor slowly chips away stone to reveal the form below it.[23] She reinforced this theme, drawing again on domestic imagery familiar to her women disciples, when she compared the maintenance of the soul to the need for constant housework to keep a home clean.[24] Yet she assured her disciples that the long years of ascetic discipline and deprivation were akin to the long months of gestation during which a fetus lacks light and "solid nourishment." The long months of gestation bring us into the light and feasting of human life; just so, the long years of discipline birth the ascetic into the light and delight of the heavenly banquet. This life with its struggles and temptations serves as a "second maternal womb" in which we are safely enclosed until we pass through the trauma of new birth into the reign of God.[25]

The Thing incessantly whispers to women their unworthiness as they are relegated to the realm of the private and the insignificant. It insinuates a niggling sense of their inferiority when their work is made invisible and their voices silenced. Syncletica resisted the Thing and affirmed the Funk and somebodiness of the very bodies who wash the clothing, clean the home, and birth the children as she spoke what had been silenced and showed what had been invisible. Weaving this common work into a parable, she elevated the mundane and connected it to the sacred, making simple work and the rhythms of life an ascetic discipline of their own.

Syncletica specifically addressed the insults women bear: "You hear yourselves called mindless and stupid, poor and a beggar, weak and worthless, ineffectual in what you do and irrational in what you say, contemptible in appearance, weak in power. These insults are the sinews of humility."[26] Her advice may seem to reinforce a self-negating temptation: such insults may debase a woman so that she learns humility. But the desert ascetics did not think of humility as humiliation. It was not solely about bringing the mighty low. Instead, humility indicated a right knowing of one's place, a right estimation of one's worth; neither a prideful self-assertion nor a groveling self-negation was the

mark of true humility.[27] The insults may remind a woman not to imagine herself a god and thereby teach humility, but if those insults were
believed—if they cultivated a sense of unworthiness—then they subverted true humility. Hence, Syncletica also taught that women could
reject and overcome these insults through virtue: "But since we women
have grown wings like eagles, let us soar to the higher places, and let
us trample underfoot the lion and the dragon; and let us now rule over
those who once ruled over us."[28] Although she spoke of ruling over the
passions that distort reason when it succumbs to sin, the men who heard
her teachings might be forgiven if they thought she intended women to
throw off the rule of men.

Until her eightieth year, Amma Syncletica continued to pursue ascetic disciples of the body and to teach the large community of
women that had gathered around her. Her hagiographer reported that
she achieved stability in her soul through bodily practices, and this link
between body and soul fits with a fourth-century theology about the
nature of God. Athanasius had taught that being the image of God meant
that humankind existed as an embodied and finite replication of God's
infinite qualities. God's infinite love and justice, for example, appear
in human life in their finite forms. Because humanity is the embodied
image of God, we experience sin as a corruption of God's perfection
in both our bodies and our souls; the path to redemption, therefore,
must include both the body and the soul. Fasting helps the ascetic to
anticipate the resurrection and to overcome the ever-changing demands
of the body, just as prayer trains the soul to fix its desires on the never-
changing God. God's perfect immutability, the reality that God remains
faithful from age to age, appears in redeemed human life as individuals
acquire a stable center of personality. As Syncletica grew in deification,
her soul gave up the flux and fecklessness typical of human life and
increasingly displayed stability and purposefulness.[29]

But even the greatest ascetics suffer bodily death, and so eventually
Syncletica succumbed to illness. Beginning in her eightieth year she
was subjected to the tortuous pain of a serious illness that lasted for
three and a half years. Her hagiographer, who painstakingly recorded
so many of her words, describes how she lost her words. "The Hater

of God . . . afflicted her organs of speech to cut off her spoken word, thinking in this way to make the women gathered around her go hungry for her inspired words."[30] She lost her ability to speak; her mouth began to rot; and she breathed out a stench that overwhelmed all who tried to minister to her. In her speaking, she gathered a community. By her silence, the devil hoped to destroy that community. But the devil miscalculated: "on seeing a woman, he was contemptuous, for he failed to recognize her manly will."[31] She bore this illness as she had borne her life, with steadfast faith, so that her speechlessness became a teaching for her disciples even when her speech was no longer available to them. She experienced visions on her deathbed and was at last carried off mercifully by the angel of death and into the presence of God.

Syncletica worked within the culturally defined space of her time: she chose an ascetic life that had been defined already by others, and it appears that she was able to make that choice only through a received social status derived from her family's wealth. But within the confines of that culturally defined space, in the midst of powerful forces of the Thing, Syncletica refused stencil-drawn social roles for women, rejected the subordination of women, and subverted the devaluation of women's work. The Thing tried to shape the writing of Syncletica's story as her hagiographer asserted that her strength rested in her "manly will." But when her speaking voice can be heard through the written din of the Thing's androcentrism, we find a distinctively womanly will animating Syncletica's teaching. Teaching through images drawn from the world of women, she built a community of Somebodies in which women could teach and learn, speak and be heard, connect with other women and with the great traditions of their faith, and begin to define their own identities and cultural space.

Macrina's Funk: "Determined to Remain by Herself"

Toward the middle of the fourth century an extraordinary family resided in Asia Minor. A wealthy family with vast land holdings, it produced two of the three famous "Cappadocian Fathers," the very ones who were so instrumental in developing the orthodox formulation of the doctrine of the Trinity. But Basil and Gregory of Nyssa were not the only members of this remarkable family important for Christian history. Their eldest sister Macrina, whom they called "father, mother, and teacher,"[32] made a lasting contribution to Christian theology and spirituality as she transformed her household into an ascetic community.

Gregory, who wrote her hagiography, hesitated to call his sister a woman because, as he explained, "I do not know if it is appropriate to apply a name drawn from nature to one who has risen above nature."[33] Throughout the biography Gregory consistently portrayed Macrina as a woman who rose above her feminine nature and who conformed more and more to humanity's created constitution, which, in his view, is not sexually differentiated. Gregory argued that God originally created the full plenitude of humanity "as it were in one body,"[34] but that body was not physical and, therefore, was neither male nor female. God intended for humanity to become a well-ordered many, a society of equals living together in perfect and permanent cooperation. In this way humankind would communally bear the image of the triune God.

The unity of the Trinity, for Gregory, rests precisely in the eternal perfect cooperation of the three persons.[35] Though humanity, confined by the limits of finitude, can never achieve the perfect unity of the divine life, it approximates that life when lived in communities of harmony, peace, and hospitality. Gregory thought that individual, embodied life was a secondary act of creation, one which God undertook knowing that humankind would sin, and that such sin would prevent the purely spiritual original human creation from procreating and becoming many.[36] God therefore created human bodies, before sin entered the world, so that when it did, human beings would have a ready means for becoming many and a vehicle for redemption; for God works to refine the soul through the body, and this is why ascetic disciplines are so effective.[37]

The path toward deification renewed in humanity the image of God, a communal and sexless image. Although redeemed humanity remained embodied, Gregory expected that through ascetic disciplines human beings could achieve an approximation of that original, sexless state. As one progresses in virtue, one becomes more human, more the image of God, and less male or female. Gregory presented Macrina as a woman whose progress in asceticism brought her to conform perfectly to his own theory that humanity existed as the image of God prior to the emergence of sexually differentiated individuals. Macrina did not become male as she put off her "womanish ways"; rather, she came to resemble God who is neither male nor female.

The remarkable correspondence of Macrina's character with Gregory's theological anthropology reminds us that hagiography never aims to offer the fullest or most accurate representation of its subject. It aims to enlighten and encourage its readers and to sway them to the author's view of virtue. Compounding the problems inherent in hagiography as a genre is the fact that Macrina's vita is constructed by a man. It is difficult, nearly impossible, to get behind Gregory's construal of "woman" to find the Macrina of history, because he never intended to tell us who she "really was." In *The Life of Macrina*, and most likely in *The Life of Syncletica*, we find men writing women, men constructing and defining womankind in general through a particular woman. The text itself, insofar as it intends to define women, is an ally of the Thing. This is not to say that Gregory intended to oppress women, or that he self-consciously found Macrina, by nature of her sex, inferior in any way, but only to note that he participated in a patriarchal culture that believed the hierarchy of male over female was part of a God-intended natural order. That culture shapes its every participant and leaves its marks on their artifacts.

If the text is a construction and expression of the Thing, though, it also opens opportunities for Funk to subvert it. Gregory's obvious admiration for his sister, her clear influence on him, and the very fact of her existence as an influential woman in the midst of a patriarchal culture point to places where Funk shines through the fissures in the Thing's apparently seamless hold on the fourth-century world. We need not assume, for example, that Gregory simply saw his sister through the lens of his already fully formed theological anthropology. It is possible also that his encounter with a woman who did not fit neatly into the predefined social roles available to her led him to question the easy essentialism of his day that insisted that sex determined gender roles absolutely. Macrina assumed a leadership role as teacher, counselor, and parent that defied simple gender categorization. Perhaps this offered

Gregory a vision of redeemed life that freed persons to live into their vocations regardless of their sex.

Macrina's earliest childhood pointed forward toward her extraordinary life. During labor, her mother received a vision telling her the child would be called Thecla, the name of the Apostle Paul's legendary companion who represented the ascetic ideal to which Christian men and women had long aspired. Macrina's family was not only wealthy and influential, but also had a long history of commitment to the Christian faith. She was educated in Christian literature only and even as a young child recited psalms throughout the day. When she was twelve, the man to whom she had long been betrothed died suddenly. Macrina responded by declaring herself to be a widow, "as if," Gregory explained, "what had been decided upon had in fact really happened." Macrina therefore decided "to remain by herself."[38] Her father died soon after. Already by the age of twelve, Macrina was established in a role, that of the widow, that would afford her the freedom necessary to become religiously influential: she belonged to a wealthy, noble family, was free from marital obligations, and, because of her father's death, could become financially independent when she reached the age of majority. By declaring herself a widow, Macrina constructed a socially acceptable station for herself as an unmarried woman. She deftly twisted a predefined role to her own purposes and thereby gained a measure of self-definition and somebodiness. By arranging to "remain by herself," Macrina found her Funk.

In a pattern that would later become typical for women choosing an ascetic life, Macrina remained in her family home and carried out her ascetic practices there. Eventually having a daughter who became a consecrated virgin would be considered a great honor, and priests would direct homilies to the fathers of these virgins, exhorting them to watch over them and protect them at all times; for an entire household might be saved through the presence of one such virgin.[39] But Macrina stood at the beginning of that tradition, and rather than receive a role and definition as a consecrated virgin, she constructed that identity for herself. Rather than making a dramatic change, such as moving out into the wilderness, Macrina slowly transformed her daily life through ascetic practices, and eventually transformed her entire household into an ascetic community.[40] She humbled herself in all things and began to take on the tasks of a household servant, even going so far as to prepare bread for her mother by her own hand, work ordinarily reserved for slaves. After the death of her father, Macrina assisted her mother in managing the family's financial affairs—with such success that when her mother Emmelia distributed inheritances to the children, the estate had increased ninefold. Macrina slowly but surely became the leader of the household.

Gregory noted how remarkably unshaken Macrina remained through all of the great changes—the tragedies and triumphs—that mark a life. "Placing reason in opposition to passion," she guided her mother through her grief not only after her father's death, but also following the tragic death of her brother Naucratius, who had been killed in a hunting accident while he was gathering food for the ascetics who lived in the woods near the family estate. Throughout all of this, Macrina did not sob or "suffer in any womanish way," but instead "rose above nature and by means of her own reasoned reflections . . . lifted her mother up together with her."[41] Gregory described Macrina's impassivity as a sign that his sister had defeated the passions that threaten to overpower reason and draw the soul away from God, but even his admiration for Macrina was expressed in terms of the stereotyped gender expectations of his culture.

Eventually Macrina's influence in the family became pervasive as the entire household moved to an estate in the countryside of Annesi, which was transformed into an ascetic community. Macrina became "father, teacher, guide, mother, counselor in every good" for Peter, the youngest of Emmelia's children.[42] She convinced her brother Basil, who would become "Basil the Great," the Saint Benedict of the East, to strive for ascetic virtues. Gregory, in a moment of honesty only a sibling could achieve, tells how his brother Basil was won over:

> [He] came back from the school where he had been trained for a long time in the discipline of rhetoric. Although when she took him in he was monstrously conceited about his skill in rhetoric, contemptuous of

every high reputation and exalted beyond the leading lights of province by his self-importance, so swiftly did she win him to the ideal of philosophy that he renounced worldly appearance, showed contempt for the admiration of rhetorical ability, and went over of his own accord to this active life of manual labor, preparing himself by means of his complete poverty a way of life which would tend without impediment toward virtue.[43]

Basil went on to write a rule of monastic life that became profoundly influential in the development of Christian asceticism. Here we find the power of Macrina's speech behind the influential writings of her theologian brothers.

After the family fortune had been distributed equally among the siblings, Macrina gave her portion over to the local priest to be used for charitable purposes.[44] She eliminated differences of rank in the household by manumitting slaves, "making them sisters and equals instead of slaves and servants,"[45] and organized the entire household for constant prayer and worship. Macrina's community began to attract other women, both poor and wealthy, to the ascetic life. Her community took in impoverished orphans, the victims of famine, as well as such powerful and wealthy widows as Vetiana and Lampadion. In theory every member of the community entered and humbled herself as a slave. Wealthy women, former slaves, and famine orphans were all treated alike, undertaking the same tasks and striving toward the same goals. Macrina's community, in other words, corresponded precisely to Gregory's vision of human participation in God's triune life. The image of God in humanity, recall, is borne by the community. When people live together in harmony and cooperation, striving toward a common end, they move toward a vision of God's triune life. Just as the three persons of the Trinity live as a society of three equals made utterly one by their perfect, eternal communion and cooperation, so also human life bears the image of God and participates in the life of God when it is lived out in egalitarian societies in which unity is achieved through harmony. Again we see that Gregory's theology finds embodiment in Macrina's life and community, but we need not assume that he simply imposed his theological vision on the telling of her life. Equally likely is that his encounter with her community offered him a vision of goodness and beauty that pointed toward a divine truth.

A structure emerged from Macrina's community that provided Christian women a regular place where they might pursue their religious vocations as women. The pagan world lacked such a structure; there each woman who wanted to make an unconventional choice had to invent a place for herself independently. The emerging structure that offered Christian women an alternate life option to the path of marriage and procreation, however, did not upset conventional understandings of social status in spite of Macrina's expressed desire for an egalitarian community. Susanna Elm has pointed out, for instance, that although differences of rank had ostensibly been eliminated in Macrina's community, noble women seem to have formed a core group of leaders and that both "Macrina and Gregory remained fully conscious of the social distinctions that separate those who are noble from those who are not. Their ascetic aspirations prompted them to negate the practical effects of class distinction, but in no instance the notion of the distinction itself."[46] It is significant, in this regard, that the only women of the community whose names Gregory provided, Vetiana and Lampadion, were both of noble birth.

Gregory returned to the family estate in 380, following a synod in Antioch, to find Macrina ill and nearing the end of her life. They talked together at length, and when the subject turned to Basil, who had died by that time, Macrina lifted Gregory out of his sorrow, delivering a discourse on the soul and the Christian hope for resurrection. She then went on to retell the events of her own life, emphasizing how God had increased the family's wealth because of its great faith. And when Gregory complained to her of how he had been driven into exile by the emperor Valens, she rebuked him, reminding him both of his noble birth and of how his reputation had extended even further than his father's.

These discourses near the end of Macrina's life point to three ways in which social conventions continued to place limitations on her ability to define her own identity and to reshape her cultural space. Here we find places where the Thing is so deeply woven into the fabric of late antique society that to pull on its thread of marginalization would threaten to unravel the entire fabric of a social order that organizes the world according to insiders and outsiders, superiors and inferiors, norms and others. Macrina and Gregory seem unable to do that. The first place in this end-of-life discourse where we see them holding back from a thoroughgoing redefinition of the cultural space comes when Macrina twice reminds Gregory that they are of a noble family, though she identifies that nobility with the "standards of this world."[47] The importance of nobility enabled Gregory and Macrina to pursue their separate vocations, and this did not escape Macrina's notice even though she had relinquished her wealth and assumed the tasks of a servant. Though she may have performed the tasks of a slave, she had by no means relinquished her status as a noble. It was precisely that status that allowed her to found, order, lead, and maintain an ascetic community, even if that community received women of all social classes. The Thing that defines women as inferior also enforces a hierarchy of social status. Macrina and Gregory accepted the cultural perspective of that hierarchy even when they attempted to resist its practical implications.

Second, Macrina rebuked Gregory when he complained of his exile. His status as an influential theologian and bishop, an outspoken advocate of the homoousian position,[48] serves as a sharp reminder of the limitations placed on her own influence. Macrina may have been recognized as a great teacher and leader, but her teaching and leadership were exercised only within her own household community, while her brothers Gregory and Basil had both become public figures with power to shape official church doctrine and to construct the rule that would govern the burgeoning monastic communities. Gregory's very ability to become embroiled in public and political controversy, and to be exiled for his courageous stance against the emperor, pointed to Macrina's own confinement to the relatively private realm of the family estate.[49]

Finally, the purported record of Gregory's conversation with Macrina regarding the soul raises intriguing questions about how clearly we hear her own voice through Gregory's writing. Gregory purportedly recorded that conversation in his dialogue "On the Soul and the Resurrection."[50] His claim that the dialogue conveys Macrina's theological position and indeed her very words is problematic in light of his description of her education. Gregory had praised his mother for choosing a strictly Christian education for Macrina and eschewing pagan learning, but the discourse in question was clearly modeled on Platonic dialogues and is filled with classical allusions. Most scholars have simply assumed that Gregory used Macrina as a character in his own theological treatise, putting his words and ideas into her mouth.

In the introduction to his translation of *The Life of Saint Macrina*, Kevin Corrigan proposes that Macrina's contact with her brothers would have provided her with the informal education necessary to account for her ability to argue the position attributed to her in "On the Soul and Resurrection."[51] Growing up in a noble family, with brothers who received thorough classical educations, Macrina would certainly have been exposed to the ideas and language of Platonic philosophy and classical learning. Platonic dualism provided the operative cosmology of the day, and Macrina could scarcely have been unaware of it. It would be natural for her to map her own developing theology onto these ideas. But of course Gregory did not attempt a verbatim account of his conversation with Macrina, so it also would have been natural for him to express the essence of the conversation using forms and language most familiar to him and most likely to convey her point persuasively to others. To separate the Macrina of history from Gregory's construction of her is, in this case, wholly impossible. But to blithely assume that she simply served as a mouthpiece for Gregory's own lofty ideas is to further the maginalization of fourth-century women.

As Macrina's life drew to a close, Gregory reflected that her final words revealed that "she had transcended the common nature . . . [and] seemed no longer to be a part of human realities." He likened her to an angel who had freed herself from "the life of flesh" and whose "thinking . . . remained impassible, since the flesh did not drag it down to its own passions."[52] The vita concludes with two miraculous healing narratives that confirm Macrina's angelic status. The first narrative recounts how Vetiana and Lampadion assisted Gregory in preparing his sister's body for burial. Vetiana pointed out to Gregory a small scar on Macrina's breast, the only remnant of a tumor that had been healed.[53] Vetiana explained that Macrina had been too modest to seek the help of a physician but had instead wept as she prayed that God would heal her. This is the only instance when Macrina is reported to have wept. Her tears mingled with the dirt to form mud; when she applied this mud to the tumor, she was healed. A second account of miraculous healing was reported to Gregory during his journey back to the family estate following Macrina's funeral. Along the way, he encountered a garrison commander who told him how Macrina had healed his daughter of an eye infection. After he and his wife had visited the community and were telling each other everything that had happened while they were separated—he had gone to the men's quarters, she to the women's—his wife remembered that Macrina had promised to give her an ointment to treat the child's eye. But after a meal, she had left, forgetting the ointment. Just as they were about to turn back to retrieve the forgotten ointment, a nurse noticed that the child had already been healed.

By the time of her death, Macrina, who began with the intention "to remain by herself," had established a community that would become the pattern for women's communal asceticism throughout the East. Christian asceticism had entered a period of concentrated growth and experimentation in the fourth century. Patterns of ascetic life that would later become institutionally structured were still in their formative stages. During this dynamic, unsettled stage, Macrina took remarkable steps to define her own identity and to create a space in which other women could join her in defining their own identities. Later church authorities would curtail the freedom and experimentation of these days. Macrina's community, for instance, seems to have had no official ecclesiastical oversight, and therefore no male authority figure. It included both men and women, and though Peter seems to have had special oversight of the men, Macrina was clearly the acknowledged leader of the entire community. In the decades that followed, monastic rules were written for women's communities that required priestly (that is, male) oversight and that forbade both sexes from living within a single community. Susanna Elm argues that it was a common feature of women's asceticism in Asia Minor and Egypt during this period to construct communities that depended on living within a conventional but modified role.

Macrina followed this pattern by constructing a new role for herself, that of the virgin widow, out of the other roles available to her. In doing so she gained for herself space to be Somebody, space for Funk to resist Thing, space for women to shape and determine their own identities and vocations, space to speak an identity and a theology that would only later be written.

SPEAKING FUNK, WRITING THEOLOGY

The thought patterns of the fourth century were thoroughly androcentric. Pagan and Christian leaders alike assumed that to be human was to be male and that women were somehow derivative and inferior to this male norm. Given the overwhelming power of patriarchy, it is something of a miracle that women created theology at all, that any managed to escape the construction of "woman" in texts and contexts in order to speak their own identities. Some women carved out unconventional roles for themselves by accepting these norms. Amma Sarah certainly seemed to accept it when she declared that her ascetic discipline had made her male. Other women chose to "become male" by disguising themselves as men and living in the desert or even in monasteries as such; their true identities were only discovered at death, when all would exclaim over their discipline and humility. There are many such stories of women living as men and of being praised for overcoming their feminine nature. There are, of course, no hero tales of men who courageously lived as virtuous women and overcame their masculine nature.

All of the stories of women living as men, however, like Sarah's response to her hecklers, rest on an acceptance of the androcentric norm. But Syncletica and Macrina offered a different path, one that carried them away from unworthiness and objectification. By choosing to remain by themselves, by choosing not to be defined through their relationships with men, and by speaking their own identities, both women became more authentically connected to their own womanhood. They managed to rise up and resist the definitions of "woman" available in their time. And, in doing so, both women built communities in which women connected with one another to tell their own stories and author their own lives. They did not give Funk to others; Funk cannot be given, but it can be cultivated in communities where women are invited to share their visions of God.

A womanist analysis of the written lives of Syncletica and Macrina—written lives of women who spoke—raises significant questions about how written texts interact with living, speaking women in communities of faith that defy the acceptable definitions of "woman" available in a given era. What happens to the words of those who are by sex, race, class, or sexual orientation "other" than the dominant culture when those words encounter the mode of expression—writing—endorsed as bearing authority by that culture? Womanism itself often draws on the songs and stories embedded in the oral traditions of African-American communities. What happens to the vitality and orality of those traditions when they become fixed on paper? Womanist theology, even when it is written, often resists the fixedness of dominant theology by expressing itself in terms not traditionally part of the theological lexicon. Funk and Thing, somebodiness and unworthiness: these are not the modes of expression in which questions of sin and salvation have been explored in the dominant, written strands of Christian theology. They are not words that make claims to universal truths. But they are words that make sense of a world from within a particular community.

Perhaps it is significant that Syncletica and Macrina did not write. Perhaps their chosen mode of expression, speech, indicates something about how they imagined theology ought to be done. There are profound implications for theology if the spoken word takes primacy and the written word serves only as a secondary mediation of teaching and learning best encountered face to face, mouth to ear. Speech as primary means that all theological formulations take the form of encounter, that they are always tethered to the particularity of a moment when *this* speaker and *that* listener are engaged with one another in an intimate way. Syncletica and Macrina never offered words for all people in all times; they offered "a word" for members of their community, known to them as sisters who lived and labored together.

Speech as primary means that theology takes the form of a conversation where every claim is provisional and open to reformulation through dialogue. One does not enter Syncletica's or Macrina's community to become a spectator. One comes to listen to a great teacher, but also to find a voice and speak back, to enter the conversation. So too, theology—even written theology—that emerges from speech must express itself in a way that invites response, correction from other perspectives, and reformulation. It is natural in the course of conversations for ideas to emerge and change, for participants to interrupt one another, to challenge and question one another. Theology that acknowledges its roots in speech will celebrate its provisional, communal, and perspectival nature.

The conversational nature of speech as the primary means for making theology also highlights issues of social privilege that can be eclipsed by the technology of the written word. Who is authorized to speak and to teach? In some ways, speech is the great equalizer. Anyone may raise her voice and speak out. Anyone with a "vision of God" may gather a community. In other ways, though, the social contexts in which theological speech is typically generated create expectations about the proper form of speech, which questions matter, and whose voice may be heard. Academic classrooms and conferences, typical spaces for theological speech, are often governed by a sense of propriety that can constrain precisely the free flow of conversation that the primacy of speech ought to encourage. The womanist insistence on the authority of traditions that have been marginalized challenges precisely those social contexts in which theological speech has typically been generated.

A womanist analysis of the lives of Syncletica and Macrina illumines ways in which the forces of dominant culture seek to define and constrict women as theologians, but also the liberating power of speaking and hearing to build communities that embody alternate modes of living faithfully. Syncletica and Macrina lived and taught in ways that questioned and reinterpreted the meaning of "woman" in their time. But their lives were recorded by men with their own theological agendas. In this essay, I have sought to interpret their speaking—and their having-been-written—through the womanist concepts of the *Thing* as the power of the dominant society to define and construct women's identities and the *Funk* as the Spirit-fueled capacity of women to defy such othering. Perhaps hearing their authentic somebodiness invites us to find, speak, and write our own Funk.

6

"A MOOR OF ONE'S OWN"
Writing and Silence in Sara Maitland's *A Book of Silence*

Leigh Pittenger

For fiction, imaginative work that is, is not dropped like a pebble upon the ground . . . fiction is like a spider's web, attached ever so lightly perhaps, but still attached to life at all four corners. . . . When the web is pulled askew, hooked up at the edge, torn in the middle, one remembers that these webs are not spun in midair by incorporeal creatures, but are the work of suffering human beings, and are attached to grossly material things, like health and money and the houses we live in.

— Virginia Woolf, *A Room of One's Own* (1929)

I am sitting on the front doorstep of my little house with a cup of coffee, looking down the valley at my extraordinary view of nothing. It is wonderful. Virginia Woolf famously taught us that every woman writer needs a room of her own. She didn't know the half of it, in my opinion. I need a moor of my own. Or, as an exasperated but obviously sensitive friend commented when she came to see my latest lunacy, "Only you, Sara—twenty-mile views of absolutely nothing!"

— Sara Maitland, *A Book of Silence* (2009)

In her influential 1929 essay *A Room of One's Own*, Virginia Woolf argued that the creative process depends on material conditions. Likening fictional works to spiders' webs, "attached to life at all four corners," she insisted that, in order to write fiction, women needed financial independence and a "room of one's own." She posited that literary history had not yet produced a female Shakespeare because, traditionally, few women had possessed a private space, at least a temporary refuge from social expectations and demands, where a woman might nurture her creative imagination and give birth to her own voice.

Sara Maitland evokes Woolf's ideal of a room of her own in her autobiographical account of her midlife journey into silence, *A Book of Silence*. The narrative opens with Maitland's exuberant description of her view from the solitary house that she built on the Scottish moors. By referencing Woolf, Maitland cues readers that her pursuit of silence is linked with her identity as a writer. Indeed, she even suggests that, in finding a "moor of her own," she has surpassed Woolf's ideal. Maitland paints the "moor of her own" as Woolf's room of her own writ large, suggesting that she has reached the pinnacle of achievement for a woman writer.

Despite the self-satisfied tone of Maitland's opening passage, however, it hints at an underlying tension between her pursuit of silence (specifically a contemplative practice of silence, informed by her reading of Christian mystics) and her identity as a feminist short-story writer and novelist. While Maitland describes her austere, silent life as "wonderful" and fulfilling, she is aware that her friends view it as "lunacy." Not only is her pursuit of extreme silence countercultural, it also contradicts the privileging of speech that many feminist writers since Woolf have taken for granted. As the narrative progresses, the author reveals that she is particularly disturbed by a letter from her friend Janet Batsleer that accuses Maitland of turning her back on the hard-won privilege of speech. Batsleer even couches her argument in theological terms, evoking the Gospel of John: "In the beginning was the *Word*. . . . All silence is waiting to be broken."[1] Maitland rebuts this letter at different points in the narrative; but as a sense of tension between contemplative silence and feminism unfolds, so does a profound tension between silence and *writing*.

Maitland finds that the more deeply she enters into contemplative prayer, the more she loses her capacity for fiction writing. Though she had wanted to become simultaneously Virginia Woolf (whose silence resulted in great fiction) and Catherine of Siena (whose silence led to intense experiences of God), Maitland's experiments with silence lead her to the conclusion that these two models of silence are incompatible. After investigating both models and observing their effects on her writing, she feels that she must choose between them. In the end, she chooses to commit to contemplative silence even though it means abandoning her fiction.

Thus, by the book's end, Maitland's "moor of her own" no longer seems like "a room of one's own" writ large. On my reading, Maitland's "moor of her own" calls into question Woolf's ideal for women writers, suggesting that the value of contemplative silence surpasses that of creative writing, though such silence may well result in a different *kind* of writing. Indeed, while Maitland gives up fiction writing, she does not give up writing altogether. Instead, she embraces a new task as a writer—that of writing silence. As she explains, "I wanted to be both a silence dweller and a writer. I wanted to write silently, somehow to *write silence*. I did not know how it could be done; I did not even know if it could be done. But I very much wanted to try to find out."[2]

In this essay I explore how Maitland's experience of silence affected her both as a theological writer and as a feminist writer. In particular, I interrogate why Maitland's experience of silence leads her to insist on an irreconcilable contradiction between contemplative silence and feminist fiction of the type that she had previously written. For feminist theologians who value women's writing as a rich source of theological reflection, what possibilities and limitations are suggested by Maitland's attempt to *write silence*? What (if anything) does *writing silence* offer that fiction does not? I conclude by suggesting ways in which Maitland's attempt to *write silence* might be fruitfully put in conversation with other feminist thinkers, namely Luce Irigaray and Beverly Lanzetta, who have also recently explored the possibility of retrieving silence to enhance women's experience of the divine.

"I Had It All and It Was Not Enough"

Why did Sara Maitland feel, at age fifty, that she needed to set out on a journey into extreme silence, and what did she hope to find? In the book's opening chapter, Maitland asserts that we all live, increasingly, in "a noisy world," and that Western culture shuns and fears silence. On a more personal level, Maitland indicates that her "love affair" with silence had come as a surprise to her, as she had always led an active, "noisy" life. She had been raised in a large, boisterous family, had received an Oxford education, had participated actively in the feminist and socialist movements of the British seventies, had married an Anglo-Catholic priest, and had raised two children. Moreover, she had achieved professional satisfaction as a writer, having published several short-story collections and novels (including *Daughters of Jerusalem*, winner of the Somerset Maugham Award in 1978) and some works of theological nonfiction (including *A Big-Enough God: A Feminist's Search for a Joyful Theology*).[3] Yet she says that she was looking for something more:

> When things changed and I started not just to be more silent, but also to love silence and want to understand it and hunt it down, both in practice and in theory, I did not feel I was running away from anything. On the contrary, I wanted *more*. I had it all and it was not enough. Silence is additional to, not a rejection of, sociability and friends and periods of deep emotional and professional satisfaction. I have been lucky, or graced; in a deep sense, as I shall describe, I feel that silence sought me out rather than the other way around.[4]

Here, Maitland portrays silence as the icing on the cake of an already fulfilled life.

However, though Maitland stresses that she was not seeking silence as an escape, she does indicate that some important shifts were taking place in her life and her psyche around the time she began her journey into silence. She admits that the shift to Thatcherism in England (and its visible effects in the populations served by her husband's ministry) led her to feel somewhat despairing about society. Meanwhile, she had also become dissatisfied with Anglo-Catholicism and converted to Catholicism. (She does not give much information about this shift, other than to say that Anglo-Catholicism had become more misogynistic, humorless, and joyless.) She had also begun to struggle with her writing; as she puts it, "As a writer I ran out of steam. I lost my simple conviction that stories, narrative itself, could provide a direct way forward in what felt like a cultural impasse."[5] Moreover, her marriage ended in divorce and, shortly afterward, her youngest child left home for college, which left Maitland to live alone for the first time.

While going through the divorce, Maitland moved away from London and bought a house in the tiny village of Warkton, outside Kettering in Northamptonshire, where she discovered, to her own surprise, that she experienced silence not as a lack or an absence, but as a positive presence. Unexpectedly, too, she found herself praying more frequently and more silently, until she reached the point that she wanted a more intense experience of silence than she could obtain in Warkton. She wanted to venture to the furthest extreme—to become, as suggested in a desert hermit story from the fourth century C.E., "wholly a flame."[6]

Maitland set out to spend forty days and forty nights on the Isle of Skye, drawn by a landscape that, as she puts it, "worked in a kind of harmony with my prayers."[7] She went to the Isle of Skye with four conscious purposes. She wanted, first, to develop a better understanding of silence and to prove that it was not necessarily "waiting to be broken"; second, "to deepen [her] growing sense of the reality of God, and the possibility of being connected to that reality"; third, to recover a sense of confidence and purpose in her writing, and to prepare herself for new work; and fourth, to enjoy a kind of honeymoon period with silence, falling ever more deeply in love.[8]

The time spent on the Isle of Skye initiated a journey of several years as Maitland experimented with different types of silence in different settings and read all the literature that she could find about others' experiences. She studied the accounts of adventurers, musicians, psychoanalysts, Buddhist monks, Christian monks, Quakers, and poets. She read the writings of both men and women—though she noted that women's writings on silence are rare and that they are therefore especially interesting. Maitland's own book is not so much a "book of silence," then, as it is a book of silences, as one of her primary observations is that silence is surprisingly multiple. Different types of silence have noticeably different effects on her sense of self and her writing.

SILENCE, FEMINISM, AND WRITING

Having described her experience of silence as a positive presence and not simply a lack, Maitland addresses her friend Janet Batsleer's accusation that she has turned her back on the hard-won privilege of speech. For many feminists like Batsleer, the word "silence" has inescapably negative connotations. Maitland cites Batsleer's letter as follows:

> Silence is the place of death, of nothingness. In fact there is no silence without speech. There is no silence without the act of silencing, some one having been shut up, put bang to rights, gagged, told to hold their tongue, had their tongue cut out, had the cat get their tongue, lost their voice. Silence is oppression and speech, language, spoken or written, is freedom . . . .
>
> [The silence of the oppressed] is a place of non-being, a place of control, from which all our yearning is to escape. All the social movements of oppressed people in the second part of the twentieth century have claimed "coming to language" and "coming to voice" as necessary to their politics . . . In the beginning was the Word. . . . Silence is oppression. It is "the word" that is the beginning of freedom.
>
> All silence is waiting to be broken.

Maitland says respectfully, "She is nearly always right. But this time I was sure along my pulses that she was wrong, and I decided I wanted to prove it."[9] Because Maitland does not seem able to explain to her own satisfaction why Batsleer is wrong (at least not right away), the letter haunts the entire narrative. Even when Maitland does not allude to the letter directly, the narrative sometimes reads as Maitland's attempt to justify her chosen way of life in response to a feminist critique.

Batsleer's letter helps Maitland clarify one point at the outset: that there is an enormous difference between *imposed* silence and *chosen* silence. By no means does she want to suggest that traditionally marginalized groups should feel satisfied with silence imposed on them as

a form of social oppression. Maitland makes clear that when she celebrates the deep satisfaction and joy of a life of silence, she refers to
chosen silence. Furthermore, she observes that she has chosen not just
silence but also a landscape, and that these two choices are inextricably
bound. As Maitland puts it, "My ideas about silence had a landscape
as well as an interior dimension. This is probably merely an aesthetic
choice, but I was free to make that choice, and what called to me was
space, wide wild space . . . . For me the terrain of silence is what I have
since come to call the Huge Nothing of the high moorlands."[10] Though
Maitland states that her choice of landscape is probably merely aesthetic, her description suggests otherwise. The wild and open landscape
of the Scottish moors offers her a sense of liberating expansion and total
freedom.[11] While Batsleer associates freedom with speech, Maitland
increasingly comes to identify freedom with silence. As she describes
her experiments with silence in different landscapes (the Isle of Skye,
the Sinai desert, the hills of Galloway), it becomes clear that different
landscapes profoundly shape her experiences of prayer and writing in
different ways—but all of them offer a sense of freedom.

The Catherine of Siena/Virginia Woolf Conflict

Despite Maitland's emphasis on the *chosen* nature of her silence and
on her sense of landscape-inspired freedom, Batsleer's assertion that
"all silence is meant to be broken" is not easily laid to rest. It lingers
beneath the surface of a conflict that emerges between Maitland's two
most cherished desires—to enter deeply into contemplative prayer and
to renew herself as a fiction writer. As she puts it, she wanted to become
Catherine of Siena and Virginia Woolf simultaneously. At the beginning
of her journey, she expects the silence, the solitude, and the landscape to
make this ideal possible for her, and she expresses a sense of incomprehension when a conflict emerges. She finds that as her practice of silent
prayer intensifies, it erases her ego boundaries and disrupts her sense of
time and narrative, making fiction writing impossible. Maitland writes,

> I could not understand what was happening. When I set out on my
> journey into silence, I had a very well-imbedded assumption. I was a
> writer and a pray-er; through a disciplined practice of silence I would

get better at both. It is a commonplace, almost a cliché, that silence and solitude are good for the creative artist and particularly for writers . . . . So it had seemed perfectly reasonable to me that I could go and lurk up on a high moor, put in the disciplined practice of concentration and meditation, and thus become both a better, more prolific imaginative writer and more safely and intensely engaged in the life of prayer.

To put it at its simplest I was now being proved wrong.[12]

Aware of numerous literary figures who have practiced silence and solitude as a means of enhancing their creative imagination, Maitland puzzles over the diminishment of her capacity for fiction writing. She begins to suspect that prayer and creative writing are rooted in two different types of silence undertaken for contradictory purposes: one, the silence of prayer or mysticism, designed to annihilate the ego in the experience of ineffability; the other, the silence of the writer, designed to shore up the ego so that one feels equipped to invent new and fantastic worlds. Contrasting Woolf's "room of one's own" to Catherine of Siena's "little secret room" or "hermitage of the heart," Maitland observes, "The vocabulary and imagery are markedly similar; the projects are radically opposed. Woolf seeks solitary space in order to escape from the social pressures on women and establish a secure identity and voice; Catherine seeks the same space in order to empty herself of ego and merge her identity with, lose her self in, her God."[13] Although these two practices of silence may initially appear quite similar, Maitland observes that their different effects on a person's sense of selfhood also affect a person's writing. For Maitland, fiction writing depends on a thriving ego, which contemplation undermines.

Unwilling to surrender her identity as both a writer and a person of prayer, Maitland decides to test her hunch that contemplative silence and Romantic silence are incompatible models by embarking on two separate pilgrimages. First she goes to the Sinai desert to intensify her experience of contemplative silence, to recreate the experience of the desert fathers and mothers. Then she goes to the Galloway region of Scotland in pursuit of the "bliss of solitude" described by Wordsworth.[14]

Maitland describes both pilgrimages as positive, joyful experiences — but undeniably different in their effects. The time that she spent in the Sinai desert gave her a "vast, loving and awestruck sense of God," as well as a conviction that God *is* silence.[15] In contrast, the time that she spent in Galloway, taking long, daily walks in the hills, filled her imagination with stories, and she found herself writing prolifically. Although both journeys were pleasurable, Maitland concludes that different combinations of landscape and intention led to different — even opposite — effects on her writing.

Maitland had set out on these pilgrimages seeking an answer to the question, "Is it possible to have both — to be the person who prays, who seeks union with the divine *and* to be the person who writes, and in particular writes prose narratives?"[16] The conclusion that she reaches is that it is not. She feels she must choose between being either Catherine of Siena or Virginia Woolf — characterized by either a permeable self that emerges from the experience of prayer or a boundaried self that is capable of writing fiction. Maitland admits that though she has always loved stories and is grateful to have earned a living by telling them, her experience of contemplative prayer has fundamentally altered her perspective on her propensity toward storytelling. Awed by the vast beauty of silence, Maitland comes to view her narrative impulse as "an intolerable arrogance and even weakness": "It came between me and the true silence of the moment — that rush to narrative seemed little more than chitter-chatter."[17]

Maitland ventures a critique of feminism from this changed perspective. She suggests that the feminist movement has perhaps relied rather uncritically on the ideal of Romantic silence, underpinned by notions of the self coming to individuality through voice. Looking back at the development of the feminist movement, she suggests that feminist consciousness-raising groups might have done better to sit in silence (akin to the Quaker model of gathering) rather than prioritizing the desire to come into language.[18]

On my reading, Maitland's narrative invites feminist writers to consider a countercultural model, the contemplative model of silence, as an ideal. As she points out, Western culture clearly holds more respect for the boundaried self, the independent, creative individual. Maitland does not want to claim that the permeable self necessarily offers a better model. But she does invite readers to question ingrained Western assumptions about the superiority of the boundaried self. If Western culture recognizes that something is lost to the self without borders (i.e., independence, creative thought, individual achievement), Maitland suggests that something is also lost to the self that cannot pour itself out to the infinite. Evoking the examples of Simone Weil and Thérèse of Lisieux as women who have practiced the deliberate obliteration of ego, Maitland admits that the model of self-abnegation appeals to her. Referring to Thérèse of Lisieux's image of herself as a divine "plaything" and Weil's image of herself as a divine "door slave," Maitland observes that both women viewed themselves as possessing "no rights, no independence, no instrumentality, no true personhood. . . . They both buried themselves in a dark silence and stayed there waiting for God."[19] Many readers will be repelled by these images: "I am very much aware that this sort of spirituality is repugnant to many people. But it is not repugnant to me. It is challenging and somehow thrilling. It is also terrifying. I do not know who I would be if I gave myself away, silenced my own words and sat waiting on God in the darkness."[20] Maitland's admiration of women who embraced such utter self-abnegation suggests that her feminism, as represented by the "moor of her own," presents a radical alternative to the version represented by Woolf's ideal. However, this affirmation of women's self-abnegation, with little attention paid to the extreme physical or mental anguish suffered by both Simone Weil and Thérèse of Lisieux in their historical contexts, does little to reassure readers who share the concerns raised by Janet Batsleer's letter—that silence is, after all, a place of nothingness, death, or nonbeing. Far from reconciling the tension between contemplative silence and feminism (that is, feminism as an expression of concern for women's physical, psychological, and spiritual flourishing), here Maitland's reflections heighten that tension. It is fair to ask whether Maitland, in questioning traditional Western assumptions about the value of boundaried selfhood, actually romanticizes a model of self-abnegation that has proven to be quite destructive to women.

"God Is Silence": Theological Implications

Maitland makes it clear that her practice of silence is primarily informed by readings from the Christian mystical tradition. (After experimenting with Zen Buddhist practice at one point, she returns to contemplative prayer because she is strongly motivated by the desire to imitate the kenotic self-emptying of Christ on the cross.) Moreover, her desire to *write silence* is also informed by the Christian tradition. It places her in the lineage of women mystics like Julian of Norwich and Teresa of Avila, who have been described as "cartographers of the soul."[21] Having abandoned fiction, Maitland claims a new vocation as a writer—"to encode silence, so that out there in all that noise, people can access it and love it."[22] Thus *A Book of Silence* is not merely an autobiography, but a work of theology.

As a cartographer of silence, Maitland introduces readers to the literature of the mystical tradition and affirms, by presenting her own experience, that a real and life-transforming encounter with God is possible for contemporary women through certain intentional practices: praying silently, reading the Bible and the mystics, and attending to the beauty of the natural world. However, Maitland does wrestle with certain aspects of Christian theology, particularly the Genesis creation story. In a chapter titled "Silence and the Gods," Maitland interrogates the notion emphasized by her friend Batsleer that "In the beginning God *said*, God spoke." Linking the Genesis creation myth with what she calls the more recent creation myth posited by scientists, the story of the big bang, Maitland suggests that the latter is merely another, perhaps less eloquent, version of the former. In both stories, a loud noise erupts from the silence of the void and establishes the order of the universe. Maitland reads this pair of narratives as reflecting Western culture's "primal myth about creative activity," a myth that links speech not only to creation/creativity but also to *dominance*:

> Creation happens when silence is broken; when someone speaks, when the formless and meaningless void is pushed back by sound or word. This particular mythological *structure* in all its diverse forms has proved so successful in terms of colonization, scientific description

and prediction, political stability and military power that it is difficult to notice what a very unusual and odd myth it actually is. . . . According to the foundation story of [Western religions], you have rights and powers over everything you name. By naming it you make it and what you make is yours.[23]

Maitland criticizes this model for imparting a dualistic conception of language and silence, privileging language as "good" and meaningful while rejecting silence as nothingness, void, or absence—"waiting to be broken." To challenge this paradigm, Maitland researches creation stories from non-Western cultures, offering a sampling of myths from the Maori, Norse, Egyptian, and Cherokee cultures. To her delight, she finds numerous stories that offer radically different views of how creation came into being. As varied as they are, these myths "get the show up and running" without the interruption of silence by speech or noise. Instead, "Gods, Prime Movers and their newer scientific substitutes, create the origin of matter by ingesting, by brooding, by birthing, by killing, by withdrawing, by defecating, vomiting and masturbating, by fucking, by desiring, by self-mutilation and even quite simply by mistake."[24] Maitland emphasizes,

> It is hard to see what most of these stories have in common, except for the things they do not have in common with the verbally creative, highly intellectual, monotheist God of the Children of the Book. They represent a different way of seeing, a different way of telling about what can only be imagined. For example, the current story, the one we call the Big Bang, could equally well have been named the Tiny Egg, but it was not. And that is not accidental.[25]

By presenting these various creation myths, Maitland aims to show that Batsleer's letter is rooted in a Western conception of language and creation that might well be challenged. Maitland not only disagrees with the claim that "All silence is waiting to be broken," she also disagrees with the image of God as "Word." In fact, she suggests the opposite—that God actually *is* silence. She writes,

> Perhaps God *is* silence—the shining, spinning ring "of pure and end-
> less light." Perhaps God speaking is a "verb," an act, but God in perfect
> self-communication, in love within the Trinity, is silent and therefore
> is silence. God is silence, a silence that is positive, alive, actual and of
> its "nature" *unbreakable*. . . . Far from "all silence is waiting to be bro-
> ken" perhaps all speech is crying out "like a woman in travail" to be
> reabsorbed into silence, into death, into the liminal space that opens
> out into the presence of the everlasting silence.[26]

Maitland's position that *God is silence* marks a significant theological
shift. God's silence is loving, relational, dynamic—not only *not* longing
to be broken, but absolutely unbreakable. While God may still *speak*,
this speech is a mere interruption of sorts; it is not linked in a fundamental way to creation and creativity. This theological critique not only
challenges a normative Christian understanding of God and creation,
but, as Maitland emphasizes, it also challenges the dominant assumptions about language and creativity that underpin Western culture as
a whole, including the assumptions upon which many creative writers
have relied.

Maitland's narrative suggests that as her theology shifts from an
understanding of God as "the Word" to God as silence, her sense of
vocation as a writer also changes. After her experience of intense silent
prayer leads to the loss of her ability to write fiction, she reexamines
the conception that she had previously held of herself as a "co-creator"
with God:

> I began to understand more seriously what George Steiner had meant
> when he described artists as "rival creators." I had always thought
> that this was rubbish—and that God wanted us, rather, to be co-cre-
> ators. I was learning, with different degrees of acceptance, frustration,
> willingness and resistance, that I could not *be silent* and at the same
> time be creating new words and new worlds. Silence has no narrative.
> Silence intensifies sensation, but blurs the sense of time.[27]

Maitland reaches the conclusion that instead of being either a "co-
creator" with God or a "rival creator," her vocation is to "write silence,"

or to "encode silence." She suggests that this kind of writing departs from narrative and becomes more akin to poetry or music. Offering the image of writing as participation in a heavenly choir, she suggests, "Perhaps a writer's job is finally cooperative, creating the words for that eternal choir, so that the endless song of 'Holy, holy, holy' never becomes boring."[28] In this type of writing, Maitland conceptualizes herself neither as George Steiner's "rival creator" with God nor as "co-creator" in the way that she had previously thought. Participating in a song of praise, her writing becomes a form of prayer itself.

SILENCE IN CONVERSATION

As I see it, one of Sara Maitland's important contributions in *A Book of Silence* is her unique development of the conversation that Virginia Woolf began about the necessary conditions of women's writing. Her narrative suggests that Woolf was right about one thing at least — that the writing process is profoundly influenced by the rooms and houses (and, Maitland would add, the landscapes) that writers inhabit. Maitland invites writers to recognize the importance of *silence* — that is, specific forms of silence, chosen with conscious intention — as one of these necessary conditions. And, though the author gives up fiction writing and aspires to *write silence* instead, *A Book of Silence* remains a work "attached to life at all four corners." As Virginia Woolf clarified at the end of her famous essay, it is not important that women write *fiction* necessarily, only that they *write*. Addressing her female audience, Woolf said,

> I would ask you to write all kinds of books, hesitating at no subject however trivial or however vast. By hook or by crook, I hope that you will possess yourselves of money enough to travel and to idle . . . For I am by no means confining you to fiction. . . . By [writing other types of literature] you will certainly profit the art of fiction. For books have a way of influencing each other. Fiction will be much the better for standing cheek by jowl with poetry and philosophy.[29]

I suggest that *A Book of Silence* will "profit the art" not only of fiction but also of feminist theology. As an autobiography and a work of theological reflection, it raises several questions about the effects of silence on women's writing as well as its effects on women's sense of selfhood and their experience of the divine. Maitland's discovery that contemplative silence is incompatible with the silence that inspires fiction writing is provocative for those of us who have tended to view women's writing as an essential key to spiritual liberation. On the one hand, Maitland *lives* in accordance with Woolf's ideal, earning a living through exercising her own agency and voice—writing numerous books, living independently in her location of choice, and traveling hither and yon in pursuit of her dreams. On the other hand, what she *writes* undermines this agency and voice, suggesting that an intense experience of God as silence, while profoundly nourishing in some ways, comes at a great cost—the cost of a sense of self and the capacity to create new worlds through fiction. In her attempt to write silence, Maitland celebrates silence even while she breaks it. Though all mystical writers have experienced this dilemma to some degree—the paradoxical nature of trying to describe silence, of trying to communicate ineffability—Maitland imparts a mixed message as to whether the experience of intense silence is ultimately nourishing or damaging to women writers. Significantly, Maitland's *A Book of Silence* emerges at a time when other prominent feminists, such as Luce Irigaray and Beverly Lanzetta, have also begun to reevaluate the positive value of silence for women in relation to the divine. Though a full discussion of their work is beyond the scope of this essay, I wish to briefly suggest some ways that Maitland might be put in dialogue with them. In short, both Irigary and Lanzetta describe silence as nourishing for women without going so far as to affirm the disintegration of self and voice.

Luce Irigaray's "Silent Constituting Pause"

Maitland's insistence that silence is not a meaningless void but rather a positive, meaningful presence offers a point of correspondence with Luce Irigaray's description of the "silent constituting pause."[30] Given her background in continental philosophy and psychoanalysis, Irigaray's discussion of silence emerges in the context of her work on sexual difference and the need for a feminine divine. Irigaray suggests that language in its present form is problematic in that it does not respect difference (especially sexual difference); it deprives the "other" of sub-jectivity. She says that human beings have yet to learn to speak with one another in ways that are truly loving, communicative, and respectful. The "silent constituting pause," then, offers a space of hospitality and welcome to the other; it is a listening space in which the other is allowed to emerge. Though it differs from speech, silence is still *communicative.* Irigaray writes, "The first word we have to speak to one another is our capacity and acceptance of being silent. It would be the first wave of recognition addressed to the other as such."[31] She also uses maternal imagery to describe this "wave of recognition"; silence is the space of "conceiving" or "begetting."[32] Irigaray does not simply reverse the hier-archy, privileging silence over speech. Rather, she suggests that employ-ing these silent constituting pauses can help human beings achieve a new form of loving communication (made up of speech, silence, and gesture) that would allow men and women to preserve subjectivity while welcoming the other.

Irigaray's advocacy of silence is linked too with her emphasis on the need for a "feminine divine" for women to come into full subjectiv-ity. Irigaray tries to retrieve positive spiritual images from the Catholic tradition as well as from Eastern religions. From Catholicism, Iriga-ray retrieves the figure of Mary, mother of Jesus, as a positive model for female subjectivity. Focusing on the annunciation story, Irigaray celebrates Mary not as the procreator of the Son but as a "woman fig-ure capable of being faithful to herself." For Irigaray, Mary offers a model of "the possibility of returning to oneself, to preserve one's inte-riority . . . and also the way to welcome the other unto oneself, while respecting him/her."[33]

In her appreciation of silence and her respect for women's interi-ority, Irigaray's work corresponds with Maitland's. However, a closer comparison of these two thinkers would be warranted because the kind of silence that they describe is not quite the same. Irigaray seems to describe a kind of silence that Maitland refers to as "psychoanalytic silence" or a "listening silence," which she respects as "a strange and beautiful thing," though she does not practice it.[34] In the psychoanalytic context, the analyst offers a silent space in which the client strives to articulate his or her own story or truth. Maitland sees this practice as incompatible with contemplative silence, as it continues to privilege language as the primary characteristic of subjectivity. In Maitland's view, the contemplative model offers a much more radical alternative to the dominant patriarchal structures that privilege speech as domination.

Beverly Lanzetta: The Via Feminina

As Sara Maitland wrestles openly in *A Book of Silence* with a sense of tension between her contemplative practice and her feminism, she seems to suggest an alternative vision of feminism, one that does not privilege speech as the primary characteristic of subjectivity. Might it be possible to read Maitland's commitment to *writing silence* as an expression of "contemplative feminism," as described by feminist theologian Beverly Lanzetta?

In her book *Radical Wisdom*, Lanzetta describes contemplative feminism as a healing alternative for women who have suffered "spiritual wounds" from the violence and subordination imposed upon them by patriarchal religions. Mystical texts and practices, especially the writings of women like Teresa of Avila and Julian of Norwich, offer a way of "un-saying" patriarchal norms that have construed women's relationship to the divine in limiting or harmful ways. Lanzetta acknowledges the validity of feminist suspicion of mysticism, recognizing that classical mysticism can also "stifle women beneath the voices of the fathers" and can "appear to be another ploy to re-inscribe the inferiority of women" (the concern expressed by Janet Batsleer's letter in Maitland's narrative).[35] But Lanzetta defines contemplative feminism as a "third way" between the *via positiva* and the *via negativa*, departing from certain features of classical mysticism in important ways. For example, Lanzetta claims that rather than trying to transcend difference (whether difference of gender, class, or race), the *via feminina* recognizes and embraces difference. Like Maitland and Irigaray, Lanzetta emphasizes that silence offers itself as a positive and meaningful presence. As she puts it, solitude and silence are "food": "They are necessary for the nourishment of the whole person, and for the actualization of the deepest possibility of a spiritual life."[36] She suggests that in the light of the mystical experience, the criteria that define feminism might shift. She defines feminism less in terms of social outcomes than in "inner freedom."

Lanzetta's emphasis on "inner freedom" does not promote any sort of quietism. She emphasizes that contemplative techniques not only empower women spiritually but also have a wider "revolutionary power." More than just an experience of the divine, mysticism "is, in fact, a far more powerful, seditious, and existential condition of *deconstruction* and *disruption* of everything and anything that stands in the way of the original freedom of God and the person."[37] This observation aligns with Maitland's description of contemplative practice: it offered her a wide freedom, but it also unraveled her faith in assumed cultural norms. Her contemplative practice stands as a challenge to conceptions of language and creativity that are aligned with appropriation, mastery, and dominance.

Conclusion: Living and Writing "in the Presence of Reality"

I suspect that some feminist readers, especially those who feel attracted to both contemplation and writing like Maitland, will remain somewhat troubled by her insistence that a room of one's own and a moor of one's own are rooted in two fundamentally incompatible models. As she observes, much feminism has accepted the Romantic model of selfhood and writing without questioning it or conceiving the possibility of other models. By exploring silence and trying to *write silence*, she follows a relatively unexplored path for women's writing in our time. Putting Maitland into conversation with Irigaray and Lanzetta offers avenues for exploring further the ways in which contemplative silence can be positively reclaimed for feminist writers.

Despite Maitland's depiction of a strong tension between her model and Woolf's, the very fact of her writing *A Book of Silence* suggests at least one common element: both writers found themselves living in the presence of an invigorating reality, and they wanted to communicate it to others. After all, Woolf understood writing to be so important precisely because writers live, more than others do, "in the presence of reality":

What is meant by "reality"? It would seem to be something very erratic, very undependable—now to be found in a dusty road, now in a scrap of newspaper in the street, now in a daffodil in the sun. It lights up a group in a room and stamps some casual saying. It overwhelms one walking home beneath the stars *and makes the silent world more real than the world of speech*—and then there it is again in an omnibus in the uproar of Piccadilly. . . . Now the writer, as I think, has the chance to live more than other people in the presence of this reality. It is his business to find it and collect it and communicate it to the rest of us. . . . So when I ask you to earn money and have a room of your own, I am asking you to live in the presence of reality, an invigorating life, it would appear, whether one can impart it or not.[38]

Both Woolf and Maitland recognize that living in the presence of reality demands courage—the courage to depart from cultural norms, to take a risk. However, Maitland offers a different vision from Woolf's—an unusual vision for an accomplished feminist writer of our time—of what ideals must be surrendered and what "lunacy" must be pursued to live in the presence of reality. Maitland's own pursuit led her to surrender her ideals of autonomous selfhood and "voice" (as in the power to write fiction, to create new worlds), but in doing so she found a new voice (the inspiration to *write silence*) and a vast unlimited sense of freedom.

Maitland ends *A Book of Silence* with an emphasis on uncertainty. She acknowledges that her plan to live alone in an austere landscape, venturing ever more deeply into the heart of silence, is risky: "I have always known it would be risky, and I was raised in a risk-averse culture. I hope I do not underestimate the risk. But I am willing to face it. Terror and risk walk hand in hand with beauty. There is terror, there is beauty and there is nothing else."[39] Her narrative is valuable to feminist theologians because it conveys a vivid sense of this freedom and the risk involved. It invites us to contemplate the lure of terror and beauty.

WITH PRAYER AND PEN
Reading Mother E. J. Dabney's *What It Means to Pray Through*

Michele Jacques Early

It may not be your task to go
In to countries far away;
You can help the wanderer at your door
You can read, write and pray.
Some of the greatest needs in the ministry today
Are for those who use their pen;
For those who are prepared in every way
To enlighten the hearts of men.
Business is a part of a Christian's life,
How lovely when one can stand
Free from self-righteousness and strife,
And supply the church demands.
It is right that a record be kept,
In heaven they have the same.
You will not be counted with those who slept
If you continue in Jesus' Name.
Writing is wisdom from above
It has been used throughout the years;
It expresses our kind Saviour's love,
It has delivered many hearts from fears.

His presence shall go with thee,
He will help you to meet every test.
He will pay you for working with me.
Your aunt and sister are glad to know
You made your life worthwhile.
The staff, your friends, turn the green light Go!
Your name is on heaven's file.
Some day we shall gather over there,
In that city of your King;
You will see added stars in your crown,
You gained by using your pen.

—E. J. Dabney, *What It Means to Pray Through* (1945)[1]

Elizabeth Jackson Dabney (1903–1967)[2] was of that generation and ilk of women placed in the untenable position of mediating desire, fulfillment, and the call to a life of holiness, with what was then understood as the "proper place" of African-Americans and women. As such, she went where "free space"[3] presented itself. Her ministry of prayer—the traditional ministry for women—became a sacral home, an altar where she welcomed any and all to join her in communion with God. She found her way forward by going back to prayer and wrote to the world for which she prayed.

What It Means to Pray Through is the story of God's leading and Mo. Dabney's yielding, not so much in obedience, but to whom she was divinely called to be. It illustrates a life nuanced by suffering, faithful struggle, resistance, and reward, and the understanding that true empowerment is achieved when one appropriates the righteous and holy life. This essay discusses Mo. Dabney's writing of her life, her emergence as a writer, and the central themes in her message.

WRITING HER LIFE

In her narrative (a semiautobiographical guide to prayer), Mo. Dabney does not give the date of her birth, nor does she highlight many dates within her text. While on the one hand she aims to play down her person—not wanting to distract from the telling of God's story—she is on the other hand its progenitor. Squarely in the tradition of earlier narrative genre, her story focuses on the significance of her life of prayer for "everybody, everywhere."[4] As a lifelong member of the Church of God in Christ (COGIC), the largest African-American Pentecostal denomination in the United States, she chronicles her movement into this ministry and how God uses her to bless the world.

Information on her formative years is scant. Born in Virginia around 1903, at some early period of life she moved with her mother and two siblings to the North, perhaps to New Jersey. Katie McBurrows reports that Mr. Jackson (Mo. Dabney's father) was born into slavery in Virginia and was taken away one day to be tarred, feathered, and burned alive.[5] Neglecting to bring the fire, his captors left to obtain it. He escaped and went into hiding, during which time he met and married Dabney's mother. He died while Dabney was young, and so she knew little about him.[6] Instead, Mo. Dabney begins her story with her mother's ministry and her experience of growing up with the "family altar."[7]

Their home was known by many as a "place of consolation."[8] Mrs. Jackson, her mother, she never mentions by name. Mo. Dabney shares simply that her mother was widowed, was a noted missionary and singer, and was renowned for being "a great woman of prayer."[9] In particular her mother ministered to preachers and their wives. Taking respite at the "family altar," they brought their tired, weary, and battle-scarred persons for consolation and renewal. "The Family Altar" is the title of the first chapter of Mo. Dabney's book and signifies much about her life and her ministry. Honoring this altar represents the commitment of the whole of one's life and affirms the minister and the minister's family in the attendant suffering synonymous with ministry. Of significant note in the opening chapter, Mo. Dabney mentions she has unpleasant memories from childhood, though she chooses not to explicate them. "There was something about the suffering of ministers and their families that followed me from early childhood. It created a horrible picture in my mind. It was so dreadful I disdained the idea of being a minister's wife. I wanted to be a public speaker."[10] As a result, she vowed never to marry a minister.[11]

Mo. Dabney met and married Benjamin Henry Dabney, who studied music and worked in catering. She speaks joyously of marriage and their plans[12] prior to the revelation of his call to preach. Mentions of her biological role as a mother are intermittent in the text and incidental to other events in her ministry. The reasons for this virtual silence about her personal experiences of motherhood are not stated. She gave birth to two children. Henry was the first, whom she eventually sent to Pennsylvania College, where he earned a degree in English. The second, born during her and her husband's initiation into the pastorate, died shortly after birth. She seems proud of her son Henry, and McBurrows alludes to the grief Mo. Dabney felt at losing the second child. Mo. Dabney speaks highly of her husband and comments on his exemplary role in ministry and parenting. Perhaps the disdain she received from others for abandoning the traditional mothering role during her three-year vow[13] led her to downplay this aspect of her life.

Mo. Dabney's formative years parallel those of the Church of God in Christ. The early twentieth century was a tumultuous time, a time of persecution of African-Americans by society at large and rejection of Pentecostals within the larger Christian church community. African-Americans were still not full citizens; Jim Crow in the South and discrimination in the North translated into little hope of enfranchisement and continued fear for one's life. The subsequent years of the Great Depression and war caused even more grief and hardship. Lynching and legal segregation were the reality, but so was the rise of the New Negro and Club Women's movements. The progressive quarters of the black community and assertiveness of the COGIC Women's Department, in fulfilling its call, signaled that the potential and productivity of black life could not be entirely co-opted and controlled by dominant society. The COGIC grew rapidly, even amid persecution and rejection. Of the early pioneers of the denomination, historian Lucille Cornelius writes,

> They realized the practice and development of Christian religion, in this hectic age, was just as necessary and paramount as in the days of the early church . . . . Many miracles were performed through them

and they suffered severe persecution. They preached in brush arbors and old shacks, they were rotten egged and shot at also put in prison, but God gave the increase and blessed their labor.[14]

In these early days, men and women evangelized, spreading the gospel to create what Anthea Butler terms "a sanctified world."[15] Often, this involved husband-and-wife teams relocating to plant churches in varying states or regions. Mo. Lizzie Roberson,[16] the head of the Women's Department, would travel throughout the year by wagon and on foot accompanied by groups of women evangelists. The authoritative place out of which this ministry was done rests in these women leaders fully appropriating the title and role of the Mother.[17]

While Mo. Dabney carried the title of Mother, it is not clear whether she fully embraced this overarching metaphor as prescriptive of her ministry. But the position is one which she appreciated, and it afforded her a respected and authoritative place in the congregation while allowing her to cast for herself a different image and focus. Adopting the stance of the professional entrepreneurial woman, she focused most on education and training, the purpose of which was to help young African-American women become proficient in the professions available to them both in church and in society. This stance was also confluent with the leadership emerging with General Supervisor Mo. Lillian Brooks Coffey,[18] who became the second head of the COGIC Women's Department.

Mo. Dabney's choices were perhaps spurred by a desire to be set apart from the experiences in her earlier life and in the church. The goal of being a public speaker seems to be an express alternative to a destined call to be either a preacher's wife or a missionary, in the fashion of her mother. Public speaking requires being educated and trained to write and think critically.[19] Her desire to write was likely influenced by her environment, the writing traditions of African-American women, and the specific emphases of her church. In *What It Means to Pray Through*, however, writing emerges most prominently as an extension of her ministry of prayer.

According to McBurrows, Mo. Dabney attended college in Philadelphia. While taking a psychology class, she and her classmates visited a newly forming Church of God in Christ in the city, led by Elder Ozro T. Jones[20] (who later became her pastor and Bishop). Their plans to observe and then petition to have the church closed were cut short when, in that service, Mo. Dabney was healed from two physical conditions and received Spirit baptism. These events are confusing and difficult to reconcile with the timeline she provides in her book, as she refers neither to this event nor to her formal education. Her opposition to the church and the effect it had on her eventual ministry are not disclosed. It is possible that this event occurred during a period when Elder Jones was laying the groundwork for a local church (prior to 1925). She and Elder Dabney may have been called to work with Elder Jones when he was ready to officially establish the local congregation. In her narrative, Mo. Dabney notes only that her husband's call impacts her and devastates her to the point of becoming temporarily incapacitated. It was his acknowledgment of and resignation to the call to preach, she claims, that caused her to acquiesce and return fully to the life of the church.

After several years in ministry working under the male and female leadership in the church, Mo. Dabney writes of a nagging hunger:

> When I worked in Churches in New Jersey with my husband under pastors and women supervisors, I had a great desire to go to that place where the Christian women went in the ancient days. They prayed and found God's favor and divine righteousness; He made Himself known unto them. I grew tired of everything I knew; there was something greater for me than gossiping and tale-bearing, or making myself a busy-body in other individual's matters.[21]

This restlessness and hunger led her back more fully to the family altar. Although she had continued a life of prayer, this turning point marks the beginning of a deeper quest and experience with God. While serving churches in New Jersey, she says, she was called by Elder O. T. Jones in 1925 to work in Philadelphia: "He permitted my husband and his brother to assist him in the church work and he told me my work was to pray and write for the church."[22] She does not discuss specifically what this work encompassed. Elder Jones observed her and her husband's work in New Jersey and requested that they be assigned to him. She refers to this period as the entrée to their ministerial career (as pastor and pastor's wife) and the initiation of a vow that ushered in her prayer ministry.

The vow she made marks a pivotal point in her life. Fulfilling this vow even represents a kind of womanist turn. While traditional calls to a particular ministry are often said to be spurred by supernatural acts of initiation and/or intervention, Mo. Dabney's was quite different. In her narrative, she describes her vow as a self-initiated call to act, when God drew her attention to the conditions in the church neighborhood. Taking note of the horrid conditions surrounding their church, she asks if God will give victory to her husband's ministry and break through the bonds if she enters into a covenant with God. She asks that this happen in a way that hushes the mouths of gainsayers.[23] She later covenants to pray day and night, to meet God in prayer every day for three years at 9:00 a.m., and to shut in day and night for 3 days each week to fast and pray.

The parameters she sets for the vow and the arm twisting in which she engaged to obtain her husband's "approval" are equally telling. Devotion to the vow required that she engage in a nontraditional commitment to the work. Such would prohibit her from fulfilling many traditional domestic duties as wife and mother—and would in turn force her husband to assist with them over this three-year period. The vow would also impinge on her duties as the pastor's wife. While this specific duty is not mentioned, she does indicate that church members also objected to the parameters set, both because of their altering of traditional roles and the suspicion of influence by demonic or ungodly forces.

The necessity for arm twisting is reflective of a patriarchal orientation and the dialectic of authority operative in black Pentecostalism.[24] Mo. Dabney is required to have the permission of Elder Dabney, as her husband and pastor, to fulfill such a vow. This need for permission is considered in line with scriptural teaching that proclaims man as the head of woman and the pastor as one who watches over the souls of congregants. His repeated objections are countered with her argument that she is required to keep her promise to God. In the end, his denial would be tantamount to sin. Prayer becomes the centering act in her personal journey and prescriptive of her vocation. The vow becomes the vehicle through which and the motivation around which she ministers with others in a spiritual and professional communion.

Mo. Dabney's vow represents the opportunity for God to perform a miracle for both her and her husband, as well as for the community. For just as the parameters of the vow require nontraditional sacrifice and commitment from them both, they also promise rewards for the same. And while the dialectic of authority may lead one to subordinate personal desire to hierarchy, it also works to embolden rebellion. The covenant began around 1929. As it progressed, Garden of Prayer (their church) grew and flourished. When the covenant ended, it marked the beginning of Mo. Dabney's national and worldwide prayer ministry. Garden of Prayer hosted prayer revivals, as did other churches in the city and the country. Just as important were the "unseen revivals" carried out through correspondence[25] and culminating in the writing of her book.

MO. DABNEY AS WRITER

The writing tradition is neither strange nor strained among African-Americans. Women wrote, hampered more by milieu (the sexism, racism, and repression that pervaded the United States) than by ability or desire. Many of Mo. Dabney's particular challenges are described throughout this essay. Social constraints existed in that legal segregation, economic disfranchisement, and an absence of legal rights for women circumscribed her environment. While she was employed prior to her husband's entrée into ministry, it is never mentioned afterwards. Limited financial resources and racism relegated them to deficient housing and worship facilities. Many times they prayed in the cold, huddled together to keep from freezing. Traditional gender roles in society and the church limited the scope of her involvement and the resources available to her. Mo. Dabney and the collegial band of women staffers at times rendered services without appropriate compensation. The tenuous denominational stance on women meant that Mo. Dabney's prayer ministry was relegated to a nominal status. She struggled with a dualistic theology that both enabled and obstructed personal authority and autonomy. Though hindered by discriminatory practices and a lack of legal, social, and denominational parity, Mo. Dabney wrote. Bolstered by the tradition of her forebears and by a progressive era, she partnered with a collegial communion of believers to write a gospel for her era.

Mo. Dabney's book reflects the varied aspects and impulses of American writers. Determining the exact process and chronology of her emergence as a writer is difficult. It perhaps began with her desire to be a public speaker. It is signaled in her early work in the church and comes to full fruition as pen and prayer merge in the heat and heart of ministry.

Mo. Dabney writes only once of her early desire for public speaking as a profession. She speaks of it in reference to life goals and in terms not centered in the church. It is a preferred alternative life vision to that of a life of ministry. Much of her inspiration and desire may be spurred by freedom activity and the ideologies of the Woman's Era. At the time, African-Americans were fully engaged in the fight for full citizenship. With the abolition of slavery, American women became proponents of women's rights. The separatism and racism of the suffrage movement led African-American women to advocate for full rights in associations with African-American men and on their own. Much of their activism took place in the formation of women's clubs. Those in the leadership of the Black Women's Club Movement[26] were outstanding public speakers, writers, educators, entrepreneurs, and community activists, as well as wives and mothers. Many of these women were born during the latter part of slavery and early emancipation (1860–1885). The Woman's Era of the late nineteenth century proffered the idea that women and womanhood cannot be defined by motherhood and domesticity alone and that, unrestrained by traditional gender roles, a woman is capable of engaging any profession of her choosing and of making outstanding achievements. From New York to Washington, D.C., and across the nation, women were freed in these associations and clubs to do the work important to them. Mo. Dabney was squarely located in this milieu.

Additionally, in the period preceding her writing career, much of the concern for African-American writers centered upon themes of protest, moral living, and racial uplift. While many white women writers were protesting the restrictions posed by the patriarchally driven images and value system of the Victorian Lady, African-American women challenged the racial and sexualized stereotypes of themselves presented in American society. These portrayed women of color as immoral. Ann Allen Shockley says that, "For Black women ennobling a downtrodden race was more important"[27] than strictly gender concerns. Writing presented critical perspectives from black women themselves that documented who they were and the heights they were capable of achieving. Though Victorian themes persisted in many writings, the aim was to defend the moral character of African-American women. The New Negro Movement[28] arising in the 1920s and 1930s enabled African-Americans to publish even more. Novels and literary and political magazines expressed the creativity and political candor that acted as a stimulus for all types of African-American genres, including religious ones.

While Mo. Dabney does not explicitly speak in the language of social commentary or political protest, her writing reflects the tenor of the era. Historical events appear as subtexts. Her desire to be a public speaker, and her ambitions to own a store, to travel, and to be educated also reflect this. But the work God does through her takes center stage in her life and in her book. The larger context of women's community affirms her right to ambition, but she translates her desire within the parameters of COGIC community and beliefs.

Mo. Dabney's work in the church also signals movement toward or interest in writing. Upon recruitment by Elder O. T. Jones, her appointed tasks were to write and to pray. This seems neither strange nor monumental, since it is mentioned only once and in passing on her way to the larger story. It reflects, however, something of her having written in the context of the church. Elder Jones appreciates education and by this time has authored and published Bible study texts for the youth of the church. His tasking her to write indicates her abilities and recognized talent in this area.

Mo. Dabney also mentions her role as a writer in connection with Bishop C. H. Mason. She travelled with him, recording his prayers and their positive results in various cities.[29] He is an example of the consummate prayer warrior.[30] Bishop Mason, however, devoted himself more to preaching, praying, teaching, and organizing than to writing. Though her role may seem like a simple secretarial one, Mo. Dabney understood the significance of history and of capturing and preserving this phenomenon in writing. This work is then significant to her prayer ministry as well as to her writing task. Indeed, she notes Bishop Mason's considerable influence on and support of her ministry.[31]

It is important to note that writing was never foreign to this church or to its women members. The Women's Department, as the initial educational vehicle in the church, trained both male ministers and female leaders and congregants.[32] As part of these educational ventures, the Women's Department sponsored correspondence programs to prepare congregants to be functional in society and for ministry. Ms. Pinky Duncan organized a denominational school[33] for the protection and nurture of black Pentecostal youth, eventually sustained with the support of the Women's Department. A departmental newsletter, *The Banner*, circulated along with the general denominational news organs. Publications produced by the denomination and other like-minded materials were in wide use and form the canon of denominational religious literature. Mo. Dabney was part of this tradition and saw it as part of the work of the church.

Her writing achieves its fullest expression in authoring her book, *What It Means to Pray Through*. This book was not planned. Rather, as will be evident, she was compelled to write. Following the completion of her three-year vow, Mo. Dabney began holding prayer revivals across the country. While conducting a revival in Los Angeles, California, Bishop Mason introduced her to Miss Faye Bress,[34] who was seeking a prayer ministry of the biblical type that fueled the Azusa Street Revival.[35] Bishop Mason asked Miss Bress to write to encourage Mo. Dabney, who had seemingly experienced a negative response in this revival. This began an exchange of letters in which Mo. Dabney shared her commitment to the work and the sacrifice it entailed. After many exchanges (and unbeknownst to Mo. Dabney), Miss Bress gathered her friends[36] and together they distributed copies of the letters to Los Angeles pastors, asking them to read the letters to their congregations.

Deciding this audience was too limited, Miss Bress and her friends appealed to Mr. and Mrs. Moore, who asked Stanley Howard Frodsham, editor of the *Pentecostal Evangel,* to publish excerpts of her letters. He did so as an article under the title "What It Means to Pray Through." Interest was so overwhelming that Mr. Frodsham republished it as a tract that circulated worldwide. When Mo. Dabney returned to Los Angeles,[37] she discovered what had occurred:

> I had no idea I would ever see my name on the headlines of papers, and magazines neither had it entered my mind once that Miss Bress would publish excerpts from my personal correspondence. The Lord led her, I say it was the Lord; I have every right to believe it was in His divine plan for her to send this Gospel unto the many anxious inquirers who were languishing, conversing over what God did for Peter and John and the church in the early days.[38]

Some 35,000 letters, she says, poured in at the beginning. Eventually, as the tracts and articles were published in other magazines, she accumulated approximately three million letters from around the world—Syria, Africa, China, India, South America, Ireland, and other nations. Letter writers requested prayer, advice, and particularly information on how they too can pray through. It is these requests that prompt the writing of her book of the same title.

The above quote makes reference to Peter and John. Like their letters, hers are circulated to believing churches. Mo. Dabney's letters communicate the gospel message and demonstrate the manifest glory of the presence of God in healings, salvation of souls, answered prayers, and new community. In them, one sees the reign of God on earth. The knowledge that her letters are a modern-day occurrence of the New Testament reality is a byproduct of the response to them. Her book, *What It Means to Pray Through,* is part of Mo. Dabney's ultimate service. Following the biblical tradition, it is a canonization of the story of the movement of God in a particular time and place, and among a particular people. As were apostolic letters in early Christianity, her letters and then book function to undergird and facilitate God's work in the world. Like praying, the letters communicate believers' first work and ongoing tasks.[39] These letters represent and help fuel a movement like that at the biblical Pentecost and at Azusa Street. This canon provides a narrative connection and fills a gap between the New Testament experience and contemporary practice of faith. It is an old tradition, but a new epistle for a new time.

"Christian letter writing is not new," she writes, "but it is as old as creation. It pleased our Father to give men wisdom and knowledge how to write; there is something skillful and outstanding about it; wherever a message is directed if delivered, it will convey its meaning."[40] In communicating a message and practice that is beyond time, she cultivates in time a new reality. The wisdom and power of God enable her to write, and her own story is part of the larger story of salvation history. And like the Gospels and the Epistles, her writings convey God's message.

These varying aspects of her autobiographical narrative resemble the nineteenth-century spiritual autobiography. Such narratives speak to the history of a people from the pivotal place of the personal faith journey and document some of the realities of life as saint, as African-American, as woman, as community member, and as global citizen. The aim is to demonstrate the sacred purpose of one's life and of a given people (whether church, cultural, or racial group, etc.),[41] while also connecting with the milieu of Sanctified[42] women of her day.

Joanne Braxton notes some of the salient features that help connect Mo. Dabney's book to this tradition. Commenting on the narratives of enslaved fugitives and Sanctified ladies, she classifies them as narratives of vision and power:

> Like *Pilgrim's Progress* or John Woolman's *Journal* spiritual autobiographies by black Americans, both men and women, center on the quest for spiritual perfection in an imperfect world. For these Americans, the autobiographical act was a form of spiritual witnessing; their narratives record a journey characterized by trials, temptations, and finally triumph. . . . In addition to documenting trials, temptations and triumphs . . . spiritual autobiography illuminates sex-specific aspects of black women's early intellectual history and their quest for self-definition and self-determination, especially in the case of free black missionary women.[43]

Though she comes of age during the later Pentecostal Movement, Mo. Dabney displays the markers of these Sanctified women. In the missionary-like narrative she labels a gospel, she is led by God in her spiritual quest. Like theirs, her quest originates as a self-determining act, in that it does not proceed from an external irresistible source. She is the initiator of the ministry covenant. While she makes no reference to spiritual perfection, there is allusion to the necessity of pleasing God. *What It Means to Pray Through* witnesses to the power resident in the relationship between God and the believer committed to a sanctified life.

Writing enables her to fulfill her initial goal (of being a public speaker) as it transmits and magnifies her voice. Thus, she does not abandon the intellectual goals of her early life; instead, they shift. In this narrative act her theology emerges, bringing together the disparate aspects of her reality in her story. Her focus on the power of God in the life of the believer illustrates the possibility of a moral life and the sanity of holiness in a society ridden with war, prejudices, sin, suffering, and injustice. The writing aim is fulfilled by presenting true personhood from a divine perspective and illustrating the fact that it is God who prescribes the inherent value of and defines the parameters of one's life.

WHAT IT MEANS TO PRAY THROUGH

For Mo. Dabney, the medium is entirely about the message: what it means to pray through into God's glory. Her book communicates a gospel message in that it illustrates (in the fashion of Paul and John) what living this gospel entails. Praying through requires faithfulness in ministry despite the suffering that will inevitably come, so that God's glory is revealed. One must dedicate oneself to prayer, no matter the condition. She comes to understand God's glory manifesting in souls saved and healed, and in building Christian community. Prayer, she believes, is as legitimate a vehicle for achieving this as is preaching. Speaking directly to her readers, she teaches, admonishes, and corrects them. Three themes are prominent in her book. A predominant theme in her early life and ministry is that of suffering. Second, egalitarianism and inclusivity mark the spirit and practice of her ministry and are emphasized in her writing. The third theme is both spiritual and auto-biographical as she yields to who she is divinely becoming.

Suffering, both as the calamity that befalls one and as intentional sacrifice, is inextricable from ministry for Mo. Dabney. As mentioned earlier, she experienced suffering in her life, in a way that causes her to abhor the idea of doing ministry. "Sometimes," she said, when you come through the fire, "it is in His blueprint; if you suffer, you shall reign."[44] With this view, one may think the fire is the only way. And while the saint is taught that there is glory and a certain privilege in her or his suffering, for Mo. Dabney it is clearly an undesirable fate. This poses a dilemma for her as she is drawn into the very thing she fears and abhors.

Her book mediates this dynamic between suffering as "universal and an inescapable fact of the human condition" and as maldistributed.[45] Delores Williams posits that a spirituality that demands suffering as satisfaction for the divine is highly problematic, especially for those who are already suffering due to social oppressions.[46] This concern is evident in Mo. Dabney's narrative. However, it seems doubtful that she sees God as desiring the saints' suffering. Rather, it is unavoidable. It is especially problematic for African-American women who must mediate the dynamic mentioned above. It creates an untenable situation of vulnerability and the possibility of submission to servitude. Compounding this situation is that theology in Pentecostalism "assumes the role of servanthood"[47] and that the *Official Manual* of the COGIC references women's ministry as that of servant or helper.[48] This attitude presents for COGIC women the possibility and often the reality of experiencing further structural and theological suppression. Mo. Dabney negotiates this context in her prayer ministry—navigating the maldistributed suffering society inflicts and sometimes succumbing to that inflicted by the church's theology.

Her book argues that one must reconcile oneself to suffer in living a holy lifestyle; it is inevitable if one is to be who God requires one to be. Mo. Dabney provides several examples of this. One tells of an incident early in the period of her vow. When she arrives at church at eight o'clock one morning she finds a note with three hearts drawn and a dagger through them, saying, "Get out of this neighborhood at once. We do not want your prayer meetings." Vowing to remain faithful, she trusts God to confront the evil. She returns the next morning to find herself being followed by three men. She writes,

> One of them started towards me; my heart was praying so loud it seemed as if it went to the bottom of my feet . . . I did not run; I called the Name of Jesus. . . . He answered my prayers immediately, for the man stopped following me. . . . Down in my soul I heard a multitude: singing "Be not dismayed whatever betides God will take care of you." . . . I never permitted myself to accuse my dear kind Father, for after all, I had made the covenant with Him.[49]

By not accusing God, she takes full responsibility and attributes this evil to satanic forces. Though God helps her, she owns this event. It is perhaps indicative as well of the idea that God does not desire suffering, rather it is unavoidable as a consequence of evil and sin. Though the conditions in the neighborhood invoked the covenant, she seems in this and other like events caught between the unavoidable suffering and the God who delivers from it. Other incidents are noted which she characterizes as an attack of Satan. She is chastised and misunderstood, and her life is threatened, yet she perseveres. This she must do to reap the rewards of the covenant. The full measure of her struggle is not shared, but enough is revealed to illustrate the extent and types of suffering attendant with praying through. Struggling also with a call she does not seek and is reluctant to answer, she seems to succumb to a guiding principle of the church—that no crown is received without bearing a cross.

Her cross also comes from her physiology and social location. She relates an incident at a prayer revival in Norfolk, Virginia: "They were looking for a tall, stout old woman; when they found out I was small in stature they were very displeased, but the Lord convinced them it was not in the age or size. He sent a revival and stirred the city."[50] The cost of answering the call presents social and financial struggles that are the result of the existential reality of African-American lives as Pentecostals in ministry. Before the covenant, Mo. Dabney was ready to give up ministry altogether because of poor building conditions, oppressive property owners, few resources, inclement weather, etc. Pentecostals were viewed negatively in society as ignorant and of a lower class and caste. Indeed, elevation into the mainstream of American life for African-Americans often meant joining the Methodists, Lutherans, Episcopalians, or Presbyterians. Her theology is written in and through her life, in tears and blood before pen hit paper.

The parameters of her vow (three years of daily prayer meetings, two of which included fasting three days per week) court a certain amount of suffering and struggle. However, the autonomy and achievement the vow affords her mitigate the suffering. Though it is extraordinarily demanding, the vow becomes an avenue of self-definition and determination. It ensures time dedicated to herself and to God, providing a mode of agency which facilitates independence, empowerment (of self and others), and self-expression. Radical relationship with and commitment to God mediate and shift the purpose in suffering. In prayer she is continuously empowered and gradually overcomes the theological matrix of maldistributed and inevitable suffering, as God assists her in reconstructing her "self" through her ministry. Prayer became the place of resistance and the means by which resistance is enabled. Suffering, though present, takes a lesser position, ceasing to be a means of generating reward; instead, suffering is something which must be overcome.

The second theme of Mo. Dabney's book emerges from her reception of an orientation pivotal in Acts 2 and in the Azusa Street Revival.[51] Egalitarianism and inclusivity signal this pivotal orientation and are a hallmark of effectiveness and divine sanction of her ministry. More importantly, they are fundamental to building unity and community. This theme occupies portions of eleven out of seventeen chapters of the book.

Anthea Butler notes that the initial phase of leadership of the Women's Department aims at bringing people in to make a sanctified world within denomination walls. This stance is oft informed by the opinion that the COGIC (and like churches) has a moral and spiritual understanding preferable to other denominations. Paradoxically, this opens an invitation to all who are in full agreement with the belief system regardless of race, nationality, or gender and also prescribes a boundary against ecumenism and inclusivity.[52] Butler notes that in the 1940s and 1950s, "COGIC turned its attention to sanctifying the world. This shift in emphasis was the result of increasing civic engagement and community involvement."[53] Mo. Dabney's ministry (which began in 1929) is then an early proponent of this later thrust. While praying souls into the denomination, her prayer ministry joined with other denominations that many in COGIC might have felt were incongruent with its explicit Pentecostal orientation. In contrast, her emphasis on egalitarianism and inclusivity is evident:

> God taught me very definitely that it was wrong and against His divine order to make a difference between His children. A child of God, a Christian, a saint, a soldier of the cross are all the same. They must live together here, and it is their obligation and duty to follow peace and love without dissimulation. When the pastors [in the city of Philadelphia] found out I was honest in my heart and not a church wrecker, many of them consented for their members to pray with me. . . . I am very careful how I speak concerning those who represent the same Christ I represent. I never tolerate anyone's teaching that one Christian is better than another.[54]

Welcoming those from other denominations affords her a range of co-laborers and a variety of associations. When seeking a building in which to pray, she says, "Ministers of the Methodist, Baptist, Episcopal and Presbyterian churches here in Philadelphia, gave largely. The business men and women of all nationalities put their hearts into the demand and responded largely to the call."[55]

From her knees she formed a cadre of entrepreneurial, professional, educated women to participate in prayer and in the writing ministry. Displaying the tenor of the black church and club women and reminiscent of literary clubs earlier, Mo. Dabney rallied these women, who weld together ministry and service with racial and human uplift. In this ministry, Mo. Dabney committed herself with others to a tradition of expressing divine intellect and excellence. These women were initially prayer warriors and students with her, and later women formed the staff needed to respond to the multitude of letters she received. Of these women, she writes, "we must have qualified workers, those who have denounced the hidden things of dishonesty, who have been robed in the robe of righteousness and praise to show forth His glory."[56] The church is a place where all aspects of one's life converge. Her sense of obligation to God and to the work helped her navigate around the false boundaries between the secular and the religious. The work required a skilled and intelligent community committed both to moral integrity and to divine social responsibility.

Mo. Dabney testifies of those from whom she learns and the community of women who labor with her. The latter part of the book is largely a tribute to them. Chapter 10 is dedicated to her mentor, Mrs. Harriet M. Ways. Mo. Dabney notes that Pennsylvania is called the Keystone State and Philadelphia the City of Brotherly Love, but that, "Among the many women who have arisen to fame by their kind, humanitarian deeds and acts of charity are: Betsy Ross, Mrs. Mary E. Tribbet, Mrs. Annie L. Blackwell and Miss Marian Anderson."[57] She adds to this list Mrs. Ways, whom she credits with a prayer ministry after which hers is modeled. Mrs. Ways started a prayer ministry in which groups of women went from church to church praying and blessing the churches spiritually and materially. Not only were souls saved and people healed, but during the Depression this ministry was able to make financial contributions to the pastors and their churches. It is out of this ministry that the Church of God in Christ was born in Philadelphia and Elder Jones was sent to pastor and continue the work Mrs. Ways began.[58] In other chapters, Mo. Dabney honors women who work with her as letter writers, prayer warriors, promoters, financial contributors, and comforters. She also acknowledges Mo. Lizzie Roberson's vision and support, which enabled Dabney to meet pastors and minister in churches in Nebraska.

Describing one of her prayer gatherings, Mo. Dabney writes, "It felt like a prayer meeting was going on. It attracted the attention of all classes, creeds and colors. There was no separation, 'Big I, or Little You,' everybody was on the same level and it was instructive to follow the young converts as they entered into a new life for the Lord."[59] A practice and ethic of inclusivity resonates throughout her writing. It was perhaps because of all that she had seen and experienced that she was particularly sensitive to rejection and unfair treatment. This experience may also inform her continuously characterizing her ministry as one that prays for "everybody, everywhere." Her writing then becomes particularly important as it extends this community beyond our borders. As an international ministry, this gospel message empowers believers, enlarges the Christian family, and promotes wholeness so that the world can pray through into God's glory.

The third and underlying theme in her book is that of Mo. Dabney becoming who she was divinely meant to be. Praying through provides that free space to be and to fulfill herself. Only God can grant the fullest possibility of self-actualization and empowerment and make the way for one to realize these materially.

In a chapter entitled "Saved for the Purpose," Mo. Dabney shares how her self-image and definition changed in the process of prayer:

> Dear Reader, it is interesting to know how we try to make ourselves known unto others by words and through the medium of prayer. Sometimes we fail utterly. I tried to present my prayer life unto others by telling them I was a "worm of the dust, a grain of sand, a door mat, and many other insignificant objects." I thought this would present a beautiful picture of humility.[60]

Objectifying her work and her "self," she comes to realize, is not humility but an insult to God. This attitude and approach stifles her ministry, what God is able to do through her, and thus praying into the glory. While the idea of being as nothing before God is not uncommon in Christian spirituality, she rather equates nothingness with nobodyness. Given the denigration of her stature and age, the accusations associating her with the demonic, and the exigencies of African-American Pentecostal life, this initial self-concept is understandable. It may also be related to her concept and experience of suffering. Choosing divine work did not translate into her knowing her "self" as sacred.

In the same conversation, however, God scolds her and impresses her to see herself as "a child of the King." God then challenges her, asking why she "did not pray out into His glory?" Stating that she is doing her best, God tells her there is new territory to be claimed, and she asks God for "more acres in prayer."[61] Consequently, she experiences tremendous growth personally and is able to facilitate the growth and achievement of others in prayer. When this shift occurs is unclear; however, it represents an event of self-reconstruction that is transfiguring, as it occurs in the presence of God. This passage, and the transformation it describes, is a key reference to her spiritual path of "praying out into God's glory." This exchange reflects a mutuality of relationship that is radical.

The remainder of the chapter testifies to one who became an inhabitant in the "new acres" God gives. Mo. Dabney shares her transformative experience as a preface to the testimony of Miss Mary Passarella, whom God sent as a co-laborer. Her story resembles Mo. Dabney's but is foremost the testimony of a benefactor of her ministry and the manifested result of praying through. Mo. Dabney includes this story to provide a specific response to letters from despondent young women struggling with dreams deferred. Miss Passarella's life is a tangible example of what the reader can achieve in faithful devotion to God. Miss Passarella prays through into God's glory, and the reader sees victory emerge from a life fraught with sacrifice, demonic attacks, and suffering.

Mo. Dabney also speaks of God's promise after the covenant to bless her, and those pastors with whom she ministers, spiritually and materially. Like Mrs. Ways, she is able to bless churches financially as well as spiritually. But the salvation of souls is the greatest manifestation of God's glory. She reports approximately 5,118 souls saved through prayer revivals, tracts, and correspondence. As mentioned earlier, the testimonies of healings that fill the last chapter of the book further evidence the manifestation of God's glory.

Mo. Dabney is indeed saved for this purpose. The predominant work ethic in the book is that of humbling herself that she might be exalted. She decides to surrender and let God make her into what she did not want to be.[62] Humility and surrender are taught in the Church of God in Christ as one's proper stance toward God; in her words, "at his feet shall be the highest place my soul shall go. . . . All exhortations elevation and honor will be bestowed upon each individual who will learn this one lesson, 'humble is the way.'"[63] Literally, it is "at his feet" on her knees in the presence of God that she partakes of her divine identity and inheritance. Surrender can be best understood as her giving of her total self to God. It is this posture that assists her in resistance. It shifts the place of authority from the external to the internal. Authority is based in one's relationship and experiences with God, facilitating the exercise of personal power. This is the double-edged sword of the dialectic of authority. While it may lend itself to subordination on the one hand, it enables the appropriation of personal power on the other.

Praying out into God's glory is not only an act of self-reconstruction, it is also communal, each facilitating the other. Patrice Dickerson says, "a person comes into being and knows herself by her achievements, and through her efforts to become and know herself, she achieves."[64] It is the Spirit that grants the power to be, and it is accessed in prayer. Mo. Dabney comes of age, maturing in the chamber of her three-year covenant and subsequent life of prayer. She grows in servanthood, acquiring the ability to free herself from servitude. As a proto-womanist, her movement anticipates Jacquelyn Grant's examination of African-American women's work experience and service. African-American women's labor history is characterized by service positions and status. Servanthood in the church and society often takes the form of servitude. Grant states that the "servant" title in the United States context contributes to women's oppression (being servants of servants) such that it perpetuates it rather than frees one from it. Where servanthood language predominates, women are not freed from servitude. In her essay, Grant proposes a moratorium on servanthood language for African-American women, opting instead for "disciple."[65] While Mo. Dabney does not make this statement explicitly, something similar occurs in the way she reconstructs herself as a child of the King and in her references to the disciples. Her documentation of the results of her ministry in *What It Means to Pray Through* also position her as an apostle of prayer. The lowly place of prayer, its assignation to a simple service position, is vindicated. Mo. Dabney is an instrument God uses to do this, by manifesting God's glory through her and in her ministry. The lowly now embodies divinity in a way that cannot be refuted.

Referencing the tradition of Paul, John, and Peter, she chooses for herself the label of a disciple and thus a coauthor of the gospel. She says that John, on the Isle of Patmos, prayed through and out into the Spirit and that this initiated his writing letters to church leaders. Like the apostles, she perseveres in public ministry, praying through the suffering and the trials into the full capacities of her being. The "glory" is also a transfiguring experience through which she becomes more fully aware of who she is, and who God is, in the presence of God. She is empowered as in the Book of Acts to participate in furthering the reign of God as her divine inheritance with Jesus' apostles and disciples. In communion with other believers, the prayer ministry is a womb, a birthing place where the glory ushers in new beings and disciples. Salvation, wholeness, and new life extend across denominations, races, and nations through prayer and pen.

The business of making people whole in body, mind, and spirit is the work of prayer and is made effective and more expansive through the gift and skill of writing. Praying through, though intense, is not defeatist in nature, but makes the way to success. Mo. Dabney's egalitarian ethic and inclusivity enlarge her perceptions of the household of faith, feeding the ecumenical spirit in which she operated. She helps further the work of women in a traditional ministry, while elevating it to a calling equal to that of the predominantly male ordained leadership. This elevation is particularly significant in a denomination that does not ordain women. By forming and training a cadre of women to be co-laborers in the writing of a contemporary gospel, their ministry together becomes a sure foundation for them and for the manifestation of the glory and reign of God on earth.

CONCLUSION

Mo. Dabney illustrates in her life the challenges facing and the creativity of African-American women, with particular reference to the Church of God in Christ. She appropriates and reinterprets church dogma and practice so that they become a means of cultivating agency and freedom. She creates for herself, other women, and the community a free space within her own church tradition, as well as in theirs. Simultaneously, this appropriation facilitates resisting oppressive and divisive forces in society. This praxis was honed in the prayer room and in her writing ministry in a reciprocal relationship with God.

God enables her to take ownership of who she divinely is. Radical relationship and commitment lend themselves to a paradigm whereby personal spiritual power bases its authority on mutual relation. Surrender (the ultimate place of one's yielding to God) nurtures a communion that refigures her "self" understanding and her vision of the future. She becomes the embodiment of the gospel in her person and in her writing.

The ongoing and tenuous dilemma posed by the dialectic of authority is mediated (though not resolved) when she claims this relationship and stands on her experience with God. It is at this juncture that mutual accountability is possible and institutional parameters seem not to occupy parity with God or Scripture. Resistance is thereby facilitated. For Mo. Dabney, prayer becomes the womb and vehicle for overcoming denominational, gender, racial, and sociological barriers to fulfilling her human potential. While she might not frame her actions as resistance (except to Satan), her evolving sense of the sacred compels her to resist what is oppositional to God.

Prayer is transformative power. Rather than being expressive of simple desire or utterance, it is "more realistic." Thus, it does not just function as a symbol of what could be, but holds within it creative power. In the intensity of life, prayer "becomes a reality; or in other words . . . it is an instrument that opens the way for the children of God to enter into God's guest chamber."[66] In the face of God, reality can change, progressively and dramatically, literally and conceptually.

In *What It Means to Pray Through*, Mo. Dabney writes to us of these reinterpretive practices that today are all too often taken for granted in COGIC community. She implores us to understand and appropriate the power prayer gives us to reshape, resist, and revision our reality courageously. Prayer should be viewed as at the genesis of and as integral to our struggles for wholeness and justice as we work out our salvation. It is essential for grounding and maintaining one's relationship with God, self, and others. Inclusive human community and divine communion are enabled when one dedicates oneself wholly to God in mutuality and respect.

8

WRITING A LIFE, WRITING THEOLOGY
Edith Stein in the Company of the Saints

Meghan T. Sweeney

Christian literature is full of "official" and "unofficial" hagiographies, stories of holy women and men, sometimes factual, sometimes not, who have tried to imitate Christ in ways that have caught attention and captivated imagination. In the hagiographies, these holy women and men are figures whose lives are structured specifically for and around their perceived Christian accomplishments and virtues, often rendering these women and men larger than life, heroic, and almost superhuman. In the hagiographies, the holy women and men overcome and transcend the ordinary failures and limitations of "everyday" personalities and foibles, in part because their failures and limitations are interpreted as part of their spiritual struggle for holiness. In the written stories, these holy women and men are rendered distant enough so as to be effective Christian role models; they're familiar enough to the reader to effect a connection, but distant enough that the saint does not become domesticated, contained, or too easily imitated.

While there have been many (sometimes quite questionable) purposes of these hagiographies, one significant and common purpose has been formational: these stories assume that Christian individuals and communities can learn about what it means to imitate Christ, to become Christ's disciples, through others' efforts to imitate Christ.[1] At the beginning of his introduction to the hagiographic *Life of the Fathers*, Gregory of Tours (c. 6th century) writes that hagiographies "could strengthen the Church . . . because the life of the saints . . . encourages the minds of listeners to follow their example."[2] These written lives, for better and for worse, provide models and maps, reassurance, familiarity, and challenge. Hagiographies are stories of discipleship, of Christians being like Christ, meant to elicit imitative responses. Connecting with and patterning one's own life on the stories of holy women and men enables Christians to enter into an imitation of an imitation of Christ as a way to enact Christian discipleship, the effect of which is to come to know and enjoy God more deeply. Christians know God by being like God. Discipleship is layered imitation, even imitation of imitation. The Apostle Paul understands this when he exhorts the Corinthians, who are having difficulty following Christ, to "be imitators of me, as I am of Christ" (1 Cor 11:1), so that they too may become disciples of Christ by imitating Paul.

The twentieth-century saint and martyr Edith Stein (1891–1942), who was inspired by Saint Teresa of Avila's writings, wrote her own stories of holy women and men. In these hagiographical writings, Stein engages and probes the concept of imitation, in effect cultivating her own discipleship, and thus her own life and personhood. By telling and writing the lives of holy others in the form of hagiographies, she writes not only a kind of Christology, an understanding of who Christ is and what he does and effects, but also a theology of discipleship that is indirectly autobiographical. That is, Stein writes her own life in words that construct and contextualize her life through the imitation of others. This imitation of holy women and men also reveals and makes real the living Christ. By highlighting the ways in which one person reads and writes about her sisters in faith, seeing herself in and as others and thus seeking to imitate them in order to better imitate and know Christ, I show how this imitation can assist an individual in her own spiritual and self formation.

EDITH STEIN

Edith Stein is a controversial figure. Described by her famous philosophy teacher, Edmund Husserl, as his best student, this Jewish philosopher became a Roman Catholic nun, was murdered by the Nazis at Auschwitz because of her Jewishness, and was controversially canonized a saint by the Roman Catholic Church in 1998.[3] In her youth Stein declared herself an agnostic, but while studying with Husserl, she decided, like many of her friends and colleagues studying phenomenology, to convert from Judaism to Christianity. What remained for Stein was choosing from between her two main options, either the German Evangelical (Lutheran) or Roman Catholic churches. In the summer of 1921, while visiting at the home of her closest friend and university colleague, Frau Dr. Hedwig Conrad-Martius, herself a convert to Lutheranism from Judaism, Stein made her choice. The conversion story goes like this:

> It happened, however, that during one of these holiday-visits both husband and wife had to go away. Before their departure Frau Conrad-Martius took her friend [i.e., Stein] over to the book-case and told her to take her pick. They were all at her disposal. Edith herself tells us: "I picked at random and took out a large volume. It bore the title *The Life of St. Teresa, written by herself.* I began to read, was at once captivated, and did not stop till I reached the end. As I closed the book, I said, 'That is the truth.'"[4]

A text-mediated relationship of deep resonance developed between Edith Stein and Teresa of Avila, the formidable and brilliant sixteenth-century Spanish nun and reformer of the cloistered Carmelite religious order.[5] How do we make sense of this strong attraction of Stein to Teresa that is mediated through writing?

Human persons sometimes have the experience at one time or another in their lives of being drawn inexplicably and feeling connected to another human being. While certainly such attractions can be analyzed by biography (e.g., similarities of age, education, gender, geography, culture, interests, economics, vocations, avocations, etc.), they cannot be reduced to or explained away by these, for certainly there are instances in which people strongly like and dislike others who seem and are quite similar to or different from themselves. With some people there is an inexplicable resonance through which an individual feels sparked and enlivened. Something of another's personhood grabs us, and we find ourselves attracted. These relationships can exist not only between and among the living in direct relationship with each other, but also between and among individuals, living and dead, in and through texts. Through this attraction and the relationship that ensues, we come to know ourselves more deeply. Stein knew herself more fully as a consequence of reading Teresa. Stein saw herself, knew herself, in Teresa.

Prior to reading Teresa, Stein's familiarity with the finer points of Lutheran and Roman Catholic doctrine seems to have been nonexistent. It's questionable whether or not, for example, she had ever been to Roman Catholic Mass before choosing Rome. Indeed, there appears to be no explicitly doctrinal reason for Stein's conversion to Roman Catholicism. In fact, somewhat oblivious to ecclesial matters, Hedwig, a Lutheran, became Edith's baptismal sponsor on New Year's Day 1922, in a pre-Vatican II Tridentine and Vatican I anti- and ante-ecumenical era when being outside the church absolutely meant no salvation in a very literal way. Focused neither on the dogma of Augsburg (1530) nor Trent (1545–1563), what seems to have mattered most to Stein were religious practices and the people who practiced them. Truth can be mediated and accessed, can be incarnated, through embodied practice. This understanding of truth emerges in Stein's earliest philosophical interests.

Stein's 1917 doctoral dissertation, *On the Problem of Empathy*, is born of her desire to better understand the human being and human experience. In this foundational text of Stein's thought, Stein investigates a fundamental tenet of Husserl's phenomenology: empathy, an act "in which foreign experience is comprehended,"[6] an act in which "knowledge of subjectivity not your own" is achieved.[7] Stein seeks to "grasp and describe these acts [of empathy] in the greatest essential generality"[8] so as to address how the knower can know the object known. Stein is not interested, at least not initially, in what empathy empathizes, but rather in the phenomenon of empathy itself: how we gain firsthand access to others' experiences and their subjectivity.

Stein argues that we cannot know something without experiencing it. Experience of what is foreign to our individual selves comes through empathy. Empathy is and enables such necessary "experience of foreign consciousness in general."[9] Empathy facilitates the knowing of the other. And in coming to know the other, we come to know the world, both the world of the other, and the world as the other constitutes it in his or her consciousness.[10] One way to gain access to the world of another, to empathize with that person, is to read experiential texts. Empathy and its resultant subjective experience can be enabled through access to the written word and the content expressed therein.

Stein's philosophical work on empathy as a truth-discovering mechanism attuned her interest in religious practices and their practitioners. Indeed, Stein's own philosophy *enabled* Teresa's influence on her by providing a basis for interpreting her empathic connection to Teresa's writings (although her philosophy did not *cause* Teresa's influence, for if empathy effected a causal relationship, then Stein would have been unduly influenced by *everything* that she read; in Stein's case, we recall her attraction to Teresa). If she did what Teresa did, both lived the same life and engaged in spiritual writing, then empathy could ground a kind of imitation by which empathized knowledge could become imitated experience and knowledge, which is and is not firsthand experience. Imitation is both one's own experience *and* the experiences of others. Teresa's *Life* and the life of love and discipleship that it conveys through Teresa's indomitable personality present Stein with the opportunity to come to the kind of self-understanding and knowledge of truth that Stein so seems to crave. In reading Teresa and how she lived her life, Stein saw and felt herself, and thus found her way to God.[11] There is an inexplicable resonance between these two women, and Stein so trusted what Teresa wrote and the person revealed therein that she declared Teresa's spiritual autobiography "the truth."[12]

Stein's early philosophy was not merely academic, but had a constructive influence on her life. It opened her to the influence of the insights of her philosophy, namely that empathy of others' knowledge matters for growth into one's own self-understanding. Arguably, Stein's conversion to Roman Catholicism was a conversion to the Carmelite life of contemplative prayer and community described by Teresa. Teresa gives Stein a structure of meaning and a way to hook into Christian discipleship, into a life in imitation of and relationship with Christ. Stein wanted to be like Teresa. Stein wanted to imitate an imitation of Christ in order that she might have the same understanding that Teresa did. And indeed, twelve years later, Stein herself entered Carmel. Teresa had what Stein wanted, and in order to gain the same firsthand knowledge of self and God that is displayed in Teresa's *Life*, Stein chose to enter into the religious practices of Teresa's lifeworld. Empathetic attention to writing and what it sparked propelled Stein to seek firsthand knowledge.

EDITH STEIN AND HER HAGIOGRAPHIES

Stein's initial understanding of her spiritual self and her God was through reading written texts. Eventually she began to write texts as a way to enhance, develop, and layer what she encountered in her reading and the benefits derived therefrom. Soon after her conversion, Stein's academic focus began to shift. Her previous attention to exclusively philosophical pursuits was redirected toward more philosophically informed theological subjects, including considerations of Thomas Aquinas (for whom she had a deep affection), John Henry Newman, and the subject of the dignity and vocation of women. Interestingly, her later explicitly and exclusively "religious" or "theological" works consist primarily of hagiographical texts, most of them about women, which seek to help humans to live fully by highlighting the exemplary lives of others. This concern was in keeping with her philosophical goals.[13] For Stein, ideas are never disconnected from the people who promoted or, more to the point, lived them.

An apparently common practice in Carmelite convents was for the nuns to compose performance pieces for special occasions. After she entered the Carmelite order in 1934, Stein was not exempt from this tradition, and because of her writing skills she was often called upon to write short pieces about holy people for a particular saint's feast day or for other festive occasions such as birthdays and the taking of religious vows. Some of the material that Stein wrote included theatrical pieces — that is, dialogues that were written to be performed. Here I provide an example from each genre, an essay and a theatrical script. These examples demonstrate how writing about others can in fact be layered imitative and autobiographical explorations of one's own understanding of theology and discipleship, and consequently constructive of one's own self-understanding.

A Short Biography: "A Chosen Vessel of Divine Wisdom: Sr. Marie-Aimée de Jésus of the Carmel of the Avenue de Saxe in Paris, 1839–1874"

Stein's essay "A Chosen Vessel of Divine Wisdom: Sr. Marie-Aimée de Jésus of the Carmel of the Avenue de Saxe in Paris, 1839–1874" was written in 1939 for an edited volume that was never published because of the onset of World War II.[14] Not surprisingly, given its title, it is about a Parisian Carmelite nun, Sr. Marie-Aimée de Jésus, who was born Dorothée (Dorothea) Quoniam, and who died shortly after Thérèse of Lisieux (the famous 19th-century French Carmelite) was born in 1873. Stein writes,

> Dorothea's call to Carmel had already occurred when she was a child. Once when she began to take pleasure in frivolous things and endanger her interior life, her mother gave her a book that contained a short biography of Holy Mother Teresa. She found herself reflected in it word for word. "This child, upon whom God had bestowed so many graces, who loved good books and religious conversations, so longed for martyrdom, and, since she could not have this, placed her hope in the life of a hermit — was that not I?" But she also saw her own image in Teresa's involvement with frivolous friends and the consequent cooling of her ardor. Teresa finds herself again during her education in a monastery.[15]

This dense passage contains the multiple, layered voices of Stein, Dorothea, and Teresa. It is at once a description by Stein of Dorothea and of Teresa of Avila. Stein tells Dorothea's story by including Dorothea's own testimony of Teresa's influence on Dorothea. This testimony includes a brief version of the story of Teresa's own conversion to Carmel in Teresa's own words. Stein is telling Dorothea's story, and Dorothea is quoting Teresa of Avila. In writing this way, Stein links herself not only to Dorothea but also to Teresa through Dorothea.

Like a hall of mirrors, Stein sets up a three-way reflection among the three women. Stein establishes a layered web of interconnection in which she identifies with and becomes part of their stories. Like Stein, who converted to Carmel and thus Roman Catholicism by reading Teresa's *Life*, young Dorothea is attracted to Carmel through a short biography of Teresa. Like Stein, young Dorothea, "who [also] loved good books and religious conversations," finds herself reflected in and attracted to the life of Teresa of Avila, who herself was also attracted to good books and religious conversations. Stein emphasizes that Dorothea sees herself in Teresa. So much so, in fact, that, again like Stein, Dorothea "placed her hope in the life of a hermit," namely in the life of Teresa, who herself was compelled by the prophet Elijah, the forefather of the hermetic Carmelites.[16] Finally, all three women were compelled to martyrdom, a hagiographical motif that shows itself repeatedly to be of great significance for Stein. Teresa, Dorothea, and Stein choose Carmel because a life in Carmel can be a difficult life of self-martyrdom.

In her essay, Stein quotes Sr. Marie-Aimée de Jésus (Dorothea) as saying, "I need Carmel . . . with its perfection and way of perfection. Carmel with its purity, its apostolate, its martyrdom."[17] Stein emphasizes that Dorothea was attracted to the perfection, to the structure of Carmel itself and to what this perfection and structure enabled. Carmel is pure, and it offered a way of being an apostle of Christ through a demanding love that asks for self-martyrdom so as to put Christ and his commandments first: to love God and neighbor. This is what Stein herself strove to do, and her time in Carmel further trained her mind and heart. When Stein had the early chance to flee from Germany to unoccupied Switzerland, she refused to do so until permission could be secured from the Swiss Carmelites for her biological sister, Rosa, to flee with her. But permission came too late, and instead they fled to a Carmelite convent in occupied Holland, where they eventually were captured by the Nazis.

Concluding her essay, Stein writes, "Nor could Dorothea consider any other Carmel than the one that seemed to be stubbornly closed to her. God's will was too clear to her. And her trust was finally rewarded."[18] Upon her conversion to Roman Catholicism, Stein wanted to enter Carmel right away. But her confessor told her to wait in order to settle into her new religion and not rush into a rash decision with a convert's (sometimes misunderstood and misplaced) zeal. Although it took twelve years of waiting, Stein was patient, and her trust was finally rewarded.

As readers who are mindful that it is Stein who has penned this quasi-hagiographic biography, we have to ask the question of whether and how Stein writes the story of Sr. Marie-Aimée de Jésus in her own spiritual and biographical image. Dramatic theological and spiritual meaning is infused into the rendering of Dorothea's life. As such, Stein is writing her own life, her own spiritual journey, giving meaning and coherence to her own existence in and through the story of another. This story is implicitly autobiographical, relating Stein's own journey and her connectedness to the journeys of her foremothers, whom she loves and respects. What Stein emphasizes in these stories tells us much about herself. Stein makes intelligible her own life by writing about Dorothea and Teresa. In so doing, she writes her own life, an act of self-definition through writing. Through obfuscated identification with the stories of others, Stein's writing gives her deeper access to herself, to her form of discipleship, and to her God.

An (Explicit) Dialogue: "I Am Always in Your Midst"

The second example of Stein writing about herself through others is "I Am Always in Your Midst," a dialogue between Saint Angela Merici, the founder of the Ursuline nuns, whose primary mission is the education of girls, and Mother Ursula, a nun named after Saint Ursula, the patron saint of the Ursulines. It was written by Stein in December 1939. Similar to "A Chosen Vessel of Divine Wisdom: Sr. Marie-Aimée de Jésus of the Carmel of the Avenue de Saxe in Paris, 1839–1874," the reader cannot help but notice the hidden autobiographical references within this explicit dialogue. Key to understanding this particular text is the German Jewish situation, for example that *Kristallnacht* had already occurred in November 1938, ushering in open and accepted German anti-Semitism, and that only two months prior to this dialogue's composition Germany invaded Poland, officially starting both World War II and the ghettoizing of Jews.

The dialogue begins with Mother Ursula in prayerful conversation with Saint Angela:

> How good it feels to become a child again
> And rest without cares in mother's arms.
> The gentle hand drives off the fever's heat,
> And every pain is lessened before the tender eyes.
> Will you now advise me what to do?
> I'll listen calmly and obey, oh so gladly![19]

Ursula describes the rest, safety, and security of being a child again in her mother's arms, and the mother's alleviation of her fever. Ursula is vulnerable, but protected and loved, free from the pain of illness. For a brief moment, she is at ease; she is held, loved, cared for. And she trusts this mother. She asks for direction and promises that she will obey.

After Ursula extols Saint Angela's own willingness to follow the call of God and to be an instrument in God's hands, Ursula discusses how God leads each person on her own path and forms these people in various ways by "gentle finger strokes" and "chisel blows," and that "we collaborate with God on his work of art."[20] Of significance is that *Stein* in German means *stone* in English, stones that are shaped through hammer and chisel. The reader gets the sense that perhaps Stein is referring to herself as one of God's many unique works of art who collaborates with God in her own self-formation. Then, picking up on a theme touched upon in "A Chosen Vessel," Ursula discusses the ways in which people do not hear the soft voice of God within, or hear the voice but do not understand where the voice is drawing them. In the voice of Ursula, Stein writes,

> Then someone else must come,
> Gifted with a finer ear attuned and keener sight,
> And disclose the meaning of the obscure words.

This is the guide's wonderful gift,
The highest that, according to a sage's word,
The Creator has given to the creation:
To be his fellow worker in the salvation of souls.[21]

In the earlier story about Sr. Marie-Aimée de Jésus, Stein had Dorothea recount the cooling of her own ardor. Although Stein's ardor cannot be "cooled" in the same way, since she was not born a Christian, nevertheless Stein went through a period of agnosticism in her youth and later required a guide to direct her religious proclivities. Teresa of Avila became her guide. In this dialogue, Saint Angela functions as leader (founder) and teacher of the Ursulines and Mother Ursula, just as Teresa functioned as leader (founder) and teacher of the Carmelites and Stein. Both Angela and Teresa, in their roles as leaders and teachers, collaborate with Christ in the salvation of souls.

This poem, however, indicates that the standard (and simpler) forms of leading and teaching will not be the means by which some souls will be saved. In a strange twist, Saint Angela finally speaks and tells Ursula to become a guide herself, to build God's kingdom, perhaps in a vineyard that demands her efforts, "Even if it be a different one than up to now, / A different one than you yourself had thought."[22] If Stein herself appears as Ursula (like Ursula, Stein had been a teacher), then Angela is telling her that what will be asked of her will be different from what has been asked in the past. Pointedly, Saint Angela says to Ursula, "Then you have one more question to resolve / To which you sought an answer tonight: / May you bind still other human beings, / To an uncertain fate?"[23] The reader is left wondering about this uncertain fate to which Ursula will lead herself and others as part of building up God's kingdom. Mother Ursula's final words are noteworthy and ominous:

How foolish now this doubt appears to me!
If God's call sounds within a soul,
When he leads it to our house's door,
And to knock hard—why should we not open
The door wide, our arms and our heart?
If he shows the way, then he also knows

That it is not a wrong track where people suddenly get lost;
No spurious way that ends in desert sands.
That step by step the road will be revealed,
I firmly believe. And in fact what is certain?
Where is "certain fate"? Yes, we see—
And it's good that we are so confronted—
How around us structures are becoming ruins
That seemed to us to have been raised for eternity.
One thing alone is certain: that God is
And that his hand holds us in being.
Then even if around us the whole world falls to wrack and ruin,
We are not ruined if we hold ourselves to him.[24]

In line 10, after chiding herself for her doubt and her resistance, it seems that Ursula (Stein?) then attempts to convince herself ("I firmly believe") of God's loving providence in which reward will be given for following the divine road.

In an almost desperate way, Ursula begins to ask, what is certain, anyway? In the midst of "wrack and ruin" in which the whole world is being destroyed all around her, she asserts that it is good that she is confronted with this situation of destruction and the question it raises for belief. "Wrack and ruin" enables the insight that true certainty comes from holding oneself to God alone, whose existence is sure and who holds humanity in being.

After seemingly aligning herself with Ursula in the beginning stanzas of the poem, it is hard not to continue interpreting Ursula as a figure for Stein as she deals at a spiritual and theological level with the Nazis' "final solution." Although Stein herself had converted to Christianity, she was under no delusion that she was safe from the Nazis. Additionally, although no longer Jewish in religion, she felt a strong connection to her Jewish heritage as well to her Jewish relatives and friends. As evidenced by a letter that she wrote in 1933 to Pope Pius XI, pleading with him to have the Roman Catholic Church speak out against the inhumane treatment of Jews, Stein had a deep sense of her own impending destruction.[25] The way in which Stein understands God asking her to participate in building the kingdom of God will require great self-sacrifice on her part, a self-sacrifice to which she may also lead others. But she seems to retain hope that if she and the others "hold ourselves to him," then they are "not ruined."

Stein and Queen Esther

The intensity and complexity of Stein's autobiographical hagiographies of others deepen in her accounts of Queen Esther, the Hebrew heroine. Whereas Stein identifies *with* Sr. Marie-Aimée de Jésus and Mother Ursula and is *like* and connects with them through the imitation of discipleship, Stein comes to identify in a more strictly mimetic capacity *as* Queen Esther who has returned in a messianic, Christ-like mode to save her people. If Stein donned the costumes of Sr. Marie-Aimée de Jésus and Mother Ursula, she donned both the costume *and mask* (persona) of Esther.[26] Stein's paradigmatic identification *as* a new self-sacrificing Esther was established in part because in the year she was born, Stein's birthday occurred on Yom Kippur, the Jewish high holy day of atonement and repentance on which sacrifice is offered to God to amend for wrongdoings. This coincidence captivated Stein's imagination and self-understanding throughout her life.

"Conversation at Night," which is a midnight encounter between the Mother Superior of a Carmelite convent and Queen Esther, originally was staged as a birthday celebration in 1941. In the short conversation, Queen Esther visits the Mother Superior and initially only hints at her identity. When Mother Superior asks the stranger, "Oh tell me! Are you she herself, the Virgin Mother?," Esther responds,

> "I am not she—but I know her very well.
> And it is my joy to serve her.
> I am of her people, her blood,
> And once I risked my life for this people.
> You recall her when you hear my name.
> My life serves as an image of hers for you."

To this, the Mother responds,

"A riddle, unusually hard to understand—
How am I to grasp it? You are a woman whom we recognize as an
   'example'?
You staked your life for your people?
And you certainly had no weapon, either, then,
Except those hands raised in supplication?
So are you Esther, then, the queen?"

Esther replies, "That is what people called me. You know my fate."[27]

In this "Conversation," there are multiple layers at play. First, as in "I Am Always in Your Midst," Stein is reflecting on the then-current fate of the Jews, as demonstrated by Esther's last statement, "You know my fate." Later in the text, Mother Superior states, "And today another Hamam [or 'Haman,' the enemy of the Jews in the book of Esther] / has sworn to annihilate them [the Jews] in bitter hate," a statement which seems like a clear allusion to the Nazis' "final solution."

Second, Stein is also pointing to the obvious possibility of the deliverance of the Jewish people (whether in this life or in death is uncertain) by Jesus' sacrifice on the cross.[28] Esther quotes the resurrected Jesus addressing the Jews of the Old Testament era, "Come to me all you who have faithfully served / The Father and lived in hope / Of the redeemer."[29]

Third, by having Esther say to Mother Superior, in reference to Mary, "My life serves as an *image* of hers for you," Esther is aligning herself with Mary as the mother of salvation because of her status as Theotokos, and consequently as the mother of all of humanity.[30] Mother Superior's response, "You are a woman whom we recognize as an *'example'*" (emphasis added) misses the fullness of the meaning of Esther's comment. Esther considers herself to be in the image of Mary, almost symbolically and iconically reflecting and pointing to Mary's person and her near-divinity. Esther is not Mary, but she is also not *not* Mary. She is a medium for Mary, both an allegorical precursor of Mary *and* an incarnation of Mary.

Fourth, in having Esther return to 1941, Stein is also making hidden claims about the role of Esther in then-current political and theological situations. Although the text explicitly links Esther with Mary, and uses the concept of image to do so, another more pointed but less

clear connection is the one between Esther and Jesus, and by extension, both of these characters with Stein. In this dialogue, Stein paints
Esther as the savior of the Jewish people who liberates them from
their bondage. Esther says, "So I grew up / Far from home and yet
protected / As in the temple's quiet sanctuary. / I read the holy Scriptures of these people, / Who were now enslaved in a strange land, and
fervently implored that a savior come to them."[31] Esther also speaks
of being chosen to be this savior, this maidservant of the Lord at the
King's palace (read: Nazi-occupied Europe) even though the task was
painful. But in return for her suffering, God promised her the salvation of her people.[32] Mother then asks Esther the *very* pointed question,
"Is this in fact why Esther has returned?"[33] Esther has returned in and
through the person of Stein. By appropriating the persona or mask of
Esther, Stein is a medium for, an incarnation of, Esther and makes her
present, re-presents her.

There are two important details to note. First, in a 1938 letter (three
years *before* she penned "Conversation at Night") Stein writes, in the
context of discussing her family trying to flee Germany,

> There is no longer any sense to saving [money] since they have to turn
> everything in when they emigrate. If only they knew where to go! But
> I trust that, from eternity, Mother [[that is, Mary]] will take care of
> them. And [I also trust] in the Lord's having accepted my life for all
> of them. I keep having to think of Queen Esther who was taken from
> among her people precisely that she might represent them before the
> king. I am a very poor and powerless little Esther, but the King who
> *chose me* is infinitely great and merciful.[34]

In this letter, Stein makes a connection between her life and that of
Queen Esther, a connection that culminates in the "Conversation at
Night" dialogue. Given Stein's reticence to discuss her own life explicitly and directly, it is probable that this mention of Queen Esther was
perhaps the first and only explicit and direct moment in which Stein
does so. Second, a few years after Stein and her older biological sister,
Rosa (who also had converted to Roman Catholicism and who had
become a Carmelite lay sister), had escaped to the Carmelite convent in

Echt, Holland, the Nazis came to arrest and deport them. It is rumored (perhaps apocryphally) that Stein said to Rosa as they were arrested, "Come, let us go for our people." Combining the story of Esther with a Christian understanding of substitutionary atonement and the salvation that it brings, in tandem with the *imago* connection between Esther and Mary, Stein seems to have appropriated the *personae* or masks of an Esther/Christ/Mary figure whose life-giving sacrifice would save the Jews and birth them into new life.[35]

In telling a contemporary tale of Esther, Stein crafts for herself, she writes, an Esther persona, an Esther mask that she puts on in order to explore the multiplicity of her identities so that she can live into her own self-understanding and discipleship. Writing and living into, inhabiting, the persona of Esther links Stein's past with her present and gives interpretive and theological meaning to Stein's life.

Stein's explicitly autobiographical writing ends shortly before her conversion to Christianity, and her published letters provide few details about her internal motivations and self-understanding. Perhaps after her conversion Stein could only understand and express herself, could only access herself and God, through her identification with the stories of the holy individuals about whom she writes.[36] Through her writing and speaking about holy women and men, Stein comes to know both God and herself. But what is most autobiographical might not always be what is most direct. By layering her written investigations through multiple figures who reflect one another, she opens hidden spaces to explore. By embedding her speech in the dialogue of her saintly characters, she creates a play of meaning that opens up interpretive possibilities. Just as Stein identified with and imitated the saints about whom she wrote, her reader is invited to participate in this holy imitation. Obfuscation and indirection in writing can prove, sometimes, to be beneficial to conveying truths precisely because such forms of writing remain open to investigation and invite the reader's exploration.

Although she continues writing apparently honest and introspective letters to friends, Stein's readers are not privy to an explicit account of her spiritual journey. These two hagiographies and the other stories that she wrote provide the best textual access to Stein's inner life. However, asserting this position is not to argue that Stein intentionally wrote her stories, or at least not all of them, in these veiled or masked autobiographical ways, as if she were trying to be cagey with her writing, hoping, yet not, that someone might identify her in the stories and figure her out. If we are moderately sympathetic toward and not overly suspicious of Stein, we can see that these stories of connections with others provide Stein with a way of interpreting her own life of discipleship, a life of imitating Christ through the imitation of his saints. Interestingly, when asked why she converted to Roman Catholicism and entered Carmel, Stein always responded with the Latin *"secretum meum mihi,"* meaning "my secret is mine."[37] Perhaps her secret, the secret of her own spiritual life story, is shared through the obfuscating yet self-revealing hagiographic biographies that she wrote.

IMITATION, CHRISTIAN DISCIPLESHIP, AND WRITING

In her philosophical emphasis on empathy, Stein understands that the individual is constructed by her community. We mirror, reflect, imitate, and become like the people around us. This structure is neither good nor bad; it is simply an inextricable part of being human. If we do not recognize this structure of imitation that is already caught up in our existence, then we will never be aware of that which we imitate. We can accept imitation as a structural component of human persons and human communities and directively harness this structural capacity. Stein does. The gospels and Pauline letters do. Indeed, imitation is at the heart of Christianity. Jesus imitates the love and generosity of his father. And those who follow Jesus are called to imitate him. Through writing about and connecting herself to the lives of others and through the resultant increased knowledge of God and self, Stein grows in her understanding of her own discipleship: she grows in love for God, for neighbor, and for self. She becomes not only *like* the Christ through empathetic connection, she becomes *a* Christ through the joy and pain of messianic imitation. Through such imitation she deepens in her knowledge and love of Christ and achieves her deepest hunger and desire. While we can and perhaps ought to argue with her understanding of discipleship, nevertheless through her performative, obfuscating yet revealing texts, Stein writes her own spiritual life in an ongoing process of becoming and discovery.

At the beginning of the essay I indicated that I do not think that all stories and the personae they portray are good. Certainly the case of Edith Stein provides an example of the contentious power dimensions of choosing "saints," as she herself is a highly contested figure whose canonization in the Roman Catholic Church was supported and criticized strongly by many factions.[38] We must, therefore, be very careful about the stories we choose to engage, precisely because of their formative mimetic power. (Indeed, in book II of Plato's *Republic*, Socrates asserts that only stories of the gods and goddesses that promote goodness and honesty should be taught, especially to children, because stories are so formative for the development of character and faith.)[39] In choosing to imitate certain stories, certain theological beliefs and practices are upheld and developed, and so the process of telling stories is fraught with theological and ethical significance. In a Christian context, perhaps only those stories that portray their personae as complex figures living God's compassionate, inclusive, expansive, liberating, challenging, demanding, discomforting love ought to be taught and imitated, for this kind of love is what Jesus demonstrates and thus seems to be the call of Christian discipleship. Fundamentally, the call of Christian discipleship is to be *like* Christ. In humans being *like* Christ, humans not only witness to the presence of the living Christ as apostles, but such practices of imitative discipleship also make the Christ present in the world. We re-present and re-member Christ and thus make the living Christ known in the world. While this foundational understanding of discipleship is valid, discipleship does not mean saccharine, pietistic imitations of Christ. In the way she chooses her exemplars of Teresa, Esther, and others, Stein inhabits her faith not through a generic "what would Jesus do" imitation of Christ, nor through a fully traditional Roman Catholicism. To the contrary, she implicitly contests a number of teachings about who Christ is, what and who the church *really* is or might be, who Mary is and her role in salvation, and how atonement is effected. By choosing as exemplars of true faith strong women, both Jewish and Christian, who in their actions and writings confound essentialized misogynistic understandings of women, Stein validates both the religious knowing and the leadership of women.[40] Stein lives her life with intelligence and creativity, inhabiting the interstitial spaces that her identification of and with women's lives, and that writing her own life through creative reflection on them, provides her.[41]

Through textual (both read and written) engagements with forbears in faith, we can participate in the self- and community-creating process of imitation by which we can grow more deeply into ourselves and into the body of Christ. We can learn about God and our own vocations, and how we can become more fully ourselves and who God calls us to be, by the saints that attract us, those we choose to imitate, and the words that we read and write about them. If imitation is indeed an unavoidable structural component of the human person, then a key question of discipleship becomes, which holy women and men will we choose to imitate? Better to imitate willfully the imitators of Christ and what they seek than to imitate inadvertently and dangerously those whose desires and habits would harm.

WRITING HUNGER ON THE BODY
Simone Weil's Ethic of Hunger and Eucharistic Practice

Elizabeth A. Webb

Simone Weil is a figure who incites much passion. Dismissed by some circles as perversely self-annihilating, embraced by others as providing vast stores of insight into suffering and compassion, very deliberately ignored by others, Weil is not a figure about whom most readers remain neutral. This passion is well-deserved; Weil wrote such provocatively self-abdicating statements as, "If only I knew how to disappear there would be a perfect union of love between God and the earth I tread, the sea I hear."[1] Weil sought to live the self-abdication of which she wrote in order to keep her focus ever on Christ and on the suffering of others. The intersection of Weil's way of life and of her thought is vividly displayed in her writings on and practices of hunger. These writings and practices in particular reveal ways in which Weil's notion of self-emptying has dangerous consequences.

Despite having misgivings about aspects of Weil's life and thought, I love her deeply. I love her for the beauty of her life and of her words. I love her for her profound love for God, her deep compassion for the suffering of others, her wide-eyed yet clear-eyed proscriptions for a more just society. And I love her for her pain—not that I love the pain in her, but I long to ease her pain, to wrap my arms around her frail body, to feed her with the compassion she could not feel for herself. Some deep, unspoken trauma seems to haunt Weil, seeping into her self-perception as it seeps into her writing. I long to protect her, and when I have written on Weil previously, I have done so.[2] Above all, I long to protect her from the violence of her own thought, to downplay that violence or write it off as deliberate hyperbole, so that Weil herself is not written off. Her diagnoses of the human condition are so beautifully and painfully right, her understanding of trauma and affliction so profoundly true, her conception of compassion so deeply compassionate. Yet at every step she cannot cease doing violence to herself. Weil writes hunger on her body as if gouging the word into her flesh with her pen. My love for Weil and for the profundity of her vision calls me to plead with her to take that pen from her flesh.

Still, what Weil has written on her body demands a reading. What I read there is not only a brilliant but ultimately self-destructive ethic of living hungrily, but also the inscription of hunger in her very words. In her writing *of* hunger, Weil longs to *elicit hunger* in her readers, she cries out for our hunger. Paul Celan wrote of the strange dialogical character of poetry, especially after the Holocaust: a poem "may be a letter in a bottle thrown out to sea with the—surely not always strong—hope that it may somehow wash up somewhere, perhaps on a shoreline of the heart."[3] Like Celan's poetry, Weil's writing, with a desperate hope, seeks a reader, a hearer, a witness, who will respond with hunger, with attention to her pain. Weil's writing, that is, calls us to hunger for *her* very restoration. It is deeply sad that Weil's writing could not also enable her own hunger for herself.

Simone Weil's refusal to eat fed her writing on the moral dimensions of hunger. Weil drew parallels between physical hunger and spiritual self-emptying: as eating destroys that which we consume, our consumptive love of the other destroys that other. The proper disposition, Weil contended, is that of hunger, an emptiness that refuses to seek possession of the other, and that even issues in the giving of the self to the other as food. That self-giving is a sacramental act, enabled by our transformation from eaters to lookers in the Eucharist. Weil's own practices of food refusal allowed her to write hunger as a remedy for the disorder of consumption. As profound as this remedy is, however, the violence of it as Weil conceives it negates the very compassion for which she argues, by reifying violence in ways that issue in self-destruction and that rule out divine compassion. Yet her own best insights help to construct an alternative to her violent narrative. Hearing the cry of Weil's voice beneath the violence, and relying on her understandings of the sacredness of human vulnerability and of the restorative efficacy of openness to another, enables us to open the way for a Eucharist of compassionate healing.

Writing Hunger on the Body

Simone Weil was born in Paris in 1909 to a comfortable family of Jewish background. According to Weil's friend and biographer, Simone Pétrement, the Weil family was intelligent, well-educated, challenging, and very close. Much mention has been made of Weil's feelings of inadequacy in light of her brother, André's, apparent mathematical brilliance, and, as Pétrement writes, the desire to be brilliant and good characterized Weil's early life. Weil was also frequently ill as a child, and the various illnesses that she suffered left her ever frail. From her teenage years on she also suffered debilitating migraines, although she would often continue working despite the pain.

Weil was educated in philosophy at the elite École Normale in Paris, distinguishing herself among her colleagues as much by her odd behavior and form of masculine dress as by her intellect. Simone de Beauvoir recalls meeting Weil at the Sorbonne when both were taking exams that would license them to teach philosophy, and being impressed by Weil's compassionate tears for the victims of a famine in China. As de Beauvoir wrote, "I envied her having a heart that could beat right across the world."[4] Weil taught in a number of girls' schools, with periodic breaks either to engage in manual labor or to recover from exhaustion. She aligned herself with various leftist causes, although she often departed from the groups with which she initially worked; most significant was her departure from Communism, as a result of witnessing the atrocities of both left and right in the Spanish Civil War.

Weil's writing encompasses such diverse areas as philosophy, politics, Greek literature, and mathematics, and became explicitly religious after 1938, when she experienced a dramatic moment of conversion. While reciting George Herbert's eucharistic poem "Love," in which Christ the host invites a guest convinced of her/his unworthiness to "sit down . . . and taste my meat,"[5] Weil was grasped by the certainty that "Christ came down and took possession"[6] of her. Weil was deeply attached to the Catholic faith, but repeatedly refused baptism, due to her deep suspicion of institutions and to the exclusivity of Catholic doctrine. In fact, Weil believed herself to be called by God to remain outside the church, "to move among men of every class and complexion, mixing with them and sharing their lives and outlook, . . . to know them so as to love them just as they are."[7] Weil died on August 24, 1943, of tuberculosis and malnutrition; the death certificate indicated the cause of death as "suicide."

From an early age, Weil exhibited a strange relationship with physicality, most significantly an aversion to food and to eating. Judith Van Herik traces Weil's childhood illnesses (a weakened condition at six months when her mother, who was nursing her, developed appendicitis; a year-long illness that followed weaning, exacerbated by Weil's refusal to take a bottle; an attack of appendicitis herself at the age of three) and surmises that these experiences impacted Weil's lifelong difficulty with eating: "Longing, distrust, rage, and pain, always associated with feeding in infancy, might have become particularly tied to nourishment in her earliest years."[8] According to Pétrement, all of the Weil family had an intense fear of microbes, and Mme. Weil insisted on frequent and thorough hand washing. Simone Weil exhibited both a fear of being contaminated by being touched and a fear that her touch would contaminate the other person. She spoke, as Pétrement writes, of her own "disgustingness,"[9] and likewise was disgusted by food that was not "absolutely fresh" or that bore some kind of imperfection.[10] At times, especially when suffering from migraines, Weil was simply unable to eat; while suffering from these headaches, for periods of five or six days, according to Pétrement, Weil was able to eat only grated raw potato, and even that she could not always hold down.[11]

Coupled with this aversion to food and sometime inability to eat, Weil also took up deliberate practices of food refusal. It is not that she engaged in periods of fasting per se; it is that she adopted an ethical stance of "refusing to eat more than." When Weil worked in an automotive factory, she refused to eat more than her fellow laborers could afford. Indeed, this solidarity with workers characterized her adult life, and she gave away much of her own salary and food to those who had less. When she dined at her parents' house, Weil would leave the price of the meal on the table,[12] refusing to accept without payment a meal that was more than others could afford. At one meal with her parents during the war, Weil stopped eating and refused to begin again until her father promised that, should a German parachutist land on her parents' terrace, he would not hand him over to the police.[13] Most significantly, when in New York (where her family had sought escape during the war) and when she was hospitalized with tuberculosis in England on her way back to France from New York, she refused to eat more than the rations allowed her fellow citizens in occupied France, claiming that she did not "have the right to eat more than her compatriots."[14]

Weil's refusal to eat was deeply troubling to those around her. Mme. Weil, who sent her daughter food but upon visiting found her cupboards empty, was especially concerned about her nutrition, and recruited roommates and restaurateurs to assist in stealth feeding tactics. A physician friend, Louis Bercher, noted that "to Simone, eating seemed a base and disgusting function," and worried that Weil "was obsessed by the desire not to eat."[15] The nurses and doctors who cared for her in London and in Ashford at the end of her life were particularly concerned, urging her to eat and growing exasperated by her refusal, although it seems clear that her body reached a point at which it simply could not tolerate much food. The certificate ruling her death a suicide stated, "The deceased did kill and slay herself by refusing to eat whilst the balance of her mind was disturbed."[16] Pétrement, however, as well as André Weil, were suspicious of the suicide ruling, Pétrement noting that Weil tried to eat even in her final days and was unable,[17] and André Weil insisting that not eating had simply become a habit for his sister.[18] Through these practices of "refusing to eat more than," Weil was writing on her body the ethic of hunger that she also wrote on the page. For Weil, physical hunger not only works as a compelling metaphor for spiritual hunger; physical and spiritual hunger are contiguous, the practice of one feeding the practice of the other. Our desire to satisfy our bodies with food is paralleled by a desire to satisfy our souls with good. But our search for our soul's good easily gets derailed, and we turn a ravenous eye on other persons to seek in them the satisfaction that we crave. Left to our own devices, we love others "as food for ourselves";[19] we love others simply as means to satisfy our own longings. As the following discussion will show, just as eating destroys that of which we make our food, so our consumptive desire for another person results in that other's destruction. We must be transformed, Weil argues, from beings who "eat" to beings who "look," from beings who consume the other to beings who simply love the other for her own sake. In other words, our souls must remain hungry.

THE SACREDNESS OF INTERDEPENDENCE AND VULNERABILITY

Weil's conceptions of eating and looking are grounded in her distinct account of human sacredness and interconnection. Weil follows a typically Augustinian trajectory in arguing that human beings are made for the good, made to pursue and ultimately exist in union with the good which is God. Weil's "Draft for a Statement of Human Obligations," written in 1943 as a proposal for the reorganization of postwar French political and social life, provides a locus for exploring these notions. The "Draft" begins with two assertions: that there is a reality outside the world, "truer" than the world itself; and that, corresponding to this reality, "at the centre of the human heart, is the longing for an absolute good, a longing which is always there and is never appeased by any object in this world."[20] Thus the human longing for good, which is central to being human, is a link between the human being and the sacred reality that transcends the world.

Weil's distinct contribution to this line of thinking is her assertion that this orientation toward God, as it is commonly shared among all human beings, inherently binds us to one another. This sacred, fundamental connection among all human beings serves as a basis for obligation. We are obligated to safeguard each other's souls because we are responsible for each other's ability to pursue the good. Whatever damages or destroys a soul damages or destroys its ability to engage in this pursuit, and therefore our fundamental connection with each other obligates us to protect and restore that ability. As Weil writes, "Anyone whose attention and love are really directed towards the reality outside the world recognizes at the same time that he is bound, both in public and private life, by the single and permanent obligation to remedy, according to his responsibilities and to the extent of his power, all the privations of soul and body which are liable to destroy or damage the earthly life of any human being whatsoever."[21] This is indeed a tall order. What is at the heart of the obligation to remedy all privations is the conviction that we are fundamentally connected with each other and with the good toward which we are oriented, and deeply dependent upon one another for each person's pursuit of the good.

In locating our sacredness in our longing for good and in our interdependence in the pursuit of that good, Weil conveys an understanding of human beings as inherently vulnerable. We are made to give and receive good; indeed, we *need* to give and receive good in order to flourish. Such vulnerability and dependence indicate that we are, indeed, quite fragile creatures. The notion that we must entrust each other with our well-being, simply as particular other beings in search of the good, places the care for vulnerable souls in rather vulnerable hands. Yet this is what gives Weil's conception of human sacredness its power. We are incredibly dynamic beings, continually striving for the good, our own as well as that of others. The trembling possibility of human being is what Weil contends is sacred about us.

Instead of embracing our vulnerability and interdependence, Weil contends, we fear it. We see vulnerability and dependence in another and we are frightened and repulsed. As Weil writes, "Men have the same carnal nature as animals. If a hen is hurt, the others rush upon it, attacking it with their beaks. This phenomenon is as automatic as gravitation."[22] Our revulsion lies in our realization that the same can happen to any one of us:

To acknowledge the reality of affliction means saying to oneself: "I may lose at any moment, through the play of circumstances over which I have no control, anything whatsoever that I possess, including those things so intimately mine that I consider them as being myself. There is nothing that I might not lose."[23]

The fear of this loss wields incredible power over us, such that we turn our attention away from the good and away from the other who needs us, and turn it instead toward a ravenous pursuit of the immediate satisfaction of our fear-colored desires. We seek to keep ourselves safe, invincible, impenetrable. In so doing, however, we not only ignore and trample the needs of the other, we actually consume the other, in a wild, desperate attempt to fill our own emptiness. The remedy for such consumption is learning to "look" rather than "eat."

Looking and Not Eating

The transformation from eating to looking can be traced in Weil's essay "Forms of the Implicit Love of God." That discussion begins with her description of the attraction we feel toward beautiful things. I am drawn to a thing of beauty, and it, in turn, offers itself to me, actually giving to me its own existence. Yet even though I then hold that beauty, I remain dissatisfied, I "still desire something." That "something," according to Weil, is to possess that beauty entirely, to make it completely and eternally mine, to *consume* it. As Weil writes, "It may be that vice, depravity, and crime are nearly always, or perhaps always, attempts to eat beauty, to eat what we should only look at."[24] We come then to view other persons not as fellow creatures who have their own orientation toward the good, but simply as objects of consumption in our own frenzied search for self-satisfaction. In our single-minded, self-centered search for happiness and invulnerability, we fail to wish for the good of the other to be increased and instead reduce others to means to our own ends. "We love like cannibals," Weil writes; "we get comfort, energy, and stimulation from the people we love. They affect us in the same way as a good meal after a hard day's work. So we love them like food."[25] Weil likens such consumption of another to rape, to the taking of the beauty of another without her consent. "What can be more horrible," she writes, "than not to respect the consent of a being in whom one is seeking, though unconsciously, an equivalent of God?"[26]

Weil seeks to overcome the desire to eat the other by simply refusing to eat. Eating necessarily entails the destruction of what we eat. Thus our consumption, Weil reasoned, is indeed a danger to that which we wish to make our food. To avoid that destruction, we must not eat, we must remain hungry. Weil means this literally, in terms of "refusing to eat more than," as discussed above, and she means it figuratively in terms of interpersonal and societal relations. Refraining from eating, physically and relationally, begins our transformation from cannibals. As Weil writes in her notebooks, "When we do not eat, our organism consumes its own flesh and transforms it into energy. It is the same with the soul. The soul that does not eat consumes itself. The eternal part consumes the mortal part of the soul and transforms it."[27] Refusing to eat transforms the soul from one who eats to one who looks. Beauty, she writes, "is not the means to anything else. It alone is good in itself, but without our finding any particular good or advantage in it."[28] Beauty is to be seen for its own sake without the imposition of my desire upon it. To look, to attend, is to empty the self of all desire to possess the object of attention. Indeed, it is to empty the soul "of all its own contents in order to receive into itself the being it is looking at, just as he is, in all his truth."[29] Looking is a truly kenotic disposition; instead of filling myself with the other, I empty myself of self, ready to receive the other without consuming her. Hunger in this sense is not desire for fulfillment but is emptiness itself. If one remains hungry, awaiting the other, one loves with the love that is God. God, Weil writes, "loves, not as I love, but as an emerald is green. He *is* 'I love.' And I, too, if I were in the state of perfection, I would love as an emerald is green."[30] Emptied of my self, I would love perfectly; I would *be* "God loves."

HUNGER AS IMITATION OF DIVINE KENOSIS

The refusal to eat, emptying the soul to attend to and love the other purely, is, according to Weil, an imitation of the kenosis that is at the heart of God's reality. When we refuse to eat, when we remain waiting in hunger, we imitate in thankfulness the self-emptying of God that gives us existence. Creation is an act of supreme generosity on the part of God, who removes divine power and even presence in order to make a space for the existence of beings who have some autonomy from God. Thus, in creation, "God abdicated from his divine omnipotence, and emptied himself."[31] Creation is therefore essentially a kenotic activity for God, an emptying of Godself, indeed, a sacrifice of Godself in order to allow humans to exist: "Every man, seeing himself from the point of view of God the creator, should regard his own existence as a sacrifice made by God. I am God's abdication. The more I exist, the more God abdicates."[32]

Christ's passion communicates divine kenosis in a particularly powerful way, as Weil posits the crucifixion as a rent within God that makes infinite love possible. The infinity of divine love requires that God's love be found even where it is farthest away, even where divine love seems most absent: "God created through love and for love. God did not create anything except love itself, and the means to love. He created love in all its forms. He created beings capable of love from all possible distances."[33] God being the only infinite reality, however, no creature could possibly love God from infinite distance; this, only God can do. To actualize the infinite reach of God's love for creation, God, in the crucifixion, embraces a tearing within the divine reality: "Because no other could do it, he himself went to the greatest possible distance, the infinite distance. This infinite distance between God and God, this supreme tearing apart, this agony beyond all others, this marvel of love, is the crucifixion. Nothing can be further from God than that which has been made accursed."[34] The crucifixion is thus the rent within God by which God's infinite love could reach infinitely, to the farthest outskirts of the divine love and beyond.

It is the afflicted, Weil contends, those who exist on those farthest outskirts, who most stand in need of that infinite reach. "Affliction" has a particular meaning for Weil. It describes a deep, radical, persistent pain, the very unmaking of a person through physical, psychological, and social suffering. As Weil describes it, "Affliction is an uprooting of life, a more or less attenuated equivalent of death, made irresistibly present to the soul by the attack or immediate apprehension of physical pain."[35] Affliction is an equivalent of death, but it is a death in life, a dying of the self brought about by the violent theft of identity which the person is continually forced to suffer: "He [who suffers affliction] is living, he has a soul, yet he is a thing. . . . The soul was not made to dwell in a thing; and when forced to it, there is no part of the soul but suffers violence."[36] Affliction overtakes the soul, enslaving it and becoming its "sovereign lord," such that "at the very best, he who is branded by affliction will keep only half his soul."[37] Shame, self-hatred, and abandonment are the constant companions of the afflicted.

Those who are afflicted, Weil argues, are most in need of the restorative presence of Christ. The utter isolation and hatred, including self-hatred, of the afflicted culminate in the sense of having been abandoned by God. Affliction, Weil writes, makes God appear to be absent, "more absent than a dead man, more absent than light in the utter darkness of a cell." Affliction effects an erasing of God's presence from a life that is made for relation; thus "[a] kind of horror submerges the whole soul." The source of all good is cut off from the afflicted person, "there is nothing to love," and she is utterly alone with the affliction that eats at her soul. The love of God, to be truly infinite, must reach especially those who experience this abandonment. The cross accomplishes this reach. Through Christ's experience of abandonment on the cross, divine love reaches to human beings who are precisely in that space: "Men struck down by affliction are at the foot of the Cross, almost at the greatest possible distance from God."[38] Divine abandonment is healed by the infinite love that "triumphs over infinite separation."[39]

Weil's conception of divine self-emptying at the creation and in the cross reveals kenosis as central to God's activity on the part of human beings. God allows us to exist by emptying Godself of power. In order to meet those who experience God's abandonment in affliction, God allows a tearing within Godself that enables a healing of the distance between those persons and the divine. This divine kenosis lays the foundation for our own. Our renunciation is to be a mirror of this divine self-emptying; by remaining hungry, by looking instead of eating, we reflect back to God and to a broken humanity the infinite kenosis that God has displayed for all.

HUNGER AND EUCHARIST: EATING THE BODY OF CHRIST

Weil posits Eucharist as a particular practice through which God enables our kenotic transformation. Despite her resistance to the institutional Catholic Church, Weil had a deep reverence for the sacraments, particularly Eucharist. Louis Bercher reports that Weil found his story of a nun whose only nourishment was the Eucharist "quite reasonable,"[40] and Pétrement contends that if Weil did desire baptism "it was above all so as to be able to receive the sacraments."[41]

Weil's longing for Eucharist was perhaps rooted in her theory of the purifying nature of the sacrament. In her "Theory of the Sacraments," Weil argues that that we cannot acquire the good that is not within us by any action of our own; we can only receive it. But in order to receive such good we must first desire no less than "pure, perfect, total and absolute good." Even then such desire is not enough. Our nature as human beings, as souls and bodies, dictates that "a desire of the soul has no reality within the soul until it has passed through the body by means of actions, movements and attitudes."[42] A physical contact with absolute good is necessary for that good to be received into the soul. Thus there must be "an object from this world which can be absolute good in terms of the flesh, as a symbol and by agreement." There must be, in other words, a physical object upon which God has established, by agreement with humanity, the reality of pure good. That object, Weil contends, is the bread of the Eucharist, by which we receive the absolute goodness of Christ into our souls through the physical encounter with Christ himself.[43] By this reception of Christ our souls are transformed.

But at the moment that the soul is about to receive the sacrament, the moment that the soul faces the reality of her impending transformation, the soul is divided. There is "the portion of truth within the soul," that desires the sacrament and the transformation it offers, and the "mediocre" portion, that responds with hatred and fear. Eucharist is therefore "a journey through fire, which burns and destroys a fragment of the soul's impurities." Each time the soul partakes of Eucharist, a bit more of that impurity is burned away. As hunger for God increases, so does the suffering of the soul at the table: "The more real the desire for God, and consequently contact with God through the sacrament, the more violent will be the upheaval of the mediocre part of the soul, an upheaval that is comparable to the recoiling of a living body when it is about to be pushed into fire."[44] The more we desire God, the more our souls are burned and refined in the fires of the sacrament, so that we leave the table in a state of "motionless attention,"[45] emptied of self-obsession and waiting to receive the other.[46]

FOOD FOR GOD, FOOD FOR OTHERS

Eucharist, then, is a journey through fire by which God consumes and refines the human soul. Indeed, according to Weil, divine consumption of the soul is the culmination of a soul's transformation from one who eats to one who looks. This transformation requires that we eaters become the eaten, not only by God, but by the afflicted. Here we encounter some of Weil's most profound and most troubling accounts of the divine. She worries that we love, as discussed above, like cannibals; we consume the ones we love for the satisfaction of ourselves. This is an inescapable aspect of human existence for Weil. What ultimately transforms us from those who eat to those who look, then, is becoming food.

We are first eaten by God. Weil writes of the beauty of the world, to which we are inexorably drawn, as "the mouth of a labyrinth." One who enters this labyrinth quickly becomes lost and disoriented, "incapable even of discovering whether he is really going forward or merely turning around on the same spot." If this person does not lose courage and continues to walk, "it is absolutely certain that he will finally arrive at the center of the labyrinth. And there God is waiting to eat him."[47] It is only by "being eaten and digested" by the divine that our cannibalism can be transformed. As Weil continues, the divinely digested person "will go out again, but he will be changed, he will have become different."[48]

That one is changed, Weil asserts, into food for others. The transformed person not only remains empty, hungry, in order to receive the other, but actually gives of her own body in order to feed others in their hunger. In her "New York Notebook," Weil prays that her body, her mind, her faculties, her love, "may all this be stripped away from me, devoured by God, transformed into Christ's substance, and given for food to afflicted men whose body and soul lack every kind of nourishment."[49] Hunger is thus both a receptivity to the other and a giving, a sacrifice, of the self. The feeding of others with one's own body is sacramental: "If I grow thin from labour in the fields, my flesh really becomes wheat. If that wheat is used for the host it becomes Christ's flesh."[50] Consumption therefore cannot be overcome until the one who looks becomes the one who feeds others with her self. The notion of the self as sacrament for another who hungers, the self as the very body of Christ given to another, has a romantic Christian logic to it. Weil expresses here a lovely idea of the interconnectedness of human beings with one another and with Christ, and of the power of a Christ-like renunciation of self for others. But as Alec Irwin argues, the centrality of violence in Weil's formulation remains. As Irwin writes, "Cannibalism won't go away; but its consequences change radically when the victim enters consciously, willingly into the process, investing it with a sacrifical character. Under these conditions, Weil argues, reversing its status as the visible mark of human enslavement, the violence of eating would become an instrument — the decisive instrument — of spiritual liberation and positive moral change."[51] The violence of eating does not disappear, but is "entered consciously" by the self for the feeding of another. Divine and human violence, therefore, are necessary in order for the soul to be open and waiting upon the other with compassionate attention. Violence is not just a tragic consequence of human existence; it is of the very nature of God.

SELF-ANNIHILATION, SIN, AND DIVINE VIOLENCE

Weil's conception of a violent God leads us to a consideration of the efficacy of her claims. Does Weil's understanding of hunger serve as an adequate remedy for the human desire to consume, and does it issue in restoration for the afflicted? While there is much in Weil's thought that is constructive, even beautiful, ultimately her inability to imagine such hunger in nonviolent terms disables the very compassion that Weil seeks to espouse. In particular, her language of self-annihilation, her displacement of vulnerability with sin in her discussion of Eucharist, and her maintenance of a violent God pose tremendous obstacles to the efficacy of her claims.

The Language of Self-Annihilation

From Valerie Saiving to Rita Nakashima Brock and Rebecca Parker,[52] feminist theologians have long argued that Christianity's language of self-sacrifice issues in innumerable harms for women: that women are encouraged by this language to lose themselves in caring for others, to accept domestic violence and sexual abuse as their "cross to bear," even to welcome these as gifts that enable them be more like Christ. Ever present in the experience of women is the danger and the sad reality of self-emptying bleeding into self-annihilation; Weil herself serves as an example of the near inevitability of this bleeding.

One can argue (as I have done in previous work) that what is annihilated through this process of fiery Eucharist and divine consumption is not the true self but an illusory self. The grasping self, the self that considers itself divinely autonomous, is a fiction, a lie, which we create in order to deny the vulnerability and interconnection that characterizes our very reality as humans, in order to allay our fear of such fragility. Weil writes, "God created me as a non-being which has the appearance of existing, in order that through love I should renounce this apparent existence and be annihilated by the plenitude of being."[53] Remaining hungry, refusing to feed that grasping self so that the vulnerable, interconnected, compassionate self can be the embodiment of the love of God, being consumed by God and by those who hunger—*this* is the annihilation that Weil seeks, an annihilation of the illusory self that issues in true joy. The annihilation of the grasping self opens the soul to the ultimate joy of communion, with God and with others. This is a significant point that Weil's logic bears out despite the limited attention Weil herself was able to give it. The assertion of my grasping ego actually issues in the loss of my self. It is the true self we lose, or at least forget, the self who is made for communion with God and with other beings and who is truly fulfilled only through this communion. It is the self who is sacred in her vulnerability that the ego effaces, seeking instead to stand on its own and finding that its independent existence is a fiction. It is the self who is made to pursue the good in mutual solidarity with all others that egocentrism tramples. It is this egocentric self that is to be annihilated.

Such an argument "saves" Weil's notion of self-sacrifice from its dangers. It reconceives self-annihilation as the annihilation of a self constructed out of fear of vulnerability and desire to control. When that illusory self is burned away by God's transformative power, there is finally room for the true self, the vulnerable and interdependent self, to emerge, and to live a life of compassionate care for others. This is a compelling argument, and a very attractive reading of the language of self-sacrifice. But it is not Weil's. Weil's ultimate wish was to have no self, not even a "true" self. Both in her eating practices and in her writings she reveals a deep desire truly to be nothing. The suffering she endured during a year spent doing manual labor in automotive factories had already convinced her that she was nothing:

> What I went through there marked me in so lasting a manner that still today when any human being, whoever he may be and in whatever circumstances, speaks to me without brutality, I cannot help having the impression that there must be a mistake and that unfortunately the mistake will in all probability disappear. There I received forever the mark of a slave, like the branding of the red-hot iron the Romans put on the foreheads of their most despised slaves. Since then I have always regarded myself as a slave.[54]

Weil is describing here her own experience of affliction, of the destruction of her very soul wrought by her experience of factory work. Weil argues that decreation, her word for the self-emptying transformation of the self, is utterly distinct from destruction: "Decreation: to make something created pass into the uncreated. Destruction: to make something created pass into nothingness."[55] Decreation, then, is the enabling of a soul to pass into the realm of God. To be destroyed is simply to become nothing.

Yet the consequences of decreation and destruction for the self are ultimately the same. The decreated self is not to lose herself in the love

of God, or even to be joyfully absorbed into Godself; she is to disappear
so that God can love God. The self simply no longer exists. Referring to
God's kenosis at creation, she writes,

> He emptied himself of his divinity. We should empty ourselves of the
> false divinity with which we were born.
> Once we have understood that we are nothing, the object of all our
> efforts is to become nothing. It is for this that we suffer with resigna-
> tion, *it is for this that we act*, it is for this that we pray.
> May God grant me to become nothing.
> In so far as I become nothing, God loves himself through me.[56]

We are meant, Weil contends, to be nothing. We are meant to become
transparent vessels through which God's love passes, imposing nothing
of a "self" that would block that love. Her many aphorisms speak again
and again of this desire to be nothing: "All the things that I see, hear,
breathe, touch, eat; all the beings I meet—I deprive the sum total of all
of that contact with God, and I deprive God of contact with all that in
so far as something in me says 'I.'"[57] "If I knew how to withdraw from
my own soul it would be enough to enable the table in front of me to
have the incomparable good fortune of being seen by God. . . . If only I
knew how to disappear there would be a perfect union of love between
God and the earth I tread, the sea I hear."[58] And this:

> Creation is an act of love and it is perpetual. At each moment our exis-
> tence is God's love for us. But God can only love himself. His love for
> us is love for himself through us. Thus, he who gives our being loves
> in us the acceptance of not being.
> Our existence is made up only of his waiting for our acceptance
> not to exist. He is perpetually begging from us that existence which he
> gives. He gives it to us in order to beg it from us.[59]

Weil does indeed insist that we seek withdrawal from our own souls,
disappearance, and nonbeing in order for God's love to pass through us.
Weil's conception of self-annihilation does not oppose an illusory and a
true self; it insists that the self simply ought not exist.

Sin Displaces Vulnerability

Weil's conception of human sacredness, as rooted in our dependence on one another to receive the good, serves as a foundation for her thought. Fear of this vulnerability leads us to seek our own protection by consuming others. Yet Weil's imagery of Eucharist as a refining fire, by which the impurities of the soul are burned away, shifts the focus from human vulnerability to human sin, indeed, human defilement. The revulsion that we feel for afflicted persons, rooted in the fear of our own vulnerability, is recast in her discussion of Eucharist into revulsion for our own sin. This sin must be purged, by the refining fire of the Eucharist and by God's own consumption of our souls. To speak of the burning away of sin, however, does violence to the sacredness of the human being, a notion that Weil seeks always to maintain. To hold a soul as sacred is to soothe her fear, to embrace the soul so that she can embrace her fragile self. Weil knows this when she speaks so profoundly about restoration of the souls of the afflicted. As she writes,

> The love of our neighbor in all its fullness simply means being able to say to him: "What are you going through?" It is a recognition that the sufferer exists, not only as a unit in a collection, or a specimen from the social category labeled "unfortunate," but as a man, exactly like us, who was one day stamped with a special mark by affliction. For this reason it is enough, but it is indispensable, to know how to look at him in a certain way.[60]

Recognizing the afflicted other simply as the person that she is, Weil argues powerfully, enables the restoration of a soul that has been trampled by affliction. But Weil forgets her own conviction that all of us stand in need of recognition; such is our condition as beings who depend upon one another for each person's pursuit of the good. Sadly, the disgust that Weil felt for herself and her body led her to desire chastisement and the burning away of all she feared in herself, disabling her ability to show herself the compassion she so readily poured out for others. The violent hunger she wrote on her own frail body bled onto the page, coloring our vulnerability as defilement.

Nevertheless, there is much to be gained from Weil's conviction of our inherent interdependence and the falsity of our autonomous selves. It *is* in the fragile connection among all human beings and in the tremulous responsibility we thus bear for one another that our sacredness is to be found. We build citadels against that vulnerability, we do look with disdain upon those whose affliction makes our own fragility all too clear. There is wisdom in Weil's calling for us to overcome our self-obsession and embrace others who stand in need of care. It is not, however, a refining fire that enables this overcoming, but rather the soothing draught of compassion received and given.

A Violent God

Weil's description of God's infinite love and kenotic activity on the part of human beings points toward a conception of God as essentially compassionate, one who enters into human suffering and suffers with us. But it is a violent God whom Weil ultimately posits. That creation and the cross constitute the rending and tearing of Godself necessitates a vision of God inflicting wounds upon Godself, doing violence to Godself, in order for human beings to exist and for divine love to be extended to all. Our very existence and restoration, therefore, are dependent upon divine violence. It is then through violence that this violent God effects the transformation of human beings. God burns the soul into refinement at the Eucharist. We are "eaten and digested" by God. The image of God chewing and swallowing human beings posits a savagery within God. That a savage God could transform our own savagery is impossible. It is not divine savagery that transforms us but divine compassion, a love that enfolds our fragile limbs in a divine embrace.

Writing Hunger and the Longing for Restoration

Why did Simone Weil write in this manner? Why, with her deep sensitivity to radical suffering and her keen, sympathetic diagnosis of the human condition, does Weil ultimately rely upon language of condemnation, violence, and self-annihilation? The answers to these questions lie in her use of aphorism. While Weil wrote a number of elegant and learned essays, much of her writing was in the form of notebooks. These notebooks, published posthumously, and collections constructed from them, consist almost entirely of aphorisms. These short, enigmatic statements reflect not simply a form characteristic of notebook writing. They are carefully written, deliberate modes of expression, meant to be enigmatic and thought-provoking. Weil's aphorisms, I contend, are hungry words. They are written in order to evoke hunger in her readers, a hunger for Weil's restoration from her own affliction. They are the "story of a wound that cries out,"[61] the story of Weil's own woundedness seeking restoration through the hungry reception of her soul by another. Weil testifies to the affliction she suffered through her factory work, as I discussed above. Whether it is due to this event alone or whether Weil was already haunted by other traumatic events, it seems clear that Weil speaks of self-annihilation, condemnation, and a desire for divine violence from out of that state of affliction. Weil's desire to withdraw, to disappear, to become nothing, reflects her conviction that she is already nothing.

The self, as Judith Herman argues, is formed dialogically; one comes to be and to know oneself only in relationship with others. From the beginning of a person's life, relationships of trust serve as the foundation on which all systems of meaning are built. Trauma shatters that sense of safety and trust. A traumatic event, like rape, torture, or war, renders the person helpless in the face of an overwhelming force, which the victim experiences as a threat to her very life. When a person experiences trauma, their sense of safety and trust is shattered, not just in that moment, but thereafter, such that the traumatized person exists in a state of continual disconnection from others. This disconnection issues in a loss of a sense of self; the survivor loses "the belief that one can *be oneself* in relation to others."[62] This self can only be restored as it was constructed, that is, dialogically. The survivor longs to tell her story in order to know herself: as Dori Laub writes, "there is, in each survivor, an imperative need to *tell* and thus to *know* one's story, unimpeded by ghosts from the past against which one has to protect oneself. One has to know one's buried truth in order to be able to live one's life."[63] But trauma resists telling; it renders the survivor unable to give a coherent narrative. The survivor struggles to find the words to speak the unspeakable. Even when the words come, the telling of trauma is still resisted by those who do not want to hear. As Susan J. Brison writes of her own experience after being beaten and raped, "each time some-one failed to respond I felt as though I were alone again in the ravine, dying and screaming. And still no one could hear me. Or worse, they heard me, but refused to help."[64] The survivor's testimony can only be integrated into a coherent life narrative, so that the survivor's sense of self is restored, if that testimony is received by another.

Weil's aphorisms read like the wounded utterances of a traumatized person. In her language of self-annihilation in particular, Weil's pain bleeds onto the page. The enigmatic nature of her aphorisms, their com-plexity and their need for careful interpretation, and their continued elusiveness, signify Weil's need for a reader to hear her cry and hunger for her restoration. Her use of aphorism implies the need for a reader to finish her thought, to help construct meaning, to restore her soul and help her (re)write the narrative of her life.

HUNGER, EUCHARIST, AND THE COMPASSIONATE CHURCH

An alternative construct that honors the beauty and profundity of Weil's thought while repudiating violence and self-annihilation is rooted in an understanding of compassion as the *power* to transform.[65] God's wound-edness signals God's power to know and attend to all human afflic-tion. This emphasis on the power of woundedness allows us to envision God's compassion as God's brokenness for and with us that empowers our transformation. The wounds of God are not self-inflicted. God is a God whose love is wounded so deeply by the suffering of God's crea-tures that God is broken by it, taking into Godself not just our pain but our very being, enveloping us in the divine compassion that offers heal-ing and strength. This is the logic that we see, for example, in Julian of Norwich's meditation on the transformative consolation offered in Christ's wounds: "With a kindly countenance our good Lord looked into his side, and he gazed with joy, and with his sweet regard he drew his creature's understanding into his side by the same wound; and there he revealed a fair and delectable place, large enough for all mankind that will be saved and will rest in peace and love."[66] God's absolute com-passion for human pain, the bountiful love of God that is pained when we are wounded, provides space within God's very self in which we can find rest and restoration.

Understanding hunger in Weil's terms as a receptivity and an openness of the self to the other, and divine compassion as the power of transformation, enables the envisioning of a church that embodies in its practice of Eucharist the compassion of Christ. God's compassion is a transformative power that encircles all who know and have known pain, and that forms us to be compassionate even as it restores what is broken. In the practice of Eucharist, over time, Christ's wounded love attends again and again to our sufferings, healing those who are pained and restoring those whose identities are shattered by trauma. Slowly our vision clears and we come to see that we *are* so lovingly embraced, even those of us who are utterly convinced of our wretchedness. As our vision, our capacity for attention, is healed, we come to see the pain of Christ's love for us, we see others around us who are in pain and who are unmade, and we find ourselves within the circle of compassion, receiving and giving the wounded love of Christ. Our wounds are not the same, but there is woundedness in all of our communities, there is at least a measure of woundedness in each of us, and by allowing ourselves to be embraced by Christ's compassion, compassion can be birthed in those wounds. As Sue Monk Kidd writes,

> When compassion wakes up in us, we find ourselves more willing to become vulnerable, to take the risk of entering the pain of others. We open our lives to them in genuine willingness to be known. We tell them our own story of suffering as a way of offering healing and hope. We feel their heart bleeding into ours; we catch their tears. We relieve their pain as much as we are able, and by relieving theirs, we relieve God's.[67]

What might Weil have written if she believed that such a communion was available to her, if rather than believing the lie of her nothingness she was enabled to know *and* be known, to heal *and* be healed?

This conception of a Eucharist of compassion seeks to retrieve Weil's wisdom from her (self-)destructive claims. But it does not ignore or dilute the deepest truth that Weil reminds us of: the close proximity of love and suffering. To love is immediately to have one's heart flayed open not only by the suffering of the beloved, but by her very being. Simply seeing my daughter's face can produce in me a painful longing that stops me in my tracks. Love inevitably involves us in suffering; love makes our vulnerability explicit, makes us, indeed, wear our hearts on our sleeves. The compassionate love that seeks to attend to the wounds of others in the very space of our own woundedness makes this abundantly clear. Perhaps this above all is Weil's contribution, her claim, her cry.[68] To love deeply, as Weil did, is to hurt deeply, as much as it is to know true joy. Something, sadly, clouded Weil's vision of this reality, preventing her from seeing herself in the same compassionate light, and leading her to seek pain rather than consolation in order that she might love more purely. Her writing, however, suggests her hope that her cry for consolation would reach "a shoreline of the heart," another soul hungry and waiting to receive hers.

Writing Eucharist

Weil's traumatized cry, her longing for that hungry soul that waits to receive her broken self, instructs us that to write Christian theology is to write Eucharist. The language of theology ought to be hungry; it ought to be utterly open, always awaiting the reception of the other. This is more than a call for humility. It is a call to speak of Christ hungrily, to receive in our writing Christ in his affliction and to receive the affliction of ourselves and others, and to wait for a new word. To write Eucharist is to give the afflicted the space to be and to speak, to be open to brokenness, and to resist the closure and enclosure of that brokenness by the too-ready imposition of words. At the same time, writing Eucharist is an offering of healing, bringing into the same place the suffering of human beings and the compassionate power of Christ. Writing Eucharist, then, is finally writing thanksgiving, for the restoration we find in Christ and in communion with one another.

Conclusion

Hunger, for Simone Weil, was a passion. Hunger was a disposition, a deeply satisfying longing not to long. Weil's hunger was suffering for and with the other, a suffering which resulted in pleasure and joy beyond knowing. For Weil, human hunger mirrors divine hunger, God's self-emptying that enables our creation and our redemption. God devours us in a fiery transformation of our shadow selves, and we become food for others. Hunger displaces and replaces the ravenous consumption that characterizes our earthly life. As Weil writes, "The hunger of the soul is hard to bear, but there is no other remedy for our disease."[69]

The hunger of which Weil writes is also the hunger that was written on her own body, in her inability and her refusal to eat. Her deliberate hunger practices fed her writing on the moral dimensions of hunger. Weil embodies the interconnectedness of physical hunger and spiritual self-emptying: just as eating destroys that which we consume, our consumptive desire for the other destroys that other. The proper disposition, for Weil, is that of hunger, an emptiness that refuses to seek possession of the other. Weil's own practices of not eating enabled her to write hunger as a remedy for the disorder of consumption. That remedy, however, suffers from the painful confusions of vulnerability and sin, of compassion and violence, of waiting for the other with love and self-imposed starvation. Again, I find myself grieving for Simone Weil's tormented body and soul. And yet I am moved beyond words by the beauty that her deeper wisdom allows. That wisdom enables us to turn our attention to our sacred vulnerability, to divine compassion as the power of transformation, and to the gentle restoration of one soul through the openness of another, and allows us to construct a practice of eucharistic compassion, which is embodied both at the table and in our writing. Such a practice embraces the close proximity of love and suffering, not in order to valorize suffering, but that we might live lives of gracious communion.

10

THE BODY, TO BE EATEN, TO BE WRITTEN
A Theological Reflection on the Act of Writing in Theresa Hak Kyung Cha's *Dictee*

Min-Ah Cho

SPEAKING IN TWO TONGUES: A STORY OF MYSELF

Writing.

I do not know when it touched me or where I was when it arrived. I do not even know why I was so haunted by it. It is as though I have had a recurring dream, since it has always been a part of my life. When I write, I feel more. When I write, I feel beautiful. When I write, I feel I am finally partaking in reality. It is not because writing is something that I can do well or something that is easy for me. Writing is painfully difficult for me, and it always makes me feel inadequate. Writing is, for me, an experience of both love and hate.

Being a "non-resident alien" in the United States and speaking and writing in my second language, however, has drawn me into a totally different experience of writing.[1] As a second-language English speaker and writer whose mother tongue is Korean, I continually brace myself for a challenge that presses on me in every waking moment, at times even in my dreams. Struggling to express my thoughts and emotions as fully and fluently as I want, I have experienced deep frustrations because I do not speak and write in "standard English." In my first couple of years in the United States, these frustrations were hard to

183

bear. I wanted to speak, write, and communicate as I did when I spoke Korean, but I always failed. Moreover, the connotations and tropes of both literary terminology and everyday language were deflected and distorted before they reached me. The multiple senses that come to life in metaphors and similes—color, taste, texture, and smell—were lost somewhere between English and Korean. For quite a long time, these frustrations dragged me into the profound fear of uttering words.[2]

Years passed, and my frustrations and fears have been moderately alleviated, although I still have difficulties penetrating the cultural meanings of some English expressions. I have become accustomed to the reality that speaking and writing always involve a process of learning and being challenged. Interesting and unexpected experiences of writing, a practice which I am now undertaking, have emerged as I have gained some familiarity with English. The more I have developed the ability to catch the nuances in the English language, the more I have found new and unprecedented hunches in my understanding of the sounds and meanings of some Korean words that had never sounded strange to me before. The two languages clash and interact with one another. They take me into a "third space" where my ideas are challenged and my old convictions are dismantled.[3]

Stumbling over the two languages occurs not only in my literal and linguistic activities. I experience similar struggles as I study theology, yet in a more metaphorical way. My ethnicity and gender have been considered as a mark of "otherness" in the long history of Christianity, and the ideologically constructed images of the Western male God always make me feel impeded and abashed. As I speak and write, my speech and writing mumble with the language manufactured in the church tradition. Such alienation at times wears a very friendly face both in the church and the academy. I have frequently been asked to represent my ethnicity and gender, by delivering "authentic" knowledge of Korea (or "Asia," more likely) and even just by being present as a marker of diversity. I feel uncomfortable with such an inquiry because I often sense that it assumes that I speak authentically and purely as a "Korean woman." I really have no idea about being and speaking as an "authentic" "Korean" "woman." I rather believe that my national and linguistic identity is a product constituted by continual exchange with other human beings and social circumstances in public spheres, and that therefore it never settles down into a discrete identity.

If my literal bilingualism is a trial that makes me uncertain of language, my metaphorical bilingualism is another trial that keeps me constantly questioning "truth." And those two trials never separate from each other. As I fluctuate between two languages, both literally and metaphorically, unresolved questions restlessly linger: what does it mean to write about the body of Christ, the Word made flesh, with my Korean female body and language? By "writing," I primarily employ the French philosopher Michel de Certeau's definition: a "concrete activity that consists in constructing on its own, blank space (*un espace propre*) — the page — a text that has power over the exteriority from which it has first been isolated."[4] Such a definition of writing is more than a production of a text. Writing is a particular kind of activity authoring and claiming one's own space. "Writing" thus includes both text as a cultural production and practice that constructs a space in which to display one's culture, languages, emotions, and anything else that defines one's context in relation to a larger society.

By the "body of Christ," I mean both the original, historical body of Christ and the church as the sacramental community called into the Eucharist. I critically adapt the French Jesuit theologian Henri de Lubac's exploration of the Pauline image of the church as the body of Christ (1 Cor 10:16). In his study of the implication of the Eucharist in the Roman Catholic tradition, de Lubac suggests the term *Corpus Mysticum* (the mystical body) for the sacramental foundation of the church. De Lubac argues that the mystery of the Eucharist founds the church's fundamental identity. I press further de Lubac's argument. The church as a sacramental community is not a mere social institution that holds the Eucharist as one of its rituals. The primary function of the sacramental community is that it offers an indwelling to individual Christians in whose life the suffering body of Christ still matters.[5] By the act of "writing the body of Christ," I mean therefore the act of making one's narrative space in relation to the church as a sacramental community.

How might I incorporate my narratives that embed my culture and language as a Korean female into the body of Christ that projects the archetype of "generic," "standard," and "normative" humanity? How might I find my words to write the body of Christ out of the dominant institutional constructions of the body that keep trying to correct me?[6] Always traversing more than one occupied territory at a time, I am in search of a proper place but remain perpetually improper.[7] For me, the question of writing the body of Christ with my unsettled subjectivity is to bring together ongoing discussions about theology and a tangible matter of life and faith.

This essay is my attempt to respond to these questions. The essay begins with rejuvenating the body of Christ, particularly his body at the sacrament of the Eucharist. The guiding metaphor of the essay is that the body of Christ is given to Christians to be *eaten* and also to be *written*. I argue that, as Christ's eucharistic body must signify radical inclusivity, the body of Christ given us to write sustains the process of unconditional speaking and writing of the divine. By writing the body of Christ, as if by eating the body of Christ, Christians incorporate their narratives into the discursive body of Christ. Suggesting a metaphorical connection between the acts of *eating* the body of Christ and *writing* the body of Christ, my essay proposes the act of writing as an assist to or extension of the eucharistic liturgy. I aim to illuminate the inherent plurality of the body of Christ and further reinvigorate that plurality by emphasizing the body's dependence on diverse human lives and human narratives.

To help make this argument, I explore a text written by an immigrant author. Theresa Hak Kyung Cha, a Korean-American writer, filmmaker, and performance artist (1951–1982), relentlessly calls us to ponder the implication of writing the body of Christ at the margins of Christianity. As exiled and fleeing from both her native country and the dominant colonial constructions, Cha's writings and artworks, her book *Dictee* in particular, thematize dislocation, loss of identity, and confusion of languages. The relationship between the writing subject and the Roman Catholic influences manifested in *Dictee* illuminates my questions above. In the course of eating and writing the body of Christ, Cha incorporates her cultural location into the body of Christ and creates another vision within the institutional construction of the body. Written from a corner of the tradition, Cha's book *Dictee* demonstrates an individual Christian's struggle to manage, subvert, confront, and negotiate dominant structures and ideologies on behalf of the provocative potential of the body of Christ.[8]

It is my hope that this essay echoes the concerns of individuals and groups who still believe in the body of Christ and want to deal with the body without losing their critical edge, who still struggle with the ideological guise of the church and nevertheless choose to live with institutional religions. This approach might resonate with those Christians who want to claim a more tangible and practicable body of Christ even while living in the obscure area between the institution and the individual.

THE BODY OF CHRIST GIVEN TO EAT AND WRITE

Take, eat, this is my body.[9]

Since these simple but powerful statements were uttered by Jesus at the Last Supper, the Eucharist has consolidated and protected the church by both providing spiritual nourishment and acting as a powerful disciplinary tool.[10] Article I of *Lumen Gentium*, one of the principal documents of the Second Vatican Council, reclaims the significance of the Eucharist by stating, "The Church, in Christ, is in the nature of a sacrament—a sign and instrument, that is, of communion with God and of unity among all men."[11] The Council reflects the institutional effort of the church to restore the sacramental tradition and to take the Eucharist as the center of practice and belief in faithful communities. The Eucharist is still an "absorbing and engaging work" that palpably affects Christians in everyday life and gathers them together to the church.[12]

Nonetheless, the consecrated bread and wine have not always remained docile to the institutional church. The Eucharist has also been the most dangerous and fractious matter that put the institution into crisis as it mixed with the bodies of individual Christians within and outside the church. The belief in the real presence of the body of Christ encompasses not only the desires of the church, but also the desires of the individual believers.[13] The body stimulates the open, eternal craving for a Christ who suffered and died for all Christians. When Christians eat the transubstantiated bread and wine from the altar, they eat and mix with the flesh of God. In the words of Thomas Aquinas, "not only the flesh but the whole body of Christ, the bones and nerves and all the rest."[14]

The effect of the body often transgressed the arena the church could measure. For example, for many medieval Christian holy women, the Eucharist was essential to their spiritual devotion. The Eucharist allowed them a personal and unmediated access to the divine. The eucharistic enjoyments and miracles empowered them to raise prophetic voices and to compete with the corrupted church hierarchy.[15] Also for the Reformers, the Eucharist was a window into different theological imaginations. The debates over the policy and theology of the Eucharist were central to the Protestant Reformation.

The cases of the medieval holy women and the Reformers evince that the eucharistic body has constantly generated ambivalence and ambiguity within the Christian tradition. Crisscrossing the border between the church institution and lay individuals, the body of Christ assimilates any human agency in faith, yet it cannot belong to any human agent. It is a favorable safeguard of faith that has sustained the institution, but it is also a forceful substance that granted the laity authority to challenge the institution. It has been the single object protected from the "heretical" accounts throughout the church's history, yet it also has planted the seeds for dangerous memories, speeches, and actions. The body erupts into the lives of Christians and metamorphoses with them toward an end no one can foresee. It always moves along with human agencies. It always is in transit, in a form of action, in a form of a verb.

Theologians from diverse Christian traditions have recognized that the Eucharist is the locus in which Christianity finds both challenges and rewards.[16] Other theologians have identified the act of writing as a kind of sacramental activity. For example, David N. Power argues that, because the eucharistic body is the same body as the Word Incarnate, linguistic activity already has its place in the Eucharist.[17] The Incarnate Word, which is now given the form of bread, was a "narrating and narrated flesh" in the discursive situations of the early Christians.[18] Power

further highlights that, just like in the Eucharist, the sacramental sacrifice is realized in the practice of writing. All the power of the living
Christ is "emptied into the written Word, the Word handed on through
writing."[19] Through both the ritual and writing, the Word continues to
incorporate with Christian lives. The intrinsic connection between the
Eucharist and writing is intensified by the fact that both were initiated
by the event of Jesus' death. His death gives rise to the ritual of the
Eucharist as well as the writings of gospel authors. It is Jesus' sacrificial death that allows both the liturgy and the sacramental language to
emerge. The Incarnate Word is given to eat and write.

The identification of a sacramental action as a linguistic event may
invite criticism. Such a gesture could run the risk of linguistic reduc-
tionism.[20] However, to understand the act of writing as an aid to the
ritual of the Eucharist is not to reduce the richness and profundity of
sacramental activity exclusively to linguistic activity. It is, instead, to
make the body of Christ more accessible and practicable by employing
the organizational and conjugative power of writing in the practice of
the Eucharist. The act of writing, alone among all sacramental activities including nonverbal activities, most directly relates to the Word
Incarnate and most pervasively delivers the effect. Rebecca S. Chopp
accurately points out,

> As the perfectly open sign we may say what Word is, in our best
> approximation, but also how it sustains the process of speaking. Here
> the Word is not that which breaks into discourse, or one that governs
> it, rather it is the full inclusivity of discourse; it creates and restores
> speech, it both allows symbols to have meaning and pushes against
> any fixed meaning. The Word/God is the sign of all signs, connected,
> embodied, open, multivalent, all the things a sign can most perfectly be
> . . . and thus, in full openness, creativity and gracefulness creates, sus-
> tains, and redeems all words in their ongoing process of signification.[21]

Such excess is enabled when the writing act is understood as a sacramental activity. The eucharistic body made to be written embodies
the words, actions, and lives of individual Christians across time and
place. Given to eat and write, the body of Christ calls forth the multiple,

concrete realities of individual Christians into the communal, discursive structure. Through both liturgy and writing, the body of Christ disseminates itself into the lives of individual Christians, and it gathers back together the scattered bodies and narratives of those who have been excluded or left on the margins of the symbolic code.

The liturgy of the Eucharist and the act of writing the body of Christ complement each other in the process of incorporating the body of Christ into the lives of individual Christians. The eucharistic liturgy is a ritual that confirms Christians' union with the body of Christ, and the act of writing subsequently is a practice that shapes the union into a discursive form. By writing, the mixture of the divine and human comes into sight and is made readable and discussable. Yet both the liturgy and writing together deny that any adequate explanation of the divine could ever be consumed or written as something accomplished. The liturgy of the Eucharist and so writing the body of Christ are the activities enforcing the process of interaction that undoes any human attempt to consume, exhaust, and dominate the divine mystery. In both activities, the body of Christ generates ambivalence, oscillating between two poles of infinite accessibility and extreme unattainability. It is this ambivalence of Christ's body which opens up the possibility of reworking and rewriting the institution and tradition. The metaphorical link between eating and writing the body of Christ helps Christians participate in this ambivalence.

DICTEE: THE TONGUE, DAUNTED, BROKEN, AND CONFUSED

Being Broken. Speaking broken. Saying broken. Talk broken. Say broken. Broken speech. Pidgon tongue.[22] Broken word. Before speak. As being said. As spoken. To be said. To say. Then speak.

Theresa Hak Kyung Cha was born in Pusan, Korea, in 1951. Her family immigrated to Hawaii and, two years later, to Northern California. Cha went to an all-girls high school at the Convent of the Sacred Heart and then attended the University of California, Berkeley. She obtained her bachelor's and master's degrees in comparative literature and another master's degree in fine arts from the university. Cha spent some years in

Paris for postgraduate work in filmmaking and theory. During the years in France, she was influenced by French literary theory, feminism, and avant-garde film.[23] Cha then returned to the Bay Area and continued making films and performing. She became a United States citizen in 1972 and the same year moved to New York. Tragically, she was murdered by a stranger in New York City on November 5, 1982, seven days after her book *Dictee* was published. She was thirty-one years old at the time of her death.[24]

Dictee is the story of several women presented in a mixture of poems, photographs, official documents, translation exercises, journal entries, and film stills.[25] Over the course of nine chapters composed in a non-linear, non-thematic arrangement of narratives, Cha takes various references from Korean history, Greek mythology, the Bible, and Roman Catholic rites and weaves them through those women's narratives. Just as Cha's genre mixture confounds clear categorical classifications for *Dictee*, so too the contents of her work refute any attempt at defining the core meanings. The crossing over manifested in both the form and contents of *Dictee* reflects Cha's social status as an immigrant woman artist/writer. She has spent her short life crossing different countries. She seems to have never felt a sense of home in any place. *Dictee* embodies the precarious status of living as a stranger in a world that never stops demanding one's origin. The conditions of displacement and loss, which are the major determinants of Cha's subject formation, emerge into the foreground in several sections of *Dictee* and flow around the stories of those women. The demand to speak and write in the second language exacerbates her sense of belonging nowhere.

If, as Gayatri Spivak says, "the will to explain was a symptom of the desire to have a self and a world,"[26] the writing subject of *Dictee* cannot explain her "being" in the world, not because she has no desire, but because she has no "proper" language to describe her being in the world. The writing subject of *Dictee* speaks in broken tongue, writes broken words. She is an exiled, immigrant woman. She cannot construct a coherent discursive body to tell her own story. She is deprived of the ability to articulate herself, for she has lost her mother tongue and has not secured any other language as her own. Cha herself writes in many places in the text as if panting, as if spitting intermittent words. She describes writing in highly abrupt sentences, as if telegraphing survival signals: "I write. I write you. Daily. From here. If I am not writing, I am thinking about writing. I am composing. Recording movements."[27] Throughout the chapters of *Dictee*, the reader hears the subject's cries and frustrations from the linguistic dislocation that estranges her from both dominant foreign tongues and her own mother tongue.

The short fragments at the beginning of the text display the uneasy relation between the subject and her languages. The fragments are written in a form of *"dictee"* assignment in both French and English. *"Dictee,"* French for dictation, prefigures that the text is about a subject who does not speak in her own language, but dictates and translates what someone else speaks. Both French and English paragraphs are interrupted by punctuation instructions literally marked as "guilemets/quotation," "point/period," "d'interrogation/interrogation."[28] The subject, here the narrator, is a woman who "had come from a far." She is an immigrant woman who has been freshly transported from her own homeland. She is sitting at a dinner table surrounded by multiple "families" ("les familles/the families").[29] She is being asked by the families about her experience on the first day in the new place:

> [O]pen quotation marks How was the first day interrogation mark close quotations marks.[30]

She tries to answer, "at least to say the least of it possible," but she finds herself unable to do it:

> [T]he answer would be open quotation marks there is but one thing period There is someone period From a far period close quotation marks.[31]

"The families" that surround the narrator perhaps represent the native people in allusion to the foreign languages and ideological constructions that besiege the immigrant woman. Being interrogated by those native speakers, the woman wants to give them an answer, but she cannot even make a complete sentence. She is afraid of the inaccuracy of her language. She is ashamed of her speech breaking apart like words out of "Pidgon tongue." The literal punctuation marks so disturbingly interrupt both French and English paragraphs that they give the reader a sense of the subject's disquietude and anxiety. She is panting with physical and mental exertion to spit a word:

> It murmurs inside. It murmurs. Inside is the pain of speech the pain to say. Larger still. Greater than is the pain not to say. To not say. Says nothing against the pain to speak. It festers inside. The wounded, liquid, dust. Must break. Must void.[32]

Feeling restless with those foreign families, the writing subject endeavors to find her mother tongue. Her yearnings for the mother tongue are found in the chapters where she talks about her mother. The mother tongue, the subject believes or wants to believe, is the word of "the very flesh and bone" and of "the core."[33] To utter such a word is to infringe upon a given language and to shake the colonialist structures; to write such a word is a "privilege" that she wants to "risk by death."[34] However, the subject is an exiled, immigrant woman. The mother tongue is unutterable and ungraspable to her, not only because political and personal circumstances conspire to keep her from uttering the mother tongue, but also because she herself feels disoriented from the tongue.

The mother tongue demands her to speak it "naturally" and "authentically," but she fails to fulfill the demand because she forgot the language. She left her homeland years ago. She feels displaced in the use of her first language. The mother tongue is alive only in her vague and fragmented memory. The grammar and syntax of the mother tongue are as unfamiliar as those of the foreign tongues. The native Korean speakers expect her to "speak" as fluently as they do.[35] They judge her nationality based on her "inability or ability to speak."[36] Once their expectation is betrayed, the natives treat her like a foreigner. In the scene describing her return visit to Korea eighteen years later, the subject painfully confesses the loss of her confidence speaking in her mother tongue: "I speak another tongue, a second tongue. This is how distant I am. From them. From that time."[37] Without granting any authority or confidence, the mother tongue only agitates her and prohibits her from settling into either the foreign country or the home country. Flow-ing resiliently through the immigrant writer's veins, the mother tongue consistently disturbs her adjustment and reminds her of the condition of displacement. It positions her outside of the constructions of colonialism and yet guarantees her no eventual security.

The writing subject of *Dictee* is located in the space where her lin-guistic activity perpetually puts her into a state of confusion and a lack of confidence. For the subject, the question of identity is no longer about the displaced ultimately finding a way to the "origin" where she is "safe." It is about an existential condition in which she must deal with ongoing fabrication and uncertainty. She has lost her mother tongue even if she is striving for it every moment; she is forced to com-municate in foreign tongues even as she knows that they will never shelter her. Both the mother tongue and the foreign tongues impose a decisive identity category on her as if requiring "documents, proof, evidence, photograph, signature" at the entry of coming into another country.[38] But the subject realizes that she is neither one of them. She is "neither one thing nor the other." She is "third thing," "Tertium Quid neither."[39] Whenever she opens her mouth, she finds herself murmur-ing inside. Whenever she speaks, she finds her words bounced back from the languages and ideologies imposed on her. Her words cannot find a home either in her motherland or in the land she inhabits. She has a daunted and broken tongue.

MIMICKING HIS BODY

Since the 1990s, this impenetrable, unlocatable subject of *Dictee* has been strenuously investigated by scholars in Asian-American feminist, film, and postcolonial studies.[40] Building on the feminist and postcolo-nial reading of *Dictee*, a theological reading is also demanded by the text. Roman Catholicism stands as one of the dominant ideological construc-tions in *Dictee* that affects both the subject's ideas and languages. Cathol-icism involves not only the formation of the writing subject of *Dictee* but also the inhibition of her desire to speak and write. Cha cites the Bible and the Roman Catholic rites and yet assimilates them with her narra-tives shaped by her colonial and immigrant experiences. Her gesture of combining those different resources not only fashions a refreshing inter-pretative tension but also relocates those canonical texts in a colonial and immigrant context. The result of retelling the traditional literatures within the colonial context is the disclosure of gaps and cracks hidden in those texts. In the course of reappropriating the rite of the Catholic eucharistic reception and the requirement of truth in the catechism, the subject reveals her ambivalent position in relation to the body of Christ. By taking the institutional construction of the eucharistic body for her use, the subject incorporates her distinct bodily and linguistic location into the institutional Catholicism and exposes the inherent plu-rality cached within.

Dictee is not a "theological" text in a traditional sense, if "theology" means a discipline that strictly insists on the grammar and teaching accumulated in the tradition. However, if "theology" is primarily reflec-tion on the divine, *Dictee* qualifies, though it may differ from the texts of "professional theologians."[41] *Dictee* is a kind of text that reflects the voice of "inarticulate longing" of a believer "who [does] not want to belong."[42] *Dictee* is particularly meaningful theologically because of its textual location at the intersection of the institution and the individual. Cha's descriptions on the eucharistic reception and catechism inquiry in *Dictee* demonstrate not only the conflicts individual Christians may face in their interaction with the institution, but also their endeavors to create their own space within the institutional construction.

The scene of eucharistic reception captures such an uneasy relation-ship between Catholicism and the subject. The Catholic rite commands the subject to incorporate her female Asian body into the body of a male God. At first blush, the scene appears as a plenary and veracious description of the Catholic rite. However, the seemingly plain descrip-tion soon displays the ironic contradiction between the male God and the subject. It eventually uncovers the subject's ostensible faithfulness to the institutional demand:[43]

> The Host Wafer (His Body. His Blood.) His. Dissolving in the mouth
> to the liquid tongue saliva (Wine to Blood. Bread to Flesh.) His. Open
> the eyes to the women kneeling on the left side. The right side. Only

visible on their bleached countenances are the unevenly lit circles of rouge and their elongated tongues. In waiting. To receive. Him.

Waiting. Nearing. Nearer and nearer to the altar of God. Infusion of the surplus perfumes, bee's wax, incense, flowers.

Place back the tongue. Now to the forehead, between the two brows or just above. Hands folded fingers laced expel all extraneous space. One gesture. Solid. For Him.

By then he is again at the other end. He the one who deciphers he the one who invokes in the Name. He the one who becomes He. Man-God. Places blessed leaves blessed ashes from the blessed palms in the left hand. Black dot of ash on the forehead. Through Hosannah Hosannah in the Highest. Through the Mea Culpa through my most grievous sin. Crucifixion to follow. Of Him. Of His Son.[44]

As Lisa Lowe points out, the irony of the passage indicates an irreconcilable distance between the subject and the body of Christ. It is first conveyed by the subject's physical location. The female communicant is "kneeling on the left side," located at the margin, where she is barely seen.[45] The frequent intervals of "waiting" during the distribution of the Eucharist augment the physical distance between the communicant and the altar. The communicant, however, patiently waits and compliantly follows the order, keeping the posture of subordination. She wants to "receive. Him." The discrepancy between the subject's body and the male God's body is accentuated by the repeated intervention of the male pronouns to designate the property of God's body: "He," "His," and "Him." The body is His, the church is His. The female communicant receives "His" body, the male body, the body of Christ, mediated by "Him" the priest: "He the one who becomes He. Man-God."

The irony of that "male identification" of the female subject at her eucharistic reception is intensified by an almost pathological repetition of the male-God pronoun displayed in the catechism scene that immediately follows:[46]

Q: WHO MADE THEE?
A: God made me
To conspire in God's tongue.

Q: WHERE IS GOD?

A: God is everywhere.

Accomplice in His Texts, the fabrication in His Own Image, the pleasure the desire of giving Image to the word in the mind of the confessor.

Q: GOD WHO HAS MADE YOU IN HIS OWN LIKENESS.

A: God who has made me in His own likeness. In His Own Image in His Own Resemblance, in His Own Copy, In His Own Counterfeit Presentment. In His Duplicate, in His Own Reproduction in His Cast, in His Carbon, His Image and His Mirror. Pleasure in the image pleasure in the copy pleasure in the projection of likeness pleasure in the repetition. Acquiesce, to the correspondence. Acquiesce, to the messenger. Acquiesce, to and for the complot in the Hieratic tongue. Theirs. Into Their tongue, the counterscript, my confession in Theirs. Into Theirs. To scribe to make hear the words, to make sound the words, the words, the words made flesh.[47]

By this obsessive multiplication of the concept of "likeness," the subject both fulfills the demand of the institution and subverts the profession of the institution.[48] As Lowe puts it, on the surface, the subject of *Dictee* concedes the institutional norms and responds to the catechism.[49] The subject acknowledges the institutional demand that forces her to "submit to the ritualized form" and avow "the requirement of truth."[50] Yet, through this "faithful" response, the subject, paradoxically, "points up the impossibility of equivalence" between the Korean-American woman and the Western male God.[51] This extreme form of repetition betrays the purpose of the repetition and reveals the absurdity of the demand itself.

The ambivalent relationship that the writing subject of *Dictee* has with the dominant linguistic constructions of divinity recalls the postcolonial theorist Homi Bhabha's discussions of "colonial mimicry." "Colonial mimicry" is one way that the colonized negotiate the colonial space. Bhabha defines mimicry as "the desire for a reformed, recognizable Other *as a subject of a difference that is almost the same but not quite.*"[52] By mimicking the colonizer's appearance and behavior, the colonized makes herself visible in the colonial space. Because the other is the site of both desires and disavowals, mimicry manifests in the behavior of the colonized to demonstrate, to imitate, and to repeat the colonial desire, the desire to be "authentic." Bhabha argues that within the economy of colonial discourse, colonial mimicry renders an "ironic compromise" by which the colonizer and the colonized acknowledge as well as repudiate each other in their encounter. Colonial mimicry, therefore, has an ambivalent effect: on the one hand, it complies with and intensifies the dominant strategic function of colonial power; on the other hand, it appropriates and registers the colonized within the colonial system as it visualizes their presence. While the colonizer is affirmed by the mimesis of the colonized, the colonized is granted limited recognitions through their mimesis. In Bhabha's words, mimicry is a strategy "that reverses 'in part' the colonial appropriation by producing a partial vision of the colonizer's presence."[53] Mimicry performs and articulates "disturbances of cultural, racial, and historical difference that menace the narcissistic demand of colonial authority."[54]

The writing subject of *Dictee* chooses the body of Christ as an object of mimicry. The eucharistic rite and the catechism now function as the sites in which the subject produces a vision of her presence within the colonial system. In relation to the Catholic rites, the writing subject of Dictee has no words to express herself. She can identify herself only by contradicting herself from the images of the male God, the sacrament of "generic humanity." She is not male, she does not resemble "His own Copy," she does not speak in "His" or "Their" tongue. She has no "original" terms to elucidate herself.[55] In order to write for herself, the precarious subject first chooses to borrow the other's language. She adapts, mimics, and repeats "His" words. However, the subject's gesture of compliance is not for a simple reproduction of the original. Her gesture intends distortion and subversion of the original. By allowing "Him" to occupy her body, she reveals "His" ironies at the very heart of "His" body. She claims that she is not "His." There is more than "His." Once the subject's language takes on a flesh by mimicking the words of the eucharistic rite and catechism, the seemingly uniform body of the institutional language reveals its inherent conflicts. The subject exposes the illusion of the generic, universal, and standard image of the body of Christ. The subject's feeble reaction grows to the point of threatening those monolithic structures of institution regarding race, gender, and language. The very weakness of the ability to defy becomes the ability to mobilize the other side of the dominance, to reappropriate the artifices of the prevailing forms, and to awake the hypnotized voices within.

Dictee's descriptions of the Eucharist and the catechism inquiry strip off the institutional desire to dominate the body of Christ. The subversive character of the writing subject rises even more conspicuously when the institutional desire to control the eucharistic rite becomes barefaced. The writing subject steps into the zone of the "prohibited."[56] The more intensely the force of control at the rites operates, the more vigorously the subject reacts to the force. The conflicts between the male God and the female subject are tense. Now the Eucharist becomes the site of disclosure. The body of Christ lays open the "crossroads of what is known and permissible and that which though known must be kept concealed."[57] By exposing the impossibility of fulfilling the institutional demand, the subject menaces the narcissistic demand of institutional authority. What follows is that the body of Christ reveals its inherent ambivalence and ambiguity, breaking off institutional control. The body of Christ offers the subject the possibility to reverse the institutional visions.

By writing the body of Christ with her own body, Cha reshapes his body as a site of excess, fusion, and transgression. The Eucharist and catechism inquiry, the most deliberately protected sites of Catholicism, are turned into the most vulnerable sites in which the subject can intervene. Those seemingly solid and homogeneous constructions of Catholicism reveal their inherent contradictions. The tense relation between the writing subject of *Dictee* and the institutional constructions challenges Catholicism as a unifying category. It produces unexpected discourses that counter and resist the institution. *Dictee* shows that even though the institutional constructions of Catholicism are closely tied to the process of subject formation, the subject takes abundant opportunities to alter the dominant constructions into a scaffold by which she can make herself visible within it.

Mixing with His Body

Dictee brings attention particularly to the way the Christians at the margin relate with the dominant tradition through the body of Christ. Along with the liturgy of the Eucharist, the act of writing is a vehicle for Cha both to contact with the discursive body of Christ and to recognize the difference between the constructed image of the male God and herself. In spite of the fixed image of God, the precarious writing subject encounters the body of Christ and eventually reveals its inherent ambivalence. This ambivalence instigates the writing subject to keep in contact and work with the dominant institutional constructions of the Eucharist. It enables the subject to see and utilize the provocative aspect of the body of Christ.

The writing subject's acts of eating and writing the body of Christ highlight the ambivalent and interdependent relationship between the dominant tradition and individual Christians. By eating and writing the body of Christ through her own body, the subject is positioned as a part of larger sociohistorical divisions within Christian discourses. The subject interjects her culture, languages, desires, and emotions into the discursive structure filled with dogmatic signs and languages. Her awareness of the difference between the male God and herself is followed by her recognition of the necessity of expressing herself and writing about herself in relation to the body of Christ. The fragmented and scattered pieces of the immigrant writer's narratives consequently enter into the web of meaning.

The recognition, however, inevitably entails violent conflicts and often pains. While the process of interaction helps Cha to see herself in relation to the tradition, at the same time it also reveals her limits and frailties. The acts of writing and eating the body of Christ, then, motivate Cha to react to the tradition either by negotiating with it or challenging against it. It is important to note that in both types of reactions, the normative and regularized character of the dominant construction of the body of Christ cannot easily be cut off. *Dictee* demonstrates that the writing subject is never free from the dominant construction in her interaction with the body of Christ. What needs to be highlighted is the process of interaction in which the subject breaks the illusive normativity and homogeneity of the body of Christ. Even though the writing subject is largely dependent on the constructive nature of the institutional languages and images, the writing subject further makes the institutional constructions useful in her creation of another vision. She reshapes the Eucharist as an open and practicable place in which she can speak and write about the body of Christ.

Michel de Certeau's discussion of the life of the individual in relation to institutionalized society helps to describe the writing subject's interdependency with the church institution. In *The Practice of Everyday Life*, de Certeau explains the relationship between the institution and the individual using the pair of concepts "Place (*lieu*)" and "Space (*espace*)." According to de Certeau, the institution holds "place," whereas the individual produces "space" in reference to the dynamic of power relations within society. Place refers to a concrete "locatedness" constituted by systems of signs, the rules and conventions of the church tradition. Space, on the other hand, is a practicable and practiced place in which this place reveals its intrinsic gaps and slippage made by individuals. Place and space cannot exist without each other. While space cannot manifest itself without the order and stability of a place, place is animated only by successive, multiple, and even irreconcilable spaces. In other words, place is realized by the individuals who create their own spaces within place, and space needs place as a reference to assign.[58]

The writing subject of *Dictee* is in perpetual need of creating her "space" in which she can speak and write the body of Christ. To create her "space" the subject must fatefully rely on the "place" in which the norms and regularities of the language are manufactured. The Catholic doctrine and ritual of the Eucharist are places that offer the subject the signs and languages through which she can express herself in relation to the body of Christ. The subject adapts and utilizes the established signs in order to communicate with the body of Christ. The institutional construction enables the drifting subject to take flesh and anchor in time, even if for a passing moment. The interaction keeps both the institution and the individual moving, changing, and crossing each other. The interaction then brings a change that affects both sides. Once the writing subject of *Dictee* and the language of the institutional church encounter each other through the Eucharist, the orderly and norma- tive nature of Catholicism offers connective motifs weaving through the fragmented nature of the immigrant subject. The scattered narratives of the subject are intertwined with the institutional means and therefore registered into the everyday life filled with religious images and motifs. Meanwhile, the interaction also instigates the institution to suffer and express what it experiences during the process. The institution is vio- lated by the subject who brings her own space into it. The disjunctive and drifting subject makes scratches and squeaking sounds on the side of the institution. It confuses and complicates the homogeneity of the rigid institutional construction. It explodes within the institutional con- struction while making a wound on it, whether critical or minor.

The interaction between the institutional church and individual Christians involves risks, particularly for individuals. Each individual has a distinct body shaped in historical, geographical, and linguistic difference, which is distinguished from the generic and normative body the institution imposes. Because the institution tends to maintain the stable and unifying configuration, it suppresses the individual that fluc- tuates and shifts back and forth without previously defined position. There is also a political disparity among individuals, besides the dispar- ity between the individual and the institution. Once the fragile indi- vidual is exposed to the obstinate institutional systems, the safety of the individual is often put into danger. Because of this perilous condition, some individuals often hide and withdraw themselves within their own ghettos, and the institution mostly casts aside those daunted individu- als. However, unless the individual faces the dangers and transgresses the limit the institution draws in the system, she has nothing to refer to, nothing to be different from. The individual would be pointless if she merely meandered around the fragmented and unsettled arena at the margins of the Christian tradition. Without the painstaking effort to speak out and write with their own bodies, individuals hardly take part in the process of reworking and rewriting the body of Christ.

Cha foregrounds the necessity of initiating this action in *Dictee*. The writing subject of *Dictee* writes in spite of her fear and insecurity. She reveals a body covered with the wounds and scars that she received from immigrant life. As she finds herself muffled by her lack of "mastery" over language, she dictates, repeats, recites, and translates. She practices the act of writing throughout the text and discloses its gaps and cracks. Instead of avoiding conflicts with the suppressing institution, the writing subject of *Dictee* employs and utilizes them. By borrowing the institutional constructions and fusing herself into them, the writing subject of *Dictee* makes her uncertain, inauthentic, unnatural body visible within the dominant tradition.

The writing subject of *Dictee* knows that the institution will never secure a refuge for her. She knows that the harder she pushes, the more forcefully she is pulled into confusion and risk. Acts of eating and writing the body of Christ make the subject painfully aware that her cultural and linguistic displacement cannot be easily resolved, can never be the same as the institution. However, this frustration is the point at which Cha believes that the acts of eating and writing the body of Christ can be propelled, pushing the writing subject to burst like "pure hazard igniting flaming itself with the slightest of friction like firefly."[59] In order to challenge and stimulate the tradition, the writing subject must take a risk. Without disclosing her vulnerability and difference, the subject cannot make herself seen and heard. Without the mobility of the subject, the institution would also have nothing on which to act, nothing to subject, nothing to move on. The writing subject of *Dictee* hardly tries to avoid the necessary conflict. Instead, she vigorously creates occasions for conflicts. She thereby invites other individual believers into this labor, particularly those who suffer from cultural and linguistic displacement and yet cannot easily detach themselves from the influence of dominant institutional religion. And she encourages them to produce the countless discourses tracing many different trajectories so that their writings create a huge inventory of differences that shatter the obtuseness of the institutional church.

DISSEMINATING AND DIVERSIFYING HIS BODY

At the close of this essay, I want to return to the question I raised at the beginning. How might I write the body of Christ with my own body, from my own cultural location, in spite of the myriad ideological constructions of the body, in spite of my own frailties and limits? By suggesting the link between the act of eating and writing God, I seek a way to attend to these questions more closely, to make them more lively, and to voice them more loudly. Sharing my anxiety with Cha, who also struggled with the body of Christ, I draw inspiration from the ways Christians make the body of Christ more troubled, expose the body to confusion, and therefore push it to draw more arduously on the motley desires of individual Christians in different life places. In the act of writing the body of Christ, the frailties and limits of individual Christians' bodily locations and languages are not mere ordeals, but precisely the necessity and contingency for shattering and challenging the dominant institutional constructions of the body of Christ.

Writing the body of Christ with my cultural location as a Korean female theologian living in the United States may put me into trouble that will never cease. But I cannot give up dealing with the body of Christ, because the body is inseparable from what I claim for myself as a Christian. For me, to deal with the body of Christ means to be part of the tradition, to communicate with other Christians, and to relate with people of other faith traditions as a Christian. To be sure, the institutional presentation of the body of Christ that employs a single, universal standard should be subject to suspicion and critique. However, the body of Christ, as we learned from *Dictee*, shows that to be part of tradition is not simply to follow the accepted norms and regulations. It is also to add my voice to others' voices and to connect the established signs and languages with my own context. The Eucharist's association with the institution can be useful because it first provides a communicative tool among Christians; and then it provides individual Christians with a space to intervene in and transform the system. Through eating and writing the body of Christ, I can emphatically resonate with my fellow Christians who also want to discover, recover, and uncover the fact that the Christian tradition cannot be dominated by a single standard. In the history of Christianity, the body has constituted a focal point that draws those tantalizing voices into the contact zone. The body of Christ is not a set of doctrines, but a practicable and writable flesh that needs to be animated by human bodies, human desires, joys, and sorrows of everyday life.

To stress the necessity of incorporating with the body of Christ, however, does not mean that the writings of individual Christians are always in need of validation or authorization granted by employing grammar and signs accumulated in the tradition. Neither does it beg favors from the church to take care of the believers at the margin or to make doctrines benevolent to these believers. Instead, it emphasizes the need for the institutional church to accept and acknowledge that the believers at the margin are part of the body of Christ. Marginal discourses allow the church to realize its borders and limits and to see itself in contact with and in fusion with other bodies within and around Christianity. The weakness of the believers at the margin, their "flaws" and "crooks" are precisely the nudge that their power lodges, as they reveal the illusion of the homogeneous institution. Even though those individuals seem passive and guided by established norms, each of them is an agent that brings divergent plurality to the institution and alters its conventional determinations. Without the individual bodies, the body of Christ remains dormant and fails to incarnate. In a secularized world, Christian beliefs and practices could no longer rely on the belief system and practice set by the institution alone. They require individual believers, who always try to create space for others and to open the closed systems of Christianity to difference and diversity.

My suggestion of the metaphorical link between the acts of eating and writing the body of Christ is meant to illuminate the mutual dependency between the divine body and the multiple human bodies, and also between the institutional church and individual Christians. It is to highlight an ensemble of processes that allows the different groups and individuals in Christianity to be treated in their own rights and to be respected for their own distinctiveness. In that process, I may find my space too. My cultural location will require me, along with other tasks that I share with my fellow Christians, to break through the decayed barrier between different cultures and languages in reworking and rewriting the body of Christ. Instead of avoiding the conflicts and trying to resolve them hastily, I may create cacophony, challenge the conventional sense, and translate emerging insights across different cultures. Walter Benjamin's understanding of the task of the translator applies to my task as well. I may cast my own language into the "spell of another" in order "to liberate the language imprisoned in a work in [my] re-creation of that work."[60] What underlies my speaking and writing as a Korean female theologian is the conflict between the fear of allowing myself to be mistaken and the desire to bend myself to accepted norms—in order to be understood. This, of course, inhibits not only me as a bilingual theologian but any theologian who strives to "write herself"—write about herself and bring herself to theological discourses.[61] Perhaps such a venture of writing will always be marked by the inevitable failure to reach truth and certainty.

Cha's presentation of the immigrant subject echoes with my fear. However, Cha never assures me that the acts of eating and writing the body of Christ will be an intermediary to empower individual Christians at the margin. The acts cannot bring us any clear and certain direction or end to which we can adhere. "There is no future," Cha says, but "only the onslaught of time."[62] The only outcome that Cha can expect from these acts is to be able to keep "moving," to move "toward the movement itself," to "extend" the journey of the immigrant and the colonized lives without ceasing.[63] The acts are exhausting and endless. To eat and write the body of Christ with fragmented bodies while keeping contact with the institution will demand an intensive labor. It is a labor which is never finished and yet can never be abandoned. However, Cha urges in the text that this labor is unavoidable and indispensable insofar as one lives near the territory of the institution. And she patiently waits for the moment in which this slow and vague movement takes shape, the moment in which she is able to be pinned to the ground of everyday life, and the moment in which the institutional language is broken up from its rigid foundation. This is the moment of resurrection Cha waits for in her book *Dictee*, when not only will her wounds be healed but also when the mummified religious language will come to life.

NOT WITH ONE VOICE
The Counterpoint of Life, Diaspora, Women, Theology, and Writing

Kristine Suna-Koro

It was on a dreary and foggy November day in 2000, somewhere within the maze of halls of the State Department's National Foreign Affairs Training Center, that an overheard remark struck me as a most expressive designation of my native language and culture as I have come to consider it in diaspora. I was invited by the Appeal of Conscience Foundation as the representative of the Latvian Evangelical Lutheran Church in America to participate in one of the annual seminars on religious life as a panelist to elucidate the religious situation in the Baltic countries for American diplomats being rotated to serve in the region. Gradually bits of conversation between two foreign service officers directly behind me filtered through the all-around chatter. Suddenly one of them exclaimed, "Wow! Azeri? But that's a *boutique* language! You really want to learn it? But you can't use it anywhere else except in Azerbaijan . . . aren't you wasting your time?" A "boutique" language!? The designation reverberated in my ears as a linguistic and geocultural homerun: aha, that's what my native Latvian is too, isn't it? Now it was my turn to say "wow." Indeed, my experience of being perceived as bizarre (being white and still an ethnic minority?) and exotic (where in the world is Latvia, Latvia . . . *what* is it? Oh, it's not Lapland and it's not in the Balkans?), and as "other" within the complex tapestry of cultural traditions in America, could not be summed up more uncannily. Now in the world of fashion industry, "boutique" means something tiny, rare, highly specialized, exotic, and, yes, even exclusive in the sense of being expensive, upscale, and trendy. But in the world of global markets, imperial formations, and dominating mega-languages such as English, Mandarin, Hindi, and French in knowledge production and consumption, "boutique" most certainly means downscaling from exclusivity into obscurity. In short, in the mundane world of cultural power plays, "boutique" usually means an exotic periphery going hand in hand with its perceived irrelevance. With this awareness in mind, I pondered over the flippant precision of the "boutique" as one of the most germane markers of my hyphenated Latvian-American identity in early twenty-first-century North America. You see, there are over twenty million Azeri speakers in Azerbaijan, Iran, and elsewhere, while there are barely two million speakers of Latvian in the world! In the context of multicultural and minority discourses, "boutique" preeminently describes the interstitial and fluid position of those small cultural and ethnic minorities. They fall, as it were, "in between" the assumed racial, geopolitical, and linguistic identifying lines of routinely canonized large-scale minorities such as, for example, the often sloppily homogenized "Latino/a" or "Asian" diasporic constituencies. Yet the actual ethnoscape of contemporary America facilitates far more complicated cultural variables than initially appear in the massive clichés of glib multiculturalism.

How does one think and write—about God, or love, or military history, or anything—in diaspora, the provisional and mobile homeland of hyphenated identities? Diaspora usually refers to the ethnic and cultural assemblages of people who have been uprooted and dispersed from their homelands by explicit or implicit political, military, or economic forces—through exile, asylum seeking, or migration—into new countries, cultures, and languages. Diasporic imaginary suggests another view of living amid differences and contemplating differences. Diasporic imaginary is a distinct way or style of perceiving the world as it is, as well as envisioning it as it ought to be. It evolves out of the inhabited experience of having lived in multiple places, having spoken multiple languages, having participated in multiple political, economic, and civic traditions. Imaginary is an amalgam of rationality and aesthetic perception, of creative imagination and bodily practice in the context of the preexisting sociocultural realities as they all together orchestrate and are in turn reorchestrated into new patterns and values of life. From within diasporic lifeworlds, differences appear intensely relative and relational, always present yet fluid, mutating, evolving, and allowing for multiple loyalties and allegiances. In the present context of globalization, which various cultures and peoples in the world experience asymmetrically and often outright inequitably, theologians are nudged ever more persistently to reflect on how a peaceful and equitable human cohabitation on our planet and in our country could be credibly imagined. In the search for alternatives to temptations to divide, ostracize, and fabricate oppressive hierarchies, can anything useful emerge from a "boutique" diasporic imaginary? How would a diasporic angle contribute to a fruitful vision of living together amid the dramatic, yet not incommensurable, differences across the interwoven terrains of culture, race, gender, language, ethnicity, class, theological orientation, liturgical tradition, and political outlook?

My itinerary in this essay is to sound out the possibilities for a theological vision of living together and writing theology amid cultural and theological encounters (and even clashes!) from the viewpoint of a culturally hybrid theological sensibility. Starting with a brief look at the present multicultural realities and my own diasporic legacy, I will converse with an unusual lineup of Latvian women theologians from within the liturgical space that I coinhabit through their writings across decades and continents. Finally, I will sketch some possible trajectories of writing theology for life as it is actually lived—at least by some of us in the diasporic enclaves of the contemporary North America—as peculiarly contrapuntal. Counterpoint in music is all about relation between several different voices and rhythms that sound together more or less harmoniously even though each of them remains independent and mutually irreducible. Counterpoint is a precious, nimble, and precarious harmony and not an indistinguishable fusion of uniformity. The sort of diasporic life I have in mind here is contrapuntal in the sense of acting, speaking, gesturing, thinking, and dreaming in more than one language simultaneously. Thus, mother and stepmother tongues and cultural experiences ceaselessly intermingle, overlap, overshadow, interrupt, and chase and flee one another. The emerging melody of life in counterpoint through thoughts, images, feelings, words, and bodily movements sounds and then also writes like a decidedly unfinished symphony of cross-pollinations fluttering among past, present, and imaginary homelands and languages.

Not Purely One Thing

Postcolonial critic Edward W. Said wrote in the early 1990s that "no one today is purely *one* thing" and that "labels like Indian, or woman, or Muslim, or American are not more than starting-points"[1] in the postcolonial world of late modernity. Postcolonial hybridity, not being purely one thing, refers to the emergence of human identities and cultures that have been formed through political, cultural, racial, ethnic, and economic cross-contamination between invasive colonialist regimes and the peoples subjugated under colonial rule and its messy aftermath. Hybridity as a sociocultural, geopolitical, and also epistemological condition generally indicates the colonially founded asymmetrical interdependence between peoples, territories, languages, wisdom traditions, and their epistemological imagination in which "these differential temporalities and histories have been irrevocably and violently yoked together."[2] Consequently it is now impossible to disentangle these intertwining yet grossly unequal trajectories. Thus, as Stuart Hall accurately observed, no place or culture "either 'there' or 'here,' in its fantasied autonomy and in-difference, could develop without taking into account its significant and/or abjected others."[3]

It is precisely in the context of migration that the reality of being "not purely one thing" obtains a pragmatic dimension today. Migration is one of the hallmarks of the contemporary world. The processes of migrancy, whether they be political exile; economic migrancy; seeking asylum from war and genocides; or family reunifications of people scattered by terrorism, persecution, or poverty, all produce cultural hybridities. Migration as an "endless motion surrounds and pervades almost all aspects of contemporary society."[4]

Recently, as the conundrum of the "undocumented" or "illegal immigrants" escalates, awareness about the United States as a multiethnic geocultural space is growing regardless of political position. According to the Census Bureau's demographic forecast, ethnic, cultural, and linguistic minorities will constitute the "majority of minorities" in America by 2042.[5] America today is becoming perplexingly aware of itself as what Avtar Brah calls "diaspora space."[6] This insightful notion denotes a crucial dimension of many societies today. Migration in all its forms fosters the emergence of diasporas of astounding cultural, religious, and linguistic variety. Due to postcolonial migration, an increasing number of Western societies are becoming "diaspora spaces": spaces that are inhabited by both migrants and those who are seen as indigenous or native to particular locations. They are spaces of entanglement wherein the genealogies of dispersion are intertwined with those of "staying put."[7] Diasporas and other floating communities of migrancy can no longer be marginalized as "them" because now "they are us,"[8] and our life together changes us all. Of course, "diaspora space" most definitely is not diaspora as such. It is what happens when a sociocultural space becomes hybrid through its diversity. It is also what happens when a discursive space becomes equally hybrid. Thus, the practices and patterns of knowing, discerning, judging, feeling, and acting become hybrid, too. What could this emergent cultural and religious landscape offer us all from a diasporic perspective?

HOMING DESIRE: ON A VISION QUEST
FOR A PLACE AND A TONGUE

As I write this essay and occasionally glance out of my window, the same two pairs of eyes frequently meet my gaze with a magisterial look of control, comfort, and possession from the windowsill of the opposite house—all the while exuding a confident air of belonging. No, not simply belonging, but rather being in charge and totally, indeed enviably, at home. Of course, the eyes are those of my Southern neighbor's two cats idly gazing at me in their invariably benevolent condescension! Sooner or later amid the crosshairs of our gazes I never fail to blink first, with quite a resignation: I do not know what or where a home, properly speaking, is, whether geographically, linguistically, or theologically. I arrived in the United States in the late 1990s to serve as pastor in an ethnic Latvian Lutheran community in suburban Philadelphia. This community, which is part of the worldwide Latvian Evangelical Lutheran Church Abroad (LELCA),[9] was looking for a Latvian speaking pastor. The ordination of women in Latvia was swiftly and single-handedly suspended in the freshly post-Communist Latvia in 1993 by a newly elected bishop after having been practiced for almost twenty years. Having been ordained in 1995 in Germany to serve in LELCA, I was looking for avenues of ministry and theological inquiry outside my homeland after graduate studies and pastoral calls in Great Britain and Germany. Lamentably, as I write this, women are still not readmitted to ordained ministry in the Lutheran Church of Latvia, hence my ordination in LELCA in 1995 and hence the decision to relocate into what a fellow female diasporic Latvian Lutheran pastor once sarcastically termed "ecclesiastical exile." Since that time, English is steadily becoming my stepmother tongue, emerging from the distant position in between the third or fourth language. Exasperatingly un-Anglo-Saxon syntax and convoluted grammar, which is materializing in this essay with virtually every sentence, is just one outcome of constant thinking in some three languages simultaneously. Then there are those exasperating moments of double (or triple, or quadruple . . . ?) consciousness in which I belong almost everywhere and then again nowhere. That happens when no place and no language feel "native" anymore. That happens when I find myself again and again in the displacement which Wonhee Anne Joh candidly describes as a

> sense of displacement due to various forms of constant departures, arrivals, and nonbelonging . . . not only connected with geographical disorientation but also with language/voice/reality. . . . Those of us who are by necessity multilingual are often left in the end with an imposed silence and feelings of inadequacy and incompetence. . . . This issue of

"my place" is challenged and forever questioned not only by the dominant society but also from those very places of origin to which I can supposedly always return. To whichever side I turn, I am constantly met with recognition and simultaneous disavowal. The recognition that both sides of the boundary challenge my identity has been both crushing and revelatory.[10]

With my hyphenated cultural and religious identity, where else could I find myself theologically if not belonging multiply, "betwixt and between,"[11] in the imaginative company of theologians like Rita Nakashima Brock, who rightly identifies the only type of integrity that is realistically open for people like me, namely "interstitial integrity"?[12] Interstitial integrity consists in "refusal to rest in one place, to reject a narrowing of who we are by either/or decisions, or to be placed always on the periphery."[13] Theologically, interstitial integrity facilitates an interlacing of diverse and sometimes seemingly incompatible traditions of doctrinal, critical, and aesthetical reasoning; biblical interpretation; and liturgy.

Diasporic subjectivity is anchored in and enlivened by interstitial integrity. It routinely lives what one cannot discursively reconcile and sleekly unite. Rather, it is being what Kwok Pui-lan calls the "border subject."[14] What is obtained through migrancy is a diasporic imaginary of "both" and "neither/nor." Multiple belongings are held together by a "homing desire"[15] within the delicate equilibrium of interstitial integrity. Diasporic subjectivity lives in and through hybridity; it is a performed hybridity which facilitates the transformational commerce of lived reality into a cognitive model. Diasporic subjectivities are Janus-faced: they are poised between overlapping cultural legacies, political alliances, and ethical imperatives as they indwell here, there, and elsewhere. My observation is that diasporic imaginary is thus more or less like a fugue in music because it entails a multiplicity of thinking, feeling, acting, speaking, and writing "voices." To borrow Marcia Mount Shoop's language in relation to motherhood, diasporic experience is a differently colored yet equally "complicated snarl of experience" with an almost endless array of tendencies, habits, hopes, and fears.[16] Thus, doing theology from a diasporic location amounts to nothing less than thinking, acting, and writing in an ensnarled way—not simply by choice but by the pull of life's existential actualities.

Diasporic imaginary is embedded in a routine lived complexity of "here and there" in which the perennial Western predicament of interacting with otherness has lost at least some of its allergic edge. But the irrepressible specter of being "not purely one thing" is not yet the whole story. As Kwok pointedly remarks, the "female diasporic subject is multiply located, always *doubly displaced*" and hence "may not easily find a language with which to speak."[17] Or write, since writing happens in a no less displaced way for diasporic subjects! On top of the slowly dispersing marginalization of women's voices in most of the "mainstreams/malestreams" of knowledge production in arts and sciences in the West and elsewhere, for a diasporic female subject the ongoing task of navigating through at least two canons of grammar, syntax, and idiomatic fluency lurks in the background of every endeavor. In this context, linguistic hybridity is not an elitist cosmopolitan luxury or a profitable intellectual commodity invested with power. Surely, sometimes hybridity is an acquired taste that originates out of an affluence of economical and cultural options—equally so in the West and elsewhere these days. But often the forces of history conscript a writer into hybridity as an embodiment of lived cultural and linguistic tensions. It is not necessarily the case that a writer consciously appropriates and cultivates hybridity because it happens to be in vogue—even though personal history and strategic appropriation can certainly intertwine in an individual or societal life. This hybridity often seems to leave the writer suspended, as it were, in a constant displacement betwixt and between words, concepts, and images that retain their "aura" of experiential grounding and meaningful depth, indeed, a certain specific and rich taste of "authenticity," only when written and spoken in a certain language. Being suspended in the linguistic hybridity of diaspora therefore entails the reluctance, nay the impossibility, to give up the depth, the taste, the "aura" of bodily memories and epistemological imagination. Words have a context- and language-specific experiential sensuality that is written into the rationality and imagination of a diasporic subject. Some words have an "aura" only in German, or Russian, or Latvian, or English. The deeper the "auras" of words, the more complex is the multivoiced snarl of language when all the particles of bodily memories and linguistic expressions converge in one linguistic system, one sentence, one verbal image. If Ludwig Wittgenstein is right that "the limits of my language mean the limits of my world,"[18] then my world as a diasporic woman has intertwined yet different limits depending on the language in which I think, write, swear, or dream. Bringing it all together into the verbal playground of the English language in this postcolonial era sometimes feels like creative yet very pedantic and targeted "poaching." Ironically, at times "poaching" through citing and adapting the words of others can create a fruitful and even liberating avenue for letting a nonnative English voice write itself out at a much fuller stretch then one could be able to muster in splendid isolation. And this is how hybridity happens: how a certain diasporic newness enters again and again into the homelands and borderlands of writing.

A Glimpse of an Unusual Postcolony: Oh, That I Had a Thousand Voices . . .

To be blunt, there is no patristic, medieval, or modern "golden age" of documented Latvian theological creativity that would consist of an internationally recognizable lineup of "greatest hits" in systematics, biblical studies, or liturgical theology. Unsurprisingly, there is no extensive written archive of Latvian women's theological creativity.[19] Even more, there are no Latvian women starring in that field of theology which the habitual masculinist monopoly still often perceives as the eccentric and marginal "mystical spirituality." Alas, there is no Latvian Hadewijch of Antwerp, or Angela of Foligno, or Elizabeth A. Johnson. After the litany of "few and far between," a brief historical excursus can provide a helpful context here.

Historically speaking, for the Baltic lands in the northeastern corner of what is today known as Europe, the "History" has indeed been a "tormented chronology."[20] Western European expansion in the Middle Ages evolved into crusade that ultimately led to the establishment of the crusader state of Livonia in the Baltic lands in the early thirteenth century.[21] Most of it happened, as an ever-popular adage has it, "by fire and sword." Western colonial "synergy of conquest, commerce, and Christ"[22] spearheaded into the deepest peripheries of Europe before it achieved its perverse grandiosity transatlantically. As Nils Blomkvist observes, "the High Medieval 'Making of Europe' was an effort of a magnitude comparable to that of the Roman Empire, and *mutatis mutandis* to some extent to the Early Modern European global expansion."[23] By 1400 a system of apartheid was functioning as a well-oiled mechanism. The crippling outcome was the territory "where two different breeds of people coexisted: a tiny, European elite, and a mass of barely Christianized 'barbarians' kept in apartheid."[24] The unholy alliance of the Christian church and the emergent European transnational commodity market produced in the Baltics a configuration of power where

> the original aim of Christianization gradually failed. In the failure to establish a functional state and the failure to merge into a nation, the European making of Livonia produced one of the first examples of a social entity that was later to be well known around the globe—the transmarine colony.[25]

The Baltic lands and peoples were appropriated into Europe by crusade and remained in colonial subjugation for centuries by various colonial powers—German, Polish, Swedish, and Russian—until shortly after the First World War. Then Baltic lands emerged from the ruins of the Russian colonial empire in 1918 as independent countries, only to suffer another colonial subjugation under the Soviet empire from 1940 until its collapse in the early 1990s.[26]

Whatever the ultimate balance of gains and losses of Europeanization of the Baltic rim (and this continues to be debated rather passionately among those Europeans formerly known as "barbarians" as well as among those Europeans who once named them so), the indigenous culture and language resiliently developed as refuge and a site of resistance for the oppressed under the conditions of colonial domination. The resilience is witnessed in the Latvian *dainas*, the lyrical two-couplet folk songs, many of which were composed and transmitted orally during the Enlightenment era. Over two million *dainas* have been collected in written format. According to Maruta Lietiņa Ray, at least 1,300 of those reflect directly on the brutal life of serfdom for the majority of Latvians, which lasted until the middle of the nineteenth century.[27] The *dainas* present a cultural and historical voice of the colonized peasant-poets, predominantly women, speaking in their despised "peasant-speak" about the experience of both oppression and resistance. The *dainas* presented the only possible form of lament, describing suffering, injustice, shame, resentment, and desire for revenge as well as sarcasm as resistance toward colonial rulers.[28] Certainly the scope of the *dainas* is not limited to the colonial engagement alone. It is rather a poetically engendered integrative worldview of the culture in the process of survival, including reflection on matters of religion, nature, sexuality, and a version of virtue ethics while struggling with realities of violence and namelessness. Karlis Racevskis underscores notable differences in comparison with the Western European "value systems" of the time in that

> the responsibility for composing, performing, and transmitting the *dainas* belonged to women. This task of giving a voice to a people's experience of life was not carried out by old men, by a priestly caste, or by artistic or philosophic elite, as has been the case in all the so-called axial civilizations. It was a project that was fundamentally disinterested since it was both communal and anonymous.[29]

Colonial entanglements shaped Latvian Christianity and its spiritual and theological sensibilities into a creolized religious outlook in which elements of indigenous wisdom traditions often commingle with Christian theological traditions, mostly Roman Catholic, Lutheran, and Eastern Orthodox. Latvian theological formation and imagination has always been shaped syncretistically as it found itself at the crossroads between differently dominant cultural, philosophical, and theological traditions. In the absence of even the most rudimentary "canon" of Christian theological tradition—Western or Eastern—available in the Latvian language, Latvian theologians always had to be literally and figuratively multilingual by necessity rather than by choice in order simply to study their subject matter. Add to that almost a half-century of the officially canonized Soviet Marxism-Leninism with its militant atheism and it is not at all surprising that, for example, the first complete translation of the Lutheran *Book of Concord* in the Latvian language was published no sooner than in 2001. All that despite the winds of the Reformation reaching Rīga already by 1521 and the followers of Martin Luther preaching in the despised "peasant-speak" Latvian for the newly minted indigenous Protestants shortly thereafter!

The enduring ambivalence of the various colonial legacies is never absent from the Latvian theological endeavors and spiritual dispositions. Most of the Latvian theological writing in the Latvian language in the past and present—by women or men—is best described as pastorally or catechetically motivated ad hoc expressions of theological creativity in sermons, lectures, or magazine or online articles. Overall, most theology in the Latvian language is still oral and communal—it is preached, taught, sung, and conversed about interpersonally, including the mushrooming cybercommunities. Strange as it may sound, the most enduring and formative presence of women's theological voices in Latvian Protestant Christianity in the homeland and in diaspora emerges not from the margins but right from the limelight[30] of the life of faith: the liturgical space of worship. The voices from the liturgical center are the resilient voices of Latvian women poets and translators whose theological thoughtworlds continue to resonate powerfully and formatively in the lives of communities of faith across geographical, cultural, and generational boundaries through the hymnody. It is to poetry and hymnody as a site of theological creativity that I now turn.

God, She Wrote . . . Well, Maybe in Translation

Women have enduringly played a prominent role in Latvian literature and poetry from the anonymous and enserfed authors of the *dainas* to the highly versatile literary scene of the present day.[31] It is no wonder, then, that women have not hesitated to express themselves prolifically in religious verse as well. In the absence of women's voices in the Latvian religious discourse in the pulpits and scholarly theology both in the homeland and in diaspora up until relatively recently, hymns have uniquely facilitated the presence of women's theological reflection literally at the center of spiritual life—in worship. The themes of the original hymn texts and translations vary widely from incarnation, to crucifixion and resurrection, to salvation, prayer, faith, sanctification, and life eternal, as well as lamentations over the brutality of history and supplications for survival of the nation throughout wars and occupations. There is no major theological doctrine or liturgical festival that would not figure in these texts. Thus I dare to call these texts theological and their authors theologians. Without pretense to be exhaustive in my brief "listening tour" among the Latvian women poet-theologians, I will journey through the landscape of sonorous theology through the Latvian Lutheran Hymnal (Dziesmu grāmata latviešiem tēvzemē un svešumā, 1992).[32]

Women have authored or translated the texts of some of the most beloved and most popular hymns across generations. For example, Minna Dzelzkalne's (Tirzmaliete) "Ved mani, Dievs" ("Lead Me God and Bless My Journey") has been a time-honored fixture throughout the church year and is often sung as a hymn of choice at baptisms, confirmations, weddings, funerals, and even national commemoration services. If there were such a thing, this hymn would make the "Latvian Top Ten All-Time Hottest Hymns" list without a doubt! It is set to the catchy tune by Jean Sibelius known as "Finlandia" and is written in the form of prayer. Theological emphases fall on the synergistic guidance of God throughout life with faith and an ethically saturated happiness that "does not make another human being suffer." The prayer constantly oscillates between an individual journey of sanctification and simultaneously being a co-worker of God for the sake of the others with whom one finds oneself on the same peregrination toward salvation, so that their native land may thrive through the cooperation of human effort and divine grace.

Among other "Top Ten" contenders are also Otīlija Baštika's (Liesma) beloved translations of Charles Wesley's "Love Divine, All Loves Excelling" (as "Dievišķīgā mīlestība") and A. B. Mansell Ramsey's "Teach me thy Way, O Lord" (as "Māci man ticēt, Kungs"), and her original christological hymn "Es zinu vārdu" ("I Know the Name"), set to the famous Ralph Vaughan Williams tune "For All the Saints"—to name just a few. Baštika's texts extoll profoundly Christocentric faith as an ever-renewed trust that through grace endures even the worst trials. For her, the presence of Christ is never invasive or coercive but rather nurturing and always hopeful.

The theme of the cross and crucifixion is prominent not only in Baštika's texts but also among other women poet-theologians. Elvīra Vankina's Lenten hymn "Krusts laistās kalna galā" ("Cross is Shining on the Mountain"), Tirzmaliete's original funeral hymn "Dzied' vēlreiz sēro dziesmu" ("Sing Again the Heartrending Song"), and Sandra Tobīs' original Easter hymn "Dūc zvani, raisās gaviles" ("The Bells are Humming, Shouts of Joy are Rising"), among others, reflect on the cross as a site of hope and light for the oppressed, the mourning, and the downtrodden. The cross is the supreme source of hope against all hope in Tobīs' Lenten hymn "Pie Tava smago sāpju krusta" ("At the Cross of Your Hardest Pain"). The brutal violence of the cross emerges as a trope for the predicament of Latvia under totalitarian occupation in the texts of lament such as Lija Kronberga's original hymn "Kungs, vaidos tā zeme" ("Lord, That Land is Groaning Where My Heart and Mind Belongs"). Participation in Christ's suffering individually or politically as an oppressed nation is portrayed as the only refuge. Through his suffering, Jesus Christ remains ultimately in redemptive solidarity with the broken lives of the subjugated and the exiled, as in Valda Mōra's original lamentation hymn "Kā puķe, vētras rauta" ("Like a Flower Torn by Wind") and Amālija Breikša's funeral hymn "Zvans kad atskan pēdējais" ("When the Last Bell Tolls").

Divine power, contrary to the brutality and force of the cross, is overwhemingly conceptualized by the women poet-theologians as grace-full, as delicate and caressing yet nevertheless incomparable to anything else in power and persuasion. The divine presence is described as a gentle caress of the human soul, as, for example, in Mōra's original Christmas hymn "Šai svētā naktī" ("In This Holy Night") and in Terēze Brence's original praise hymn "Tu, kas liec rītam" ("You, Who Willed the Morning Rise"). Latvian women's voices persistently reveal the appreciation of the depth of adversity and challenge to which only faith in action is an appropriately full-bodied answer. Melānija Fetlere's original prayer hymn set to the tune of an old Latvian folksong, "Debestēvs, mēs lūdzam Tevi, dod mums spēku pastāvēt" ("Heavenly Father, Give Us Strength to Survive"), is a supplication for both grace and perseverance not only to survive and feel God's presence "on the steep rocky paths" but also for strength "to split the hardest rocks" if necessary. This prayer is not at all about asking for an easy fare but instead for a grace-guided survival that involves serious struggle. But it is arguably the diasporic Latvian-Swedish poet Veronika Strēlerte's funeral hymn "Kāds ir, kas skaita mūsu siržu pukstus" ("There is Someone Who Counts Our Every Heartbeat") that offers a glimpse of the most characteristic trait of Latvian spirituality and religious disposition *tout court*. When it comes to reflecting on and speaking about the most profound mysteries of both divinity and humanity, and when it comes to the deepest chasms of faith in the transcendent God, deferential understatement or whisper is the most appropriate form of speech, existentially and theologically. Strēlerte's text names God mutedly and reverentially as "Someone," and "the most precious words" facing death and departing from this life are said "in whisper."

One might almost detect a certain deeply ingrained resemblance of apophatic reserve in Latvian spirituality and theological attitudes that women poet-theologians consistently and deftly express in their texts. Latvian Christianity so far has never been really boisterous in its theological or doxological temperament; it is as if it stands in the long shadow of the cross—Christ's and the nation's own, in the homeland and in diaspora, in ways too many to explore here. Latvian Christianity is inextricably overshadowed by the persistent cultural memory and history of the colonial conquest. The shadows of colonialism are long and strong in Eastern Europe. Let me mention a very recent example. In June 2009 a book burning of allegedly "pagan" literature was instigated by a charismatic, predominantly Russian-speaking Christian group, "New Generation," during the usually rambunctious Latvian indigenous Midsummer celebrations (*Jāņi*) to mobilize against what they called the resurgent pagan practices of occultism and fetishism associated with the Latvian ancient wisdom traditions. Amid the raging cultural controversy and public outrage about religious intolerance, Archbishop Jānis Vanags of the Evangelical Lutheran Church of Latvia responded to these disturbing events in a widely publicized address. In it, Vanags underscored the enduring ambiguity that continues to surround Christianity as a colonial phenomenon in the northeastern borderlands of Europe with an incisive, perhaps a bit surprising for some, sociohistorical observation:

> However, Latvia is not a religiously monolithic country and Christians must remember that they are not the only religious people here. Yes, Christians are called to share their faith with others. Let us mention, however, that the greatest harm to the Christian message in Latvia was not perpetrated by pagans, and possibly not even by Communists, but by the crusaders who had presumed to impose the good news of love by fire and sword. The wounds that they inflicted have not yet been healing in many Latvian souls. Let us not resemble the crusaders![33]

The postcolonial ambiguity regarding the original entrance of Christianity by "fire and sword" undoubtedly continues to influence not only the palpable syncretism of the creolized popular religiosity but the ongoing ambiguity in theological reflection as well. Caution, moderation, inwardness, and a particular reserve toward institutional religion characterize the Latvian spiritual outlook, in the homeland and in diaspora. Moreover, from the *dainas* onward, all things religious in Latvian are preferably spoken about in sotto voce—since that is mostly how the divine acts, speaks, and leads in the creolized indigenous traditions of spirituality, virtually never by coercive or disrupting otherworldly intervention but rather through the patient rhythms of everyday life with its ebbs and flows, and quiet transformations toward the always desired and lauded harmony with nature. Of course, that may also explain why so often it is hard to tell a Good Friday "amen" from an Easter "alleluia," if one goes only by the pitch, tempo, and volume of congregational singing.

After this brief gallop through the sonorous archive of Latvian women poet-theologians' texts in their unsystematic and dogmatically irregular ad hoc brevity and diversity, one may wonder, where exactly does their creative significance reside? And what kind of insight could their voices, mostly from the unenviable past, offer to those who write theology today in the emerging "diaspora space" of multicultural North America?

From a "Boutique" Liturgical Space to the Counterpoint of Diaspora Space

For good and often for ill, especially as far as women are concerned, liturgy is a formative space. Ideally, it can be a transformative space. Liturgy forms, can transform, but, sadly, often malforms. Gestures, postures, words, sounds, images, and attitudes that we experience in the space of liturgy can school our bodies and souls in the ways of charity, faith, hope, grace, justice, and service to incarnate the vocation to imitate Christ. However, if they are used to entrench enduring injustices even deeper and to prooftext the ever-so-tempting egoism of salvation without regard for the fate and well-being of the suffering and the oppressed, then liturgy most certainly becomes a school of blasphemy. Words, sounds, gestures, postures, and actions in liturgy inform theological, ethical, epistemological, and social dispositions of worshippers as *lex orandi* (law of prayer). Again, for good or for ill, this *lex orandi* shapes and is reciprocally shaped by *lex credendi* (the law of belief). Where both of these dimensions of theological creativity meet most directly is at the crossroads of the creed, the clearest liturgical and doxological instantiation of the doctrinal core of faith.

Now hymns, in view of their fulfilling "a supplementary function to creeds,"[34] function most definitely not as mere devotional adornments but rather as an aesthetically rich and historically specific elaboration of the theological truths encompassed in the creed. Historically, in Latvian spirituality the hymnal effectively "outsings" the Bible for all practical purposes. Music and singing are engraved in the cultural DNA of the Latvians as a spiritual practice *par excellence*—in church, at home, in mass political demonstrations, in the famous national song festivals as well as during orgiastic midsummer feasts, during all the most important events of human life from cradle to grave, on the barricades of revolutions, in the deportation cattle cars on the way to Stalin's Gulag or Hitler's concentration camps, and all the way into the ice rinks of the world hockey championships. In this context, women's theological voices are by no means marginal in the (trans)formative space of liturgy as their texts are sung, remembered, and taught to children year after year.

Certainly, as the Latvian tradition unsurprisingly shows, women had to enter the theological limelight through the back door of poetry and music up until very recently. But, as Geoffrey Wainwright argues, hymns are "sung confession[s] of faith."[35] In liturgy they function as a remarkably holistic amalgam of pedagogy and doxology. If worship, as Wainwright puts it, is "an affair of the whole person, mind, heart, voice, body,"[36] then this affair has been permeated by a polyphony of women's voices right in the center of praise *and* catechesis. The liturgical center is cracked open even when praise has to be inverted to rather sound as lament, and even when the only permitted form of catechesis for women is poetry. Hymnody is both aesthetically shaped doxology and catechesis. As far as catechesis is concerned, Latvian women poets' hymn texts have been more influential in the formation of people's spiritual lives and theological beliefs than all Latvian academic theological writings taken together. To those who grow increasingly ponderous over the occasionally tired and even trivialized theme of marginality, the "boutique" Latvian liturgical space and its women poets signal a foretaste that "the centrality of the center has been decomposed"[37] through polyvocality in yet another subtle way. These voices seem to affirm that a worthy way to decompose the often inhospitable center is by raising women's voices precisely about the most central things in life and in faith, central to all and not just women or just any particular group of women, especially when the experience of suffering is so poignant.

This route of writing theology—poetically, almost unofficially, under the cloak of gender anonymity and yet somehow slipping through the back door right into the limelight almost unnoticed—merits an ambivalent assessment. On the one hand, the Latvian women poet-theologians have honed to perfection a style of speaking of all things in relation to God that could not be described more accurately than "stealth theology"[38] as far as gender in theological enterprise is concerned. Namely, their poetic and theological touch is often camouflaged in the deep universality of lament, supplication, and adoration. Only a meticulous attention to nuance, to the subtle touches that emerge from in between the lines, reveals the subversively creative insights about the nature of divine power and divine-human relationship that sets them apart from the rest. On the other hand, stealth theology resonates with the challenge to go beyond what Teresa Berger calls the basic paradox in feminist liturgies, namely the paradox "that [feminist liturgies] ultimately underwrite a binary gender division counterproductive to the diversity of women's lives."[39] But what does the Latvian slice of internal diversity among women reveal as potentially productive for the myriad of women's writing voices today?

The voices of Latvian women poet-theologians decompose the center theologically through that slippery slope of theological writing which virtually always bypasses gender as a major marker of meaningful creativity and as a facet of liberation of utmost importance. Latvian women in their hymns neither directly address women nor identify themselves explicitly as women. Gender is not explicitly recognized or privileged as a location of poetic endeavor or theological interpretation. They pray for all, lament and intercede for all, exhort and edify all, and praise on behalf of the whole community. Frequently they sound as much like modern and Western generic (male) modern subjects in love with reclusive, deceptively genderless, and individualistic religious introspection as one can possibly imagine. After all, most of these theological voices are, strictly speaking, from a prefeminist era of the twentieth century. Yet they write with an uninhibited audacity to call on God to save, comfort, and defend all God's people as fully empowered and legitimate representatives of the community and its liturgical assemblies. Certainly, there is always a reason for caution when it comes to weighing the strategic gains and losses of this trajectory of women's theological endeavors. The occlusions of gender difference may in the end reveal nothing more than a premature and thus ultimately illusory liberation. What is arguably gained by the unsettling gender anonymity is that their voices in the liturgical and theological space may no longer be perceived quite as "boutique," as this label is applied to those occupying the niches of feminist, womanist, queer, Latino/a, Third World, etc., theologies. The gains here may not be earth-shattering, but a more open mind and less initial opposition are not to be scorned amid any righteous struggle. Quite a few theological approaches are unfortunately still often perceived as nothing more than "theme park theologies"[40] or "boutique voices"[41] by the overall Western theological main(male) stream. Unmistakably, the Latvian women's voices do remain "boutique" to some degree in virtue of their "boutique" ethnicity, but then again, *all* Latvian voices are perceived as "boutique," male or female. Additionally, the emphasis on the whole community, regardless of specific confessional adherences, resonates with the prominent themes of solidarity with all the oppressed and overall well-being of all members of the community regardless of gender in womanist and black feminist theological orientations.

It is far from unequivocally clear whether these ad hoc avenues of women writing themselves through poetry right into the tremendously influential formative space of liturgy and hymnody have brought lasting and transformative difference for the understatedly elusive voices of the trailblazer Latvian "amateur" theologians and their contemporary successors. An in-depth evaluation of their impact is beyond the scope of this essay, as is literary judgment on the poetic quality of their texts. Here, however, I would like to highlight a couple of trajectories that I find fruitful for thinking and writing theology with a diasporically "fugued" epistemological perspective in mind in the context of today's multicultural America.

The Latvian women wrote theology in an "irregular," that is, non-systematic and abundantly practical, way. Of course, that should not disqualify their texts from being rightfully considered theological. They also wrote and became popular in a manner that has been occasionally understood as "fated to unoriginality"[42] in postcolonial contexts. Quite a few of the women poets' "greatest hits" are actually creative translations of the reigning European-American religious poetic texts. Or their immensely popular original verses are set to imported popular tunes, many of them originating in the colonial centers of Western Christianity.

Historically, texts and tunes often arrived as part and parcel of the colonial subjugation and dominance of colonial super-languages — mostly

German and Russian—in all spheres of education and cultural production until well into the twentieth century when Latvia first became an
independent nation. But soon afterwards, as Latvian World War II
refugees became displaced persons and gradually immigrated to a number of Western countries, texts and tunes were strategically appropriated through the processes of hybridity in the cultures of their new
diasporic emplacement. Here surfaces a paradigmatic consternation
about the authenticity and originality of texts which have originated in
a derivative relation to the dominant Western thoughtworld through the
process of forced cultural hybridity. This consternation usually rebukes
and discounts the fruits of such cultural hybridity as unoriginal and
inauthentic "almost but not quite" in relation to the Western cultural
forms. It is often implied that the "natives" or the previously colonized
people are not capable of anything more than a pale attempt to imitate
the Western European-American cultural grandeur, from engineering
to literature and arts.[43] In response to such Western and affluently metropolitan value judgments, including certain white feminist orthodoxies,
postcolonial criticism has in turn emphasized the creative and subversively constructive nature of hybridity. Particularly, it underscores the
subtly complex process of imaginative appropriation as well as selec-
tive and critical reinvention through nonidentical repetition, sometimes
called "mimicry" in postcolonial contexts. Thus, when Tirzmaliete's
"Ved mani, Dievs" blends ostensibly seamlessly with a Sibelius melody
to become one of the indispensable identifying markers of Latvian spirituality, and when Baštika's translated "Māci man ticēt, Kungs" continues to shine as the hallmark of diasporic youth devotions and their very
Latvian Christian identity in contemporary North America, something
much more complex and ingenious is at work than simply a barren
"unoriginality."

  Hybrid discursive and imaginative habits issue in styles of creativity,
including writing poetry and theology, that habitually embody difference through nuance, through fragment, through delicate transposition
of accents, and through contextualized rearrangements of the "global"
and the "local." Translation and appropriation in the Latvian tradition
has a postcolonial stylistic parallel with what Stephanie Newell has

observed in Ghanaian popular literature to dispel the assumptions of simplified passivity and unoriginality:

> quotations from Western texts and genres are being combined with quotations from other archives of popular narratives, all of which are used as tools to cultivate and refine the authors' own didactic projects. . . . Authors are selecting quotations from diverse source-texts, and positioning the quotations within narratives in such a way that their *own* messages to local readers will be illuminated. . . . Authors incorporate a variety of "master" languages from diverse narrative forms.[44]

What emerges here is a hybrid style of writing out of a situated and localized authenticity whose integrity is interstitial. This integrity is also multi-canonical. Far from being an uninspired parroting, these styles of creativity are porous not by elitist choice but through the reality of lived everyday tensions. Their poetic is that of an inventive leakage between the dominant thought forms of the West and those traditions of creativity constituted from the underside of Western modernity. Ironically, the obsession with originality continues to lead the Western postmodern intellectual commodity market, voraciously chasing innovation and profitable exotic difference, into disappointment that the differences emerging from the various undersides of colonial modernity are not different enough! In postcolonial locations, including Latvia, and its diaspora worldwide, all enduring cultural expressions from politics to poetry are irrevocably permeated by various colonial and global cultural hegemonies. So it is useless to search there for some pure and uncontaminated "native" authenticity in content or in style behind the allegedly inauthentic mimicry of cultural hybridity, unless one fabricates such an "authentic voice" out of nostalgia, naiveté, or purely commercial interest. Quotations—literary, musical, and theological—create new meanings, albeit in an intricate, perhaps a small-scale "boutique," style. This style emerges out of cultural and linguistic code-switching[45] and immersion in cross-pollinating encounters with other epistemological sensibilities and habits of imagination and action. This is also a style that resonates with diasporic subjectivity and its multiple belongings and loyalties near and far, here and there, as in a musical counterpoint.

As Kwok has perceptively summed it up, "a diasporic consciousness finds similarities and differences in both familiar territories and unexpected corners; one catches glimpses of oneself in a fleeting moment or in a fragment in someone else's story."[46]

Finally, what inspires the voices and texts that are "not purely one thing" for those who themselves are "not purely one thing" and even for those who live among such hybrid subjects with interstitial integrities and polyphonic fidelities? The most fruitful inspiration, I submit, is the resilience and perseverance for reading throughout texts, wisdom traditions, music, cultural and theological archives, imposed and chosen, foreign and indigenous, written and oral, in original or in translation, praised and demonized, in vogue and out of intellectual fashion, but reading all of it, borrowing from it, appropriating it, quoting it when useful, reinventing and rearranging it—not just to survive, but to live and to write for life. While reading, singing, and pondering over the Latvian women poets' original and translated hymns and trying to name the overarching trait of their sporadic and creolized theological oeuvre, my memory stubbornly circled back to Margaret Miles' idiom of "reading for life."[47]

Unmistakably, survival is one of the dominating themes in virtually anything that has been written in Latvian—political, poetic, or theological. Survival is the unglamorous darling motif, understandably, in most diasporic and migrant discourses because the prospects of not surviving are only too real for too many. But what the Latvian women poets underscore from the liturgical limelight of Christian life of faith against all odds and all appearances of unoriginality is not just survival but the possibility of reading for life and writing, praising, lamenting, and teaching for life—for all, and together with all, not just themselves. As I see it, the Latvian poet-theologians perform precisely what Miles theorizes as "reading for life" being "generous reading." For Miles, reading for life, allowing oneself to be shaped, taught, and stimulated by other wisdoms, is not devoid of critical questions, while "generous reading makes it possible to appropriate *for life* a book's detachable suggestions *even though* they come from a demonstrably imperfect author or are addressed to someone other than the reader."[48] At this juncture a postcolonial twist to the theme of constructive generosity for survival and thriving life can be fittingly added: the idea of "poaching" makes the thrust of postcolonial diasporic inscriptions more specific. R. S. Sugirtharajah's hybrid image of "poaching" (the term is appropriated from Michel de Certeau) suggests an "existential impulse" and reader's self-assertion through the texts by eluding authoritarian institutional control, since "texts are always in transit between contexts."[49] Thus,

> What poaching indicates is that texts and their meanings are not final but that the texts derive their meaning in their encounter with context and reader. . . . Texts in essence are moulded by the context in which they are located. . . . Ultimately, what reading as poaching indicates is that it is not possible to finalize a text, or restrict it to one context, or predetermine its meaning.[50]

Moreover, Miles is convinced, and the Latvian women poets so virtuosic in their stealth theology would agree, I suspect, that "women and other minority people can fruitfully study and appropriate flawed cultural resources not in order to understand and forgive the privileged other but in order to appropriate critically."[51] I also salute the trajectory of constructive appropriation or "poaching," stealthy or not, for it arguably gives a name to the existential impulse of diasporic imaginary in its fluctuations between homing desires and actual homes left behind and never found.

Liturgical space is precisely an inclusively privileged location to encounter and perceptively appropriate the voices of others, hopefully without presumptive reduction. It is the hymnbooks that "in particular are most often historically, geographically, ecclesiastically and culturally variegated collections."[52] Liturgical spaces can be model "diaspora spaces," allowing a multitude of voices to sound together contrapuntally through aesthetic modalities of theology in music, movement, gesture, and visual arts. Liturgical spaces have a great and underused potential for facilitating a fair hearing of the polyphonic spectrum of theological reflection across histories and cultures. If liturgical spaces live up to their transformative potential, they can entrain sensibilities that are open toward hybridity and reciprocity—asymmetrical as it always is—for respectful and mutually enriching life together amid genuine and dramatic differences in a deeply contrapuntal way. The transformative potential of liturgy consists in transforming how we believe; how we praise, lament, grieve, and repent; and, most importantly, how we relate to the mosaic of people we encounter around us here in the multicultural North America as well as worldwide—wherever we travel in person or in cyberspace. The transformation can be nurtured in us through sound and image, gesture or word, through silent contemplation or act of monetary donation, through sharing the eucharistic communion with Christ, and, in Christ, with all those for whom Christ lived, suffered, died, and was resurrected. And yes, indeed, the transformation is never trustworthy without the less glamorous yet spiritually essential liturgy of at least attempting some *imitatio Christi* in order to be a "little Christ" to one another at least sometimes, all the gender, racial, class, ethnic, confessional, sexual orientation, or immigration status differences notwithstanding. Every liturgical space has the potential to transform toward this kind of contrapuntal life together—but not all of them actually do. Not yet.

To reiterate once more with feeling, counterpoint is the unique musical capacity to sound two or more voices simultaneously without reduction. It facilitates "the coherent combination of distinct melodic lines in music, and the quality that best fulfils the aesthetic principle of unity in diversity"[53] through the balance between independence and interdependence. As Edward Said suggests, postcolonially scored "counterpoint" is a configuration of hybridity, and it engenders the principle of noncoercive and nondominative modes of life and knowledge.[54] Said points to counterpoint as a hopeful interpretive strategy and model of social cohabitation because it expresses the imaginary of "both" wherein the oppositionality or the "contra" element is always relationally interactive, overlapping, and interdependent with the other components of the relational interface. The most fascinating feature of postcolonial counterpoint consists, I believe, of its capacity to embody and address the hybrid reality of life in which so many of us are no longer "purely one thing." Liturgical space, doxologically as well as catechetically, is a paramount location of such hybrid embodiment. It can facilitate the counterpoint of legacies, laments, praises, voices, powers, struggles, and aspirations—all sounding together transformatively rather than in a mutually allergic way. In theological inquiry, the contrapuntal strategy of praising, reading, and writing aims at "interpreting together."[55] The counterpoint of life molds into counterpoint as a diasporically embodied and embedded theological method which privileges, for all practical purposes, fruitful encounters, linkages, generous appropriations, and reinventions.

In this regard, there is much to learn from the resilient Latvian women poet-theologians, whose rather opaque voices—perhaps too stealthy for some tastes—modulate the familiar, tired, and even oppressive theological imagery, often by a whisper that may look self-effacing and unoriginal, into enduring epiphanies of grace and salvation. Most importantly, these epiphanies, as the Latvian spiritual and liturgical history continues to reveal, have not remained purely rhetorical and page-bound for a niche theological market. Far from it: as "reading for life," as poaching, as appropriations and gossamer modulations of words and images often abused and misused, these epiphanies have sustained the Latvian communities of faith throughout the upheavals, wars, exiles, and totalitarian oppression. They have upheld the hope of peace and healing in the periods of frenzied prosperity in the homeland and in diaspora, all the way into the dark crevices of fear and despair during the present fatigue of capitalist pure economic reason. Having endured so much and having stood their ground in the subtly decomposed liturgical center, the "boutique" voices of Latvian women poets continue to remind, stealthily and through a whisper, that a contrapuntal theological sensibility is not to be restrained by either canonized margins or entrenched centers but poaches boldly everywhere—to survive, to live, and possibly even to thrive.

12

EMBODYING THEOLOGY
Motherhood as Metaphor/Method

Marcia W. Mount Shoop

black ocean
blanketed fecundity
teeming void
mistaken for the nothing that never has been
dive in that black water
and break into an infested universe
of amoeba, sperm whale, and
bottom feeders no human eye will ever strain to see
floating refuse will finally offend.
Perhaps you can wonder
at resourceful plankton
or visionary barnacles
who can make plastic throw-aways into ocean architecture.
what will your eyes do
when they swim in night water?
pupils wide taking color and shape inside
only memory's vision abides

your lungs feel desperate now
 this foreign sea is death to them.
 surfacing is bursting, gasping,
 grasping for familiar chunks of wind
 closer now than that Black Ocean from above

you are being born
 some fluid, some air
 And you've floated in real water
 unsustainable fusion
now breathe and drink the
 dancing shadows of what had seemed like nothing.

—Marcia W. Mount Shoop

INTRODUCTION

What seems like nothing just might be everything, or at the very least point toward that expansive All. The givenness of motherhood makes it both an obvious and an unlikely mode of doing theology. This vocation often leaves women on the outside of the theological conversation; mothers are otherwise engaged with the sequestered, meandering work of rearing children. When this way of life has been granted space in the musings of theologians, it is often distorted by simple equations with self-sacrificial living for others. Motherhood, instead, is a promising, expansive mode in which theology can find its methodological integrity not because of some self-effacing caricature, but because it swims in the waters of entangled life with utter immediacy. Motherhood is a metaphor and method for the theological task because of the mode it embodies.

Metaphor's function is to fill out meaning with similarity and impression. It is not an equation but a suggestion for how to understand something more clearly. Theology is like motherhood and motherhood is like theology: they point toward inexpressible truth and give it concreteness simultaneously. The method that motherhood provides for theology is tangled up with this metaphorical function even as it elides theology's traditional habits of describing and writing meaning. Embodying theology invites us to swim around in strange waters and write some layer of our cellular intersections into discernible descriptions. Embodied attunement and expression create and narrate ultimate meaning. Motherhood can teach us some skills, some habits, some survival techniques that help render this immersion a theological risk worth taking.

Systematic theology traditionally forms itself around an intention that the world can "fit together" and make sense. We connect pieces of a puzzle that somehow create a discernible whole. Motherhood invites a remarkably different intentionality. Things do not necessarily fit. The connective tissue of life is not systematic but more like a black widow's snarled-up, chaotic web, and like that black ocean. The connections are dense and impossible to untangle, and they create locatedness with life-giving intention. This mode of creativity is aware, attentive, even protective, and wise to danger and brutality. Motherhood is boldly vulnerable and invites theology to embody this same orientation. Writing out of this bold vulnerability expresses the urge to create and feed vitality and new life where we can.

Embodied theology requires immediacy to our human condition. Process, relationality, locatedness, and ambiguity are the often unclaimed touchstones of our human situation in contemporary theology. Theologically embodying this fluid condition has largely been methodologically accomplished through context and location in constructive theology. The startling voices of those who speak from marginalized experiences are, indeed, concrete and revelatory embodied theologies. But locatedness can also permit distance and authorize even more marginalization in the theological conversation. Claimed location can tempt the still-audible meta-narratives of theology to trivialize the embodied truths these contexts reveal. They can become simply voices of the who and where they come from rather than being pathways to transform the mode of the theological task itself.

How can the work of theology deepen its immersion in embodied experience at the same time that we cultivate a new regard for the broader implications of these located constructions? Can the systematic yearnings of the modern theological project give way to fluid outbursts of new truth in the snarl of humanity's painful and promising condition?

In order to dig into the ultimate meaning and the divine threads in our situation, theology needs intentional and immediate proximity to the multifarious lives we live as bodies. And this proximity needs a bold intention to intuit those divine threads as they glimmer with some new clarity and transform with promising vision. Theology then becomes not so much a systematic way of thinking in ultimate terms, but intentionality rife with kindling intuitions of divine presence and purpose. Constructing and writing theology gives expression to this intuition, this intention as it seeks to point toward radical connection, a shared world.

I can think of no better metaphor and method for this theological shift from systematic product to intuitive intention than motherhood.[1] Motherhood exists in spaces in which the system is not systematic, the location is not static, and intention is entangled with a primal taste for life. Motherhood has a dizzying immediacy to life's rhythms, change, and power. It invites vulnerability and nurtures attunement and availability. What seems like throwaway time is ultimately a moment of truth. What feels like straining to see greater purpose in inconsequential things gives way to inhabiting life differently. The theological inclinations of the mundane moments that mothers inhabit offer both rich metaphors and methodological promise for embodying theology. A theological intuition emerges from my exploration of motherhood around these creative and responsive styles of existence.[2] Idiosyncrasy, ambiguity, and interdependence characterize this mode of life. And embodied ambiguity, idiosyncrasy, and interdependence have the promising capacity to create space for expression that substantively constructs even when constrained. In this constructive theological essay, I let styles of motherhood embody theology both in its method and in the truth to which it points.[3] Writing in and through this entangled mode gives birth to constructive and suggestive offspring—words that will fill out their meaning as they intersect with others, sentences that have dashes and commas where periods may otherwise have been. These are the grammatical stretch marks of writing, which is always and already connectional. Writing does not reveal a tight system or a linear thought, but instead inscribes description and suggestion for a world in the midst of being born. Deep breathing is required. And when we submerge ourselves in the birth waters, in order to find vitality we have to somehow create ways to trust the strange kind of oxygen that is there.

A THEOLOGICAL PROBLEM

When motherhood and theology come together in the task of theology, the collaboration has both great promise and a multilayered problematic. Distortions, contortions, and disembodied habits of thought challenge this invitation to embrace motherhood as metaphor and method for embodying theology.

Theologically, motherhood has been distorted in its equation with nurture and self-sacrifice. Mothers are often cast as those who "give up their lives for their children."[4] The marriage of traditional conceptions of sin and the glorification of self-sacrifice oversimplifies the experiences that mothers encounter in raising children. Motherhood has more to offer to theological conversations than orientations of self-sacrifice or an ethic of care.[5] Motherhood points to open spaces that invite us to explore how indeterminacy and ambiguity cultivate adventure and expanded possibility. These open spaces are ripe for indeterminacy to feed a style of life that is attentive if even still swimming about in murky waters.

The contortions that make this method/metaphor a challenging invitation are many. They are the twists and turns of how we understand the term motherhood itself. I deliberately use the term "motherhood," rather than mothering or maternity. I am pointing to the multilayered experiences, institutions, practices, and ideologies that intersect in being a mother. Motherhood suggests embodied styles of existence—not a static essence or ideal, or a certain set of practices.[6] By "style," I am suggesting a sustained, durable manner or mode that has both fluidity and consistency. The consistency of style is enough to be recognizable and create a collective impression. Motherhood is held together by internal inconsistency, flux, and blurred boundaries, although it rests in spaces not without structures, boundaries, and immense concreteness. Motherhood invites a vulnerability to what life has to give that nurtures attunement and availability.

The creative complexity of motherhood is often invisible in a culture that holds the productivity and profit of industry as the highest value.[7]

Mothers themselves are the site of conflicting discourses on which activities are truly important in our society.[8] Some feminists have rejected the role of motherhood and the expectations it places on women as a tool of the oppression of women (Shulamith Firestone); others have embraced it as a window into an ideal that can disrupt the patriarchal order (Sara Ruddick, Luce Irigaray, Julia Kristeva).[9] Still others have disturbed the feminist wrangling itself by asking questions that stem from different racial, ethnic, political, and economic positions (Patricia Hill Collins, Delores Williams, Marilou Awiatka).[10] The contradictions and contortions of motherhood are apparent in these attempts to theorize it.

The disembodied habits of thinking so prevalent in our Western context only deepen and complicate these problems. Theological conversations need space for deep dissonance and intuitive modes of doing theology to emerge. Legitimizing and authorizing this kind of dissonance and intuition in theology places a curious demand on our Western mentalities. Beneath the novelty of it is the deep suspicion that there is a lot to lose with such radical shape-shifting. Claiming our own complexity, idiosyncrasy, and ambiguity is also not a pleasant prospect; the payoffs for this kind of orientation are not attractive. Theology is already being pushed into a corner in religious studies; "feminizing" its methodology can only mean its academic credibility falls further from the center of the legitimate conversation. The luster of this kind of theological integrity perhaps only shines for those who have eyes for the redemptive glimmers that fleetingly glisten in these murky waters. The invitation into this black ocean means theology dives into its own claims of divine presence and purpose. The promise of this mode is that constructive belief may be transformed into lived modes of operation that in-form the theological task itself.[11] The challenge is how to welcome and claim the visceral into what is perceived as a cognitive task. "Constructive belief" engages the theological conversation with this visceral/cerebral dynamic not simply in mind but in method and mode.

THE WAY MOTHERS ARE

Mothering children is not essentially this or that way, because children and mothers are not this or that way.[12] Like the black widow's web and that black ocean, the connections, the shape, the intentions are not simply obscured by intricacy and density; they exist creatively, not systemically. This located creative intention is metaphor for the method/ mode itself. Motherhood embodies the impossibility of impermeability to harm. It knows the constancy of interruption and the wounds of knowing our children will see death. Ambiguity, idiosyncrasy, embodied interconnection, the intent to give and cultivate life in the midst of ambivalence, love, compassion, anger, cruelty, exhaustion, diminishment, and delight are the modes of motherhood and the truth to which it points for our human condition. My claims about motherhood and its capacity to model an embodied theological method indicate more general descriptions of our human experience. Our human distortions and capacity are embodied in all expressions of motherhood and so are glimmering icons of what is best about our human vocation. The embodied theological task is like that—boldly vulnerable.

Mothers mold and mark us, hold and release us, birth and differentiate us. The ghosts of our mothers swirl around us and course through our veins no matter our proximity to the geography they inhabit. And we mother with equally dense layers of idiosyncrasy. Motherhood is simultaneously like vapor and like concrete. Motherhood as metaphor is not the equation of itself, but always approximating, pointing toward that which it is and is not, even while functioning to create, disrupt, and reverberate the other and itself. This complicated snarl of experience is why motherhood can nurture embodied theology. Pregnant with meaning as well as power, motherhood gives birth to and rears much more than the children it bears. Motherhood embodies idiosyncrasy, ambiguity, and interdependence; these three loci can in-form embodied theological methods.[13]

Idiosyncrasy

I never saw my mother, to know her as such more than four or five times in my life; and each of these times was very short in duration, and at night. She was hired by Mr. Stewart, who lived about twelve miles from my house. She made her journeys to see me in the night, traveling the whole distance on foot, after the performance of her day's work. She was a field hand, and a whipping is the penalty of not being in the field at sunrise . . . I do not recollect of ever seeing my mother by the light of day. She was with me in the night. She would lie down with me and get me to sleep, but long before I waked she was gone.

—*Frederick Douglass*[14]

Tired feet moving toward that place that housed her sleeping child just so she could hold him defied the space that kept her from "being there" for her son. Frederick Douglass' mother manipulated space by holding that little body, so deeply asleep, in spite of slavery's deep chasm between her desire to mother and her ability to be present. She gave flesh to mothering by holding him in the dark. Her muscles, calluses, cells, synapses, and yearning enfleshed her indignant maternal commitment. Extended and entangled, this kind of embodied experience speaks volumes where there is such quiet. And with her hard-won moments with her son came his ambiguous memories, as if he never knew her. Douglas later wrote that she was like a stranger to him, that he never knew the "soothing presence" of a mother's care. Terrible truth and interpretation conspire with and against motherhood's best intentions. It is idiosyncratic in its assertion and malleability.

The idiosyncrasy of embodied motherhood is an example of what phenomenologist Edward Casey describes as the body's refusal to settle neatly into a dichotomy between social construction and biological determinism.[15] The body is not either/or, it is not natural or cultural, biological or socially constructed. It is an ambiguous mixture, a both/and. Mothers live in this gray area. The body learns and creates meaning on a continuum in which, on one end, the body is given to training and, on the other end, is given to preference and value. Both skill and taste "knit together image and rule," allowing the body to be both the expression of culture and its creator and transmitter.[16]

Motherhood embodies the habits of these "chosen" streams of preference and practice, but the idiosyncrasy of motherhood also mirrors what Casey calls "idiosyncratic habitus."[17] This kind of habitus is involuntary and resistant to conscious modification. Casey describes some of the symptoms of hysteria to give more concreteness to embodied practices that are not driven by conscious learning (such as swimming) or by the acceptance, however innovative, of certain standards or rules (like taste). He describes the symptoms of hysteria this way:

> Unlike skill and taste, which incorporate and display cultural and social interests and norms more or less transparently, hysterical symptoms are initially opaque even if ultimately quite significant, that is to say, *telling*. They are "ghosts" of an embodiment unknown to itself in terms of first origin and final sense: shadows cast by this origin or sense that have fallen upon the hysteric's body and on the body politic with which this body is covertly continuous.[18]

The body displays its genius in hysterical symptoms because they are at once idiosyncratic and socially conditioned. The hysteric's body does not simply mimic norms but displays what Casey calls a "style of action that is peculiar to a given hysteric's body."[19] At the same time, this idiosyncrasy reveals an internalization of social structures that shows itself in the symptoms. That is, the hysteric's body becomes a social critic in a manner (or perhaps in "mannerisms") that bypasses the ability of the conscious self to "censor" these expressions of resistance.[20] As Casey explains, "Hysterical symptoms are at once protests against the reigning social order and yet also collusions with it."[21]

How mothers value themselves and how others value mothers are dissonant spaces filled with expectations that no one can ever meet and with those we fail to recognize as important.[22] Casey's description of the hysteric's body can help us understand and recognize this idiosyncratic dynamic of human embodied experience. The hysteric is particularly helpful here because she "tells" of the body as social palate for critique and commentary in extreme relief. We can feel our way underneath intentionality, choice, discursive description, and resistance to societal values and norms.[23]

The body takes up the task of expressing that which cannot be consciously expressed.[24] This compliance occurs far beyond the realm of "choice," but instead is in the ghostly regions of the body's capacity for functioning and surviving. At the same time that the "body language" takes the body to the margins of social intercourse, it nevertheless enacts its need to be heard, its need to be a part of the "conversation."[25]

The body does not simply hold the experience in silence but gives it a new voice, one that demands attention and one that disrupts our ability to discern its language. It is a masterful rendering of relationship and survival. And it is a radical challenge to how we listen and receive the narratives of experience and context.

Sleep can be a window into this idiosyncratic habitus. Parenting "experts" and medical advice inhabit the bedrooms of most mothers. Economic context, culture, and formation all in-form choices about where and how mothers and children sleep in proximity to one another. The maternal body can become a template of this societal argument about the best practices for sleeping with or away from one's children. How and when sleep comes and is interrupted is not a simple series of choices, but an embodied rhythm of relationship, instinct, biological necessity, and learned skill. No matter the learning curve, however, for certain practices and skills, a mother may fall asleep only when she unknowingly happens upon some primal kind of comfort zone. Exhaustion and expectation, surrender and fetal memory, medical warnings and inherited wisdom all may feed the particular commentary a mother embodies with her sleep patterns. Frederick Douglass' mother gives this example in flesh and blood.

The genius of the body's capacity to embody commentary and even critique collective assumptions and expectations is not simply the fruit of trauma or pathology. Motherhood re-members and "converts" experience in such an embodied mode. Motherhood embodies this idiosyncratic mode and can wake us up to how our bodies engage in and in-form life with involuntary and utterly entangled interruptions and eruptions of our flesh and blood.[26] Like the liberating sleep of Frederick Douglass' mother, we are constantly creating commentary on the fabric of human expectation and limitation.

There is no clear origin or end in how the body both colludes with and critiques social standards. Conscious assertion may or may not be operative in the way meaning is made. This idiosyncratic mode of creating and constructing points theology toward its own meaning-making dynamic. Theological intuition is not simply a cognitive product, but it is in-formed by the idiosyncratic narratives of bodies, because theology is about human glimpses of divinity. Theology's idiosyncrasy is proper to its very nature—just as with motherhood. And the peculiar truths that theology yearns to embody do not squander its academic legitimacy, but instead grant it the integrity of a human vocation with proximity to what is really real.

Ambiguity

> My children cause me the most exquisite suffering of which I have any experience. It is the suffering of ambivalence: the murderous alternation between bitter resentment and raw-edged nerves, and blissful gratification and tenderness. Sometimes I seem to myself, in my feelings toward these tiny guiltless beings, a monster of selfishness and intolerance. Their voices wear away at my nerves, their constant needs, above all their need for simplicity and patience, fill me with despair at my own failures, despair too at my fate, which is to serve a function for which I was not fitted. And I am weak sometimes from held-in rage. There are times when I feel only death will free us from one another, when I envy the barren woman who has the luxury of her regrets but lives a life of privacy and freedom. And yet at other times I am melted with the sense of their helpless, charming and quite irresistible beauty—their ability to go on loving and trusting—their staunchness and decency and unselfconsciousness. *I love them.* But it's in the enormity and inevitability of this love that the sufferings lie.
>
> —*Adrienne Rich*[27]

The excruciating swing of mothers' dalliances with bliss and brutality provides the palate for embodied ambiguity. Motherhood teaches us not to kid ourselves into thinking ambiguity is something we can avoid. Gentle attention, lethargy, fear, hilarity, and frustration inhabit common spaces in child rearing. What results is not a cleanly coherent self, but the result of living out of entangled and contorted subjectivity—ambiguous fragmentation. This fragmentation is a way of life, and it informs the art of giving and encouraging life over time. Children challenge and shift a mother's sense of herself and her possibilities, as do all the others who make suggestions to, criticize, and provide assistance to mothers. Mothers experience the conflict between a gut feeling about her child and the directives of an "expert" on how she should mother. There is an unruly variation in how mothers mother even when provided the same information, opportunities, and resources. The needs of different children, the constantly changing needs of the same child over time, the desire for children to be able to do things for themselves, the pangs that wish they would never grow up, are held in tandem. The dilemmas of work and family, the dance of self-sacrifice and self-discovery, and the multiple approaches to child care are even more pieces of the complex array of motherhood's challenges.[28]

Children give mothers something that can come from nowhere else in life. They also take from their mothers in uniquely difficult and rewarding ways. Mother-child relationships are conditioned by the many messages that come in and out of vogue for mothering practices, by the voices of other mothers, and by the way the body sometimes seems to act on indiscernible (often called "instinctual") tendencies toward certain activities and orientations.[29] Maternal bodies both resist and respond to cultural messages about what is valued—they inhabit spaces both of disruption and ascent. These dissonant spaces feed the ambiguity of how motherhood is negotiated on all levels. Motherhood invites us to explore how this embodied ambiguity is inescapable *and* a life-giving reality. Motherhood occupies that gray area in which indeterminacy and the unknown seek relevant and substantive expression. This is also the task of theology. The play of motherhood within and outside the flux of meaning is, indeed, the mother of novelty and convention. Motherhood creates and destroys itself even as it gives birth to a language of the body that shapes and speaks the grammar of our understanding. Motherhood occupies a shifting space as metaphor's anchor of meaning, as its other, as its destroyer, and as its creator. Meaning-making comes out of this productive tension—the fragments of experience and understanding. Meaning-making is partially a function of availability to the dissonance of experience. It is also the power to create meaning out of that same dissonance. The act of writing in this mode is always and already intensely connectional. Writing births description and suggestion for a world waking up to itself. The writing itself becomes an ambiguous offering to that world—creating words to be seen, heard, and that take on a life of their own. The ambiguity of this power to make and to be shaped by life's meaning is productive, even life-giving.

The dissonant fragments of meaning can find resonance both in the brute fact that a common entity recognizes herself in them all, and in the glimmers of recognition that others encounter in these fragments. There are contradictory constellations of feeling at work in one's constantly developing construction of the self.[30] These contradictory constellations of feeling do not cancel each other out. Instead, their multiplicity finds a home in the complexity of particularity. The self is not simply always in process, but it is also constantly informed and conditioned by a myriad of feelings that do not necessarily translate into a harmonious and unified subject. Disharmony and conflict are part of what conditions subjectivity, not by decision between alternatives but through the way they coexist, fluctuate in their conditioning effect, and fashion our uniqueness. Motherhood models how ambiguous fragmentation can function creatively. Contrasts gather steam and fuel a unique kind of intuition.

Living in that ambiguous flux creates spaces that are not overdetermined by one set of experiences. These spaces are the conditions of possibility for a unique kind of intuition that is able to "live with" disharmony and contradiction. This intuition possesses itself with flexibility and the capacity to create even when constrained. The fluctuation becomes productive with the fuel of both frustration and availability. The allowance for disruption and dissonance tempers the need to control that which cannot be contrived. The ambiguity of motherhood also cuts through the illusion of an inside and an outside.[31] Ambiguity makes the body's geography fluid in where it stops and starts and who is included: a metaphor for theology in our time, to be sure.

The givenness of fragmentation, dissonance, and fluid distinction between cognition and physicality invite theology to find its stride in the academy in its own distinctive way of including an array of human experience. Thinking about God is not, therefore, a strange participant in intellectual conversations, but it is a truth-telling partner in inquiry about what it means to be human. The methodological opportunity is in the willingness of theologians to dive in to such ambiguous waters with a commitment to recognize divine indwelling when we see it.

Interdependence

In our young minds houses belonged to women, were their special domain, not as property, but as places where all that truly mattered in life took place—the warmth and comfort of shelter, the feeding of our bodies, the nurturing of our souls. There we learned dignity, integrity of being; there we learned to have faith. . . . This task of making homeplace was not simply a matter of black women providing service; it was about the construction of a safe place where black people could affirm one another and by so doing heal many of the wounds inflicted by racist domination. We could not learn to love and respect ourselves in the culture of white supremacy, on the outside; it was there on the inside, in that "homeplace," most often created and kept by black women, that we had the opportunity to grow and develop, to nurture our spirits.[32]

—bell hooks

The creation of homeplace embodies the tangle of otherness and its formative power. bell hooks describes the life-giving possibilities of our entanglement with others who tell us who we are and are not, clear spaces for us to grow, and urge us in a direction of healing. Motherhood orients us to others by its very nature as it is open to the adventure and the nurturing capacity of our entanglement with otherness. Its mediating role facilitates interconnection as well as differentiation. It communicates the ingenious way that meaning is produced out of immediacy to snarls of interconnections. It has the power to be available to all that is, and to be assertive and malleable in its metaphorical function.

Motherhood functions in close proximity to the needs of children—the mess and stress, the tenderness and bliss, the fleeting nature of it all. Always negotiating another, always inhabiting that space that complicates otherness itself, always working to create life's meaning, motherhood is an embodied metaphor for human ambiguity and idiosyncrasy. And it models the necessity and givenness of interdependence.

Motherhood is vulnerable to otherness because it is defined by it. A mother is created out of relationship with an "other." Theology can be enriched by such a necessary entanglement with difference. The metaphors of motherhood's body language fill out meaning, not with control but by being conducive to, available to, life's complexity.

The meaning-making is not passive, but productive, disruptive, and resourceful enough to accommodate shifting meaning. Motherhood communicates styles of existence that embody this dynamic of flexibility and indeterminacy and its power to give life and assert itself in the ongoing process of meaning-making. Consider some of motherhood's embodied metaphors of such interdependence.

The dynamics of nursing and milk supply "speak" the fluidity of the geography of maternal bodies. For most new mothers, their milk will often come in more quickly after their babies are born if they have more skin-to-skin contact with their babies. The experience of the flesh of a baby next to the flesh of his mother helps create a healthy breastfeeding bond. Many women who nurse experience milk letdown at given intervals according to the feeding patterns of their child. Some women can hear the cry of another baby, not even their own, and their milk will let down. Still others report being able to express milk from their breasts in various circumstances months after their children have been weaned. Some feel milk let down when their children are ill; still others experience it when they begin thinking of having another child.

Many mothers experience breastfeeding as relaxing and joyful. Research tells us that there are actually pleasure-inducing hormones that are released into the body during breastfeeding. Some scientists have connected this hormone release to an increased tendency to be nurturing because of how it calms the nursing mother and makes her more responsive to her baby's needs and less prone to stress.[33] Research shows that these same hormones can be released when a mother is exposed to "familiar sights, sounds, and activities associated with breastfeeding."[34]

The voices and silences of this language can also translate for some women into an insurmountable kind of stress. Milk production can be compromised if there is stress or distraction for the mother. For reasons not completely understood by medical science, some women report being overcome with nausea when their baby latches on.[35] Others are unable and/or unwilling to breastfeed because of previous sexual abuse or other body issues.[36] For some of these women, breastfeeding becomes a physical impossibility.

The body language of nursing is one of connections—flesh to flesh, hormonal, spiritual, emotional, a cellular connection that defies space. Nursing mothers occupy spaces literally entangled with the bodies of children. These spaces are negotiated in an enfleshed, albeit mysterious, mode. Initiative and surrender work with considerable force throughout the body, speaking its indeterminacy and capacity for novelty with great clarity. This body language has so much mystery and wonder that we are unable to completely parse out the why and the how of its functioning. This language and these spaces of meaning-making are the ambiguous and idiosyncratic intersections of many factors of connection.

Maternal bodies occupy space in this way. Boundaries are fluid; availability for and attunement to connection are what nourish life. Maternal bodies are determined in their surrender and embrace and in their resistance to flesh and blood connection. The more open the space for connection and the more available the body is for entanglement, the greater the opportunity for life to be nurtured. It is a lively orientation to what feeds abundant life. The necessity of such entanglement points to a promising truth for how we do theology. We need difference to invite the richest possible visions to emerge.

The necessity of connection for motherhood to thrive embodies the importance of interdependence. Multiple mothers are not just other mothers, but they are the complexity of interconnection that mothers require to care well for children. The level of complexity of these connections communicates how crucial connections are for idiosyncrasy and ambiguity to bear their best fruit. When forced to function in contexts of relative isolation, maternal feeling is reduced to feeding on only a thin layer of connection. It ekes out its particularity from what is there. The triviality that comes from isolation does not destroy feeling, but it truncates its best possibilities. This triviality is an affront to the nature of feeling and its need for multiple connections.

The distinctive reality of multiple mothers means that as mothers we are never alone in how we mother and that we should not be alone if we are to mother well. We are always already in the company of multiple mothers. They are the "voiceless" voices, the imprints, and the bodily memories of motherhood as well as the "othermothers" who help

us along the way.[37] Multiple mothers mark us from innumerable generations, expectations, and situations of motherhood that have played their
part in the processes of history. Ann Belford Ulanov describes how we
internalize and externalize the mothering we experienced. She achieves
this description by exploring the dynamics of a child's relationship with
the most hands-on parent in the family system, who she calls the "transformational object." Ulanov says, "The system of care for us by this
'transformational object' becomes a major part of our own self-care system. We know these rules and styles of self-care and self-relating, but
we do not rescue them into thought. We are not specifically aware of
them. We do them; we do not think them."[38]

The maternal body is constantly brushing up against an enfleshed
determinant of its confinement and possibility. Maternal bodies hold
children and therefore embody a sense of space that can be particularly sensitive to what surrounds it. This extensive and entangled bodily
experience is apparent in the care of an infant. Holding a child brings
with it particular gestures, postures, and horizons. What exists to hold
the baby other than the maternal body—from partner to car seat to crib
to papoose to sling—extends the mother's embrace to expand her sense
of space and possibility. A baby's willingness to be held by other "arms"
than her mother's extends the breadth and freedom of the maternal
body. The desire of maternal bodies to hold children is a response to
how space is both defined and confined for mothers. Maternal bodies
respond and resist with embodied palpability. Will she pick up her child
or let him cry, will she carry her child with a contraption other than
her arms? Will she negotiate her body's ability to hold, to steady, and
to carry? These gestures, decisions, and tendencies are not transparent
in how and why they are carried out as they are; they are the result of
a dizzying array of factors and features that maternal bodies carry with
them in their care of children.

How and why and when a mother holds a child is the palpable and
phantasmal playing out of how she was held, of how the baby responds
to certain positions, of how she has been instructed to hold, of how she
is comfortable holding, of how she believes she should hold, of how
circumstances shape her ability to hold, of what else there is to hold,

and the constant response and resistance of her body to all of these factors and more. Mothering is not simply an activity in which cognition translates into action. Mothering is expressed through the way the body is constantly conditioned by all else that is. This conditioning process is one that begins from the very earliest stages of life. There is an endless regress to the connection maternal bodies have to their inheritance of the past.

The power to create and disrupt meaning in such an embodied mode indicates how motherhood taps into the productivity of the margins of existence. The productivity of such liminal space creates out of idiosyncrasy and ambiguity. The capacity for social criticism feeds a capacity for resistance. This mode of life is also redemptive. The capacity for redemption shows itself in the work of resistance and liberation that bell hooks conveys in her description of homeplace above.[39] The fragments of oppression and resistance reveal this dynamic of existing in and giving life out of disharmony and fragmentation. Motherhood may sometimes be the only location of resistance to the ways culture denigrates certain groups or practices. This resistance is an indeterminate space where a possibility exists for disruption of the powers of racism, sexism, materialism, secularism, fundamentalism, poverty, and any other system of oppression.[40] This "culture of resistance" and its capacity for survival in racist systems translate fragments into a kind of "double life" in which one appears to be open and forthcoming in the dominant culture in order to remain invisible to that same culture.[41]

The spaces of motherhood become the tools for justice and resistance to oppression.[42] Motherhood creates space for overturning the standards of the broader culture. It functions to fill out and change meaning out of fragmentation and complexity. It creates and disrupts meaning by virtue of the way it negotiates its location, its orientation. The theological task can be enriched by such a creatively critical mode. The goad to redeem tethers this mode to the proper nature of theology. This style of embodied interdependence means theology can search for ways to describe modestly universal truths even as the irreducible particularity of how we make meaning is embraced. And redemption is not provisional, but empowered to find novel expression.

CONCLUSION

The idiosyncrasy, ambiguity, and interdependence that motherhood embodies reveal the body's capacity for creativity and zestful experience. It is not in spite of but because of the vagaries and risks and indeterminacy of embodied life that there is the possibility of being fruitful, productive, and life-giving. A thread of providence occupies these places as the consistent offer of zest and beauty. It is the creative and confusing play of the body that means we can live in and operate out of this complexity in a life-giving mode. Motherhood, like theology, points to the ambiguity of its own grammar.

And so theology becomes intention—the intention to let questions unfold in the framework of this web of connection, vulnerability, devotion to life and love, and intuition of the thick intersections of divine possibility and presence. Theology's task is to illuminate our human condition and to point toward our capacity for redemption. Theology searches for expressions of divinity by swimming about in these waters of who we are and how we can flourish. Motherhood reveals that same immersion in the stark truths and beautiful unfoldings. Writing theology, like birthing, embodies the intention to create even when constrained. Writing theology feeds on difference and seeks to connect in a fluid rhythm of creation and responsiveness. The three loci I describe, idiosyncrasy, ambiguity, and interdependence, flow into and out of each other. The descriptions are fertile for some unforeseen connection. These descriptions are not closed, not finished. This mode of writing theology generates and creates more like a pulse than a final product.

Enfolded in motherhood are all the strange comforts, the impossible dreams, our familiar, our ordinary, and what we need to flourish. We swim in these waters from the very first twitches of our own conception. And we live into motherhood, our mothers and other mothers, the tenderness and the brutality of mothering, the distorted ways we fight our demons and embody the demons of those we love. We see ourselves: the things we wish we were, the things we hate that we are, the places we were not loved enough, and the spaces where there were always provisions.

There is flux and there are bodies that are forever tangled up in ours. There is the expectation of and delight in love, kindness, safety—and the hard tragedy of disappointment, danger, and diminished humanity. Bold vulnerability emerges as a promising theological mode with a keen eye for the redemptive thread, the providential promises in the midst of it all. Indeed, theologians are ever watchful for transformative currents, for habits of thought and life that invite divine intentions to find expression when we "breathe and drink the dancing shadows of what had seemed like nothing."

13

POSTSCRIPT
Wounded Writing, Healing Writing

Wendy Farley

It is a gratifying privilege to conclude these papers with my own reflections on what has been accomplished. I have been inspired by the recovery of so many theologians whose ideas, lives, and eloquent writing deepen our understanding of what the Christian tradition has been and can be. In the ancient desert, in convent and beguinage, in academic communities, and in homes surrounded by children, women reconstruct Christian thought and practice so that the radical vision of the gospel is continually vivified.

One of the themes that is simmering in these papers is the way in which women's writing is prohibited, conscribed, and even impossible within a patriarchal context. Levinas reminds us that the supreme violence is the supreme gentleness: repression that no longer requires the instruments of force because we have become the secret police inside our own heads. As we read Mechthild of Magdeburg, Simone Weil, Emily Dickinson, or Mother Dabney, we ask how much of this writing is contorted by the "gentle" policing not only of writing but of thought and desire. What tortured songs bleed through self-effacing prose? What bolder expressions of the divine beauty of God-bearing women remain unthought, unthinkable? It is impossible not to grieve over the holocaust of women's wisdom that is part of the collateral damage of Christianity. Like women who need only be knocked around once in order to learn the art of repression, women writers learned well the lessons of Marguerite Porete. This "false woman" bore tenacious witness to the nondual love of divinity and was burned in a Paris square in 1310 for her trouble. As we consider our own writing, we might continue to wonder how much of this gentle violence continues to shape our thought. Even if the civility of tenure review and the impossible compromises of maternity have replaced the pyre, the contortion of word and desire continues to mutilate our writing.

This maiming is represented in this volume by the stories the contributors tell, but also by the absence of women who had been part of this project from the beginning. It would be disingenuous to conclude this volume without acknowledging the voices that had not found their way back to speech in time to be included here. Their loss is silent witness to absence. I am sad that the wisdom of these women has not found its way into this volume. I am inconsolable at the absence of women's wisdom in the shaping of Christian thought.

My own writing has been mutilated by the efficiencies of gentle and less gentle violence. It entered a tomb—or perhaps it was a womb—when I found myself unable to read for several years, a symptom of traumatic stress disorder. It was demoralizing—a weak word!—it was devastating to think that my life as a scholar was over and that writing had become impossible for me. I was accustomed to a style familiar to readers of this volume: going to the library, checking out as many books as I could carry, reading them, and then exchanging them for another pile of books. My footnotes were more copious than my text. But this writing is impossible for someone who cannot read. Without other scholars, without the props and insights of male writing to underwrite my own, it seemed absurd to write. It was excruciating to give up my understanding of myself as a scholar, to give up the authorizing methods that permitted me some small place at the table. I had to proceed with no real hope that I would be able to return to scholarly writing. I had to rely only on what was already in my head, as if I had journeyed into the wilderness and there was no resource beyond what I could carry with me. "Only what was in my head." I read my own writing and wonder if it sounds familiar. As if decades of study and teaching, of living and praying were nothing, as if no amount of training could ever be adequate to justify my writing. But I did write. I wrote as my self-understanding, my resources, my intellectual home—as essential to me as my own breath—were burned to ash. I wrote without the approval of my authorizing voices, without even my own approval. But I did keep writing. It burned my skin. It authorized itself.

My story is woven together with this volume because the work of these scholars helped me to better understand the importance and healing power of women's writing. These chapters do not compile tales of woe but tell stories about power. We are reminded of the vitality of women's theology throughout history and of its vitality in this generation of women scholars. Meghan opens a window onto Edith Stein, whose brilliance bleeds through the masks she wore. Like so many of us, she uses other women's stories to tell her own. More provocatively, she uses the stories of harmless women to include in salvation history the story of the Jews, a people destined for hell by Christian theology as well as by Nazi practice. A trace of Stein's own participation in Christ's sacrifice can be gleaned from the way she tells other women's stories: pentimento. Min-Ah repaints our understanding of the body of Christ, expanding it beyond what is institutionally permissible to include Theresa Cha, an icon of the outsider and so a particularly potent icon of Christ. We hear of Mother Dabney and Phoebe Palmer, who "reshaped the theological scripts they were given" (Shelly), using the language of self-abnegation and the violent imagery of the cross to defy their "wretched choices" and participate in the "glory and reign of God in the earth" (Michele). We are invited to appreciate the wisdom that emerges from contradictory and sometimes disturbing practices: Weil's fasting, Maitland's silence, Dickinson's solitude. This is a wisdom that "enables us to turn our attention to our sacred vulnerability, to divine compassion as the power of transformation, and to the gentle restoration of one soul through the openness of another, and allows us to construct a practice of eucharistic compassion, which is embodied both at the table and in our writing" (Elizabeth). We see how women have made different decisions about how to "face reality" (Leigh): post-Christian, bisexual Virginia Woolf in a hard-won room of her own, Amma Sarah in the desert of her asceticism, Simone Weil in soldiers' camps and hospital beds where she adored a Christ whose church was not catholic enough for her to accept the honor of its baptism. We learn to hear the wisdom of Latvian women who conscript music for their theological writing. Hymns and folk tunes that fly under the radar of seminary curriculum restructure faith with news of love and hope. We do not think of these women as theologians or even as writers, and yet they build up religious culture that is assaulted not only by patriarchy but by colonialism and exile.

These women's lives were laced with difficulty made more intense by the limits imposed simply by their womanhood: "precisely because the female body itself signified a state of subjection" (Emily). And yet they embraced a life of funk, of trickster agility that wrote of women and their bodies as "worthy of respect and delight" (Kendra). They dance in bodies that "seemed like nothing," and yet remain "watchful for transformative currents" (Marcia). Our authors help us see that in Macrina, in Lalleśwarī, in Angela of Foligno we encounter "great teachers who empower us to find our own voices" (Kendra). But the voice we discover here is a writing voice. We still live in the world of patriarchy, exile, and racism. We still negotiate the ambiguities of motherhood, the mixed blessings of life as a sexual minority, the impossible crosscurrents of multiple identities. The authors of this volume allow us to appreciate how important this writing voice is. It is not the same as our speaking voice and gives only indirect hints at our biographies, our brokenness, or our constraints. Writing is a kind of fantasy of freedom that flies farther than our daily lives might go. It allows us to dwell, for a while, in a room in our minds in which theological women come together to give each other news of freedom. Our hysterical bodies move more freely. Our faith takes wings. We join the "cadre of women to be co-laborers in the writing of a contemporary gospel" (Michele). We witness to the incarnational truth that "all flesh has potential to become divine and to issue forth in words, spoken and written" (Emily).

We put down our pens and return to a church that feeds us little scraps of truth, smaller scraps of respect. But we know it is not the only truth and that the dignity of our flesh shines as bright as a thousand suns. Turning experience into words transformed Angela from an embarrassing clot of screams into a serious contemplative and leader of contemplatives. It follows the arch of Lalleśwarī from abused wife to adored saint. These women wrote themselves into health and wisdom, into ever deeper confidence in their divine nature. Writing is an underground railroad we women create for one another. The authors of this volume show us this power and participate in it. In what they wrote and that they wrote, this cloud of witnesses invites you, dear reader, to pick up your pen: "do not fear: write" (Michelle).

We are all part of this lineage of writing women, called forth by Lady Love to say what we see and to draw down our wisdom into words. The Holy Spirit calls us forth to incarnate the divine Word. The Divine Feminine invites us to eat and write God. Like Eve, we are invited to imitate the divine by being mothers of the living, choosing wisdom over obedience, creating reality with our words, and embracing the joys and pains that this choice brings.[1] We find a way to tell the story of theology by looking at stories outside the tradition, in confessions of depression and survival.[2] I think Wesley Barker is right to point us to the community we form as writing women, a community which possesses no blueprint for living with difference but which creates a space in which every woman's voice finds welcome.[3] This is the body that must bear our perplexity, confusion, and irresistible longings. Let us encourage one another to silence the secret police inside our heads. Let us be more obedient to our own wisdom than to the fathers. Let us keep faith with those who have gone before and with one another. I will give Marguerite Porete, our patron saint, the last word:

> Place all your fidelity
> In those things which are given
> By Love, illuminated through Faith.
> And thus you will understand this book
> Which makes the Soul live by love.[4]

CONTRIBUTOR BIOGRAPHIES

MIN-AH CHO received her Ph.D. from Emory University in 2010. She is assistant professor of theology and spirituality at St. Catherine University. Her research interests include medieval women's mystical literature, feminist theologies, postcolonial theories, and Asian/Asian–North American religion and culture. She is particularly interested in ways in which individual Christians reshape and reconstruct the influence of traditional church institutions in their cultural contexts.

WENDY FARLEY received her Ph.D. from Vanderbilt University in 1988 and has taught at Emory University since then. She has written several books, including *The Wounding and Healing of Desire* and *Gathering Those Driven Away: A Theology of Incarnation from the Margins.* She lives with her partner, Maggie, while watching her three children fly from the nest one by one.

EMILY A. HOLMES (Ph.D., Emory University, 2008) is assistant professor of religion at Christian Brothers University in Memphis, Tennessee. Her research focuses on the incarnation, theological language, and women's writings, and she is the author of articles and chapters in the areas of feminist theology, French feminist theory, and medieval women's spirituality.

KENDRA G. HOTZ is assistant professor of religious studies at Rhodes College, where she teaches courses in theology, church history, and healthcare ethics. She also serves as theologian-in-residence at the Church Health Center in Memphis, Tennessee. She has coauthored four books exploring the theological dimensions of religious practices: *Shaping the Christian Life: Worship and the Religious Affections*; *Transforming Care: A Christian Vision of Nursing Practice*; *What Do Our Neighbors Believe? Questions and Answers from Judaism, Christianity, and Islam*; and the forthcoming *Dust and Breath: A Christian Perspective on Faith and Health.*

MICHELE JACQUES EARLY earned her Ph.D. in theological studies from Emory University in 2003. In 2004 she joined the faculty of the Samuel DeWitt Proctor School of Theology at Virginia Union University in Richmond, Virginia, teaching courses in systematic and womanist theology. Since 2006 she has directed the Doctor of Ministry Program. Her research interests, articles, and presentations focus on womanist perspectives in Pentecostalism.

MARCIA W. MOUNT SHOOP received her Ph.D. from Emory University in 2003. She is ordained to the Ministry of Word and Sacrament in the Presbyterian Church (U.S.A.) and has served churches in Illinois, Florida, California, and North Carolina. She is currently an independent scholar as well as a mother. She preaches, teaches, and leads retreats throughout the church and beyond. Her book, *Let the Bones Dance: Embodiment and the Body of Christ*, explores the disembodied ethos of mainline Protestantism through the lenses of rape, pregnancy, and motherhood.

LEIGH PITTENGER earned her Ph.D. in the Comparative Literature and Religion Program in the Graduate Division of Religion at Emory

University in 2011. Her research explores women's writing, imagination, and ethics, and her dissertation focuses on Hannah Arendt's conception of understanding as a practice of moral imagination. She has taught courses in English and religious studies at Middle Tennessee State University and Rhodes College.

SHELLY RAMBO received her Ph.D. from Emory University in 2005. She is assistant professor of theology at Boston University School of Theology, and her research and teaching interests focus on religious responses to suffering, trauma, and violence. She recently received grants to explore an ongoing dialogue between feminist theologies and practical theology. She is author of *Spirit and Trauma: A Theology of Remaining.*

KRISTINE SUNA-KORO received her Ph.D. from Emory University in 2010. She teaches theology at Xavier University in Cincinnati, Ohio, with a focus on historical theology through sacramental, postcolonial, and diasporic discourses. In 1995 she was ordained to pastoral ministry in the Latvian Evangelical Lutheran Church Abroad, and has served diasporic Latvian Lutheran communities in Great Britain, Germany, and the United States. Her scholarly and pastoral interests overlap in her teaching and publications on women in opera as a sensual mode of theology as well as reading as a transformative theological and spiritual practice.

MEGHAN T. SWEENEY teaches at Boston College, primarily in the undergraduate PULSE Program for Service Learning, an interdisciplinary program offered through the Department of Theology and the Department of Philosophy. She received her Ph.D. in 2006 from Emory University. Her primary research interest is theological anthropology, and she has authored and edited articles and volumes in this area. She is actively involved in parish ministry in the Episcopal Diocese of Massachusetts, where she is in the ordination process for the priesthood.

MICHELLE VOSS ROBERTS (Ph.D., Emory University, 2006) is assistant professor of theology and culture at Wake Forest University School of Divinity. She is the author of *Dualities: A Theology of Difference* and a number of articles in comparative and feminist theology. She is the former cochair of the Comparative Theology Group of the American Academy of Religion, and she received the Elisabeth Schüssler Fiorenza New Scholar Award from the *Journal of Feminist Studies in Religion* in 2010. Her current research investigates religious experience from the perspective of classical Indian aesthetic theory.

ELIZABETH A. WEBB received her Ph.D. from Emory University in 2004. She has held positions at Augustana College (Illinois), Rhodes College, and William Jewell College, and is currently teaching courses at Avila University in Kansas City, Missouri. Her scholarly work centers on trauma and compassion, Eucharist, and theology and literature. Her non-scholarly work centers on teaching in her Episcopal parish and mothering the loveliest creature ever to walk the face of the earth.

NOTES

Acknowledgments

1   Teresa de Lauretis, "The Essence of the Triangle or, Taking the Risk of Essentialism Seriously: Feminist Theory in Italy, the U.S., and Britain," in *The Essential Difference*, ed. Naomi Schor and Elizabeth Weed (Bloomington: Indiana University Press, 1994), 21.

Chapter 1: Introduction

1   Barbara Johnson, "Writing," in *Critical Terms for Literary Study*, ed. Frank Lentricchia and Thomas McLaughlin (Chicago: University of Chicago Press, 1995), 39–43.

2   See Jacques Derrida, *Of Grammatology*, trans. Gayatri Chakravorty Spivak (Baltimore: Johns Hopkins University Press, 1974); and *Writing and Difference*, trans. Alan Bass (Chicago: University of Chicago Press, 1978).

3   Some of these pairs can be traced to one of the founding moments of Western metaphysics in the Pythagorean table of opposites in Aristotle's *Metaphysics* 986a in *The Basic Works of Aristotle*, ed. Richard McKeon, trans. W. D. Ross (New York: The Modern Library, 2001).

4   See Plato's myth of the origin of writing in *Phaedrus*, trans. Walter Hamilton (London: Penguin Books, 1973), 274–77.

5   David Tracy, "Writing," in *Critical Terms for Religious Studies*, ed. Mark C. Taylor (Chicago: University of Chicago Press, 1998), 385 and 391.

6   Tracy, "Writing," 389.

7   Tracy, "Writing," 390.

8   Tracy, "Writing," 391.
9   For two different approaches to the role of writing in Christianity, both informed by postmodern philosophy, see Mark C. Taylor, *Erring: A Postmodern A/Theology* (Chicago: University of Chicago Press, 1984); and the work of scriptural reasoning in Peter Ochs, ed., *The Return to Scripture in Judaism and Christianity: Essays in Postcritical Scriptural Interpretation* (Eugene, Ore.: Wipf & Stock, 2008).
10   Johnson, "Writing," 48.
11   Quoted in Johnson, "Writing," 48. See also Henry Louis Gates Jr. and Kwame Anthony Appiah, eds., *"Race," Writing, and Difference* (Chicago: Chicago University Press, 1986); and Henry Louis Gates Jr., *The Signifying Monkey: A Theory of African-American Literary Criticism* (New York: Oxford University Press, 1989).
12   Hélène Cixous, "The Laugh of the Medusa," in *New French Feminisms*, ed. Elaine Marks and Isabelle de Courtivron, trans. Keith Cohen and Paula Cohen (New York: Schocken Books, 1980).
13   Hélène Cixous, "Coming to Writing," in *"Coming to Writing" and Other Essays*, ed. Deborah Jenson, trans. Sarah Cornell et al. (Cambridge, Mass.: Harvard University Press, 1991), 23.
14   Johnson, "Writing," 48.
15   For example, Marguerite Porete's *Mirror of Simple Souls* was at one time attributed to Ruusbroec, and Angela of Foligno was thought to be a Franciscan pedagogical "trope" invented by an anonymous male author.
16   For example, medieval women writers commonly invoke body-related imagery of food and illness in their texts. See the work of Caroline Walker Bynum, especially *Holy Feast and Holy Fast: The Religious Significance of Food to Medieval Women* (Berkeley: University of California Press, 1987).
17   See Mikhail Bakhtin, *The Dialogic Imagination*, ed. Michael Holquist, trans. Caryl Emerson and Michael Holquist (Austin: University of Texas Press, 1981); and Laurie Finke, *Feminist Theory, Women's Writing: Reading Women Writing* (Ithaca, N.Y.: Cornell University Press, 1992).
18   Cixous, "Coming to Writing," 52.

Chapter 2

1   Lynn Japinga, "Fear in the Reformed Tradition," in *Feminist and Womanist Essays in Reformed Dogmatics*, ed. Amy Plantinga Pauw and Serene Jones (Louisville, Ky.: Westminster John Knox, 2006), 6.
2   Japinga, "Fear," 2.
3   Simone de Beauvoir, *The Second Sex*, trans. H. M. Parshley (New York: Vintage Books, 1989), 167.
4   Patricia Hill Collins, *Black Feminist Thought: Knowledge, Consciousness, and the Politics of Empowerment* (Boston: Unwin Hyman, 1990), 5.

5   Japinga, "Fear," 6.

6   Emmanuel Levinas, "Freedom and Command," in *Collected Philosophical Papers*, trans. Alphonso Lingus (Dordrecht: Kluwer Academic Publishers, 1993), 16.

7   Japinga, "Fear," 4.

8   Carolyn G. Heilbrun, *Writing a Woman's Life* (New York: Ballantine Books, 1988), addresses customary silences in relation to gender particularly well. Even outside of gender concerns, writing has its own perils. See, e.g., Ralph Keyes, *The Courage to Write: How Writers Transcend Fear* (New York: Owl Books, 1995).

9   A more exhaustive comparison of these women's teachings and experiences can be found in Michelle Voss Roberts, *Dualities: A Theology of Difference* (Louisville, Ky.: Westminster John Knox, 2010).

10 Translations of Lalleśwarī's *vaakh*s, which I number K1, K2, and so on, follow Nil Kanth Kotru in *Lal Ded, Her Life and Sayings* (Srinagar: Utpal Publications, 1989). For the best scholarly overview of her life and work, see Jai Lal Kaul, *Lal Ded* (New Delhi: Sahitya Akademi, 1973).

11 The earliest legends about Lalleśwarī date from at least two hundred years after her life and are, therefore, unreliable as historical sources. The hagiographies are useful from a hagiographical and theological point of view, however, for they retain the spirit of what people found remarkable about her.

12 This tale derives from the seventeenth-century hagiography of Nund Rishi, the *Nūrnāma* (S. S. Toshkhani, e-mail to the author, June 30, 2006).

13 Kotru, *Lal Ded*, vii–viii. This, the earliest documented story about Lalleśwarī, derives from Bābā Dāwūd Mishkātī's "The Secrets of the Pious" (1654). Kaul, *Lal Ded*, 2.

14 Kaul, *Lal Ded*, 17. The first written appearance of this oral legend is in Anand Koul, "Life Sketch of Lalleśwarī—A Great Hermitess of Kashmir," *Indian Antiquary* 50 (1921): 306–7.

15 Kaul, *Lal Ded*, 3.

16 Jaishree Kak Odin, *To the Other Shore: Lalla's Life and Poetry* (New Delhi: Vitasta, 1999), 44–45.

17 B. N. Pandit, *Aspects of Kashmir Śaivism* (Srinagar: Utpal Publications, 1977), 44.

18 Odin, *To the Other Shore*, xi.

19 I elaborate upon these factors in greater detail in Voss Roberts, "Power, Gender, and the Construction of a Kashmir Śaiva Mystic," *Journal of Hindu Studies* 3, no. 3 (2010).

20 Alexis Sanderson, "Śaivism and the Tantric Traditions," in *The World's Religions: The Religions of Asia*, ed. Friedhelm Hardy (London: Routledge, 1988), 159. Also see Gavin Flood, "The Śaiva Traditions," in *The Blackwell*

Companion to Hinduism, ed. Gavin Flood (Oxford: Blackwell, 2003), 213, for a discussion of the absorption of the Trika school into the householder life.

21   For an overview of this concept in various Hindu traditions, see Andrew O. Fort and Patricia Y. Mumme, eds., *Living Liberation in Hindu Thought* (Albany: State University of New York Press, 1996).

22   As a contemporary example, the spiritual genealogy of the last modern adept in the tradition, Swami Laksmanjoo (d. 1991) has been traced directly to Abhinavagupta, and thereby to one of the founders of Kashmir Śaivism, Somānanda. John Hughes, *Self Realization in Kashmir Shaivism: The Oral Teachings of Swami Lakshmanjoo, with Foreward by Lance Nelson* (Albany: State University of New York Press, 1994), xxviii.

23   Kotru, *Lal Ded*, x–xi; cf. Koul, "Life Sketch," 302.

24   Pandit, *Aspects*, 44. Disagreement circulates around the possibility of Sufi figures under her influence. Pandit mentions only the "worthy disciple Sheikh Nuruddin [Nund Rishi]" (238); and while Shashi Shekhar Toshkhani and others accept her instruction of this young Sufi saint, they vigorously deny the historical possibility of legends showing her being *influenced* by Muslim saints. See Shashi Shekhar Toshkhani, ed., *Lal Ded: The Great Kashmiri Saint-Poetess* (New Delhi: APH Publishing, 2002), 40–45.

25   See Gavin D. Flood, *Body and Cosmology in Kashmir Śaivism* (San Francisco: Mellen Research University Press, 1993), 292–93.

26   Sanderson, "Śaivism," 167. For a detailed discussion of the main branches of initiation (*dīkṣā*) of males in Śaiva traditions, see Flood, *Body and Cosmology*, 220–28.

27   Interviews of Omkar Kaul, S. N. Bhatt, and S. S. Toshkhani by the author, March–April 2006. Lalleśwarī herself attests that her guru told her only "one word" (*vachan*, K21). The only possible support I have found for the unlikely idea that she underwent the prolonged tutelage of the guru-disciple relationship lies in a saying in which she recalls asking her guru repeatedly about the nature of the Absolute (K24).

28   Kaul, *Lal Ded*, 12–13. In another strategy, Anand Koul proposes the following rumor as a derivation for her name: upon her renunciation of home and clothing, the flesh of her stomach (*lal*) grew to hang loose so that it covered her genitals. Koul, "Life Sketch," 304.

29   These illustrations are available at P. N. Razdan, "Gems of Kashmiri Literature and Kashmiriyat," accessed March 2006, http://www.koausa .org/KashmiriGems/LalDed.html.

30   Kotru, *Lal Ded*, viii. This statement is true enough, for she teaches that the true *jīvanmukta* moves beyond the point of being attached to miraculous powers: "To stop running waters and to cool raging fire, / the accursed

practice of levitation, / or to milk a wooden cow— / In the final analysis
these are all acts of fraud" (K112).

31 See Kotru, *Lal Ded*, vii.

32 Odin, *To the Other Shore*, xi.

33 Paradoxically, Lalleśwarī's disruption of the householder life as a female
renouncer, though unorthodox, offers a window into an undercurrent of
ambivalence toward social institutions in her tradition discussed in Flood,
"Śaiva Traditions," 200.

34 Odin, *To the Other Shore*, 53.

35 Odin, *To the Other Shore*, 31.

36 Citations follow Mechthild of Magdeburg, *The Flowing Light of the Godhead*,
trans. Frank J. Tobin (New York: Paulist Press, 1998).

37 Elizabeth A. Andersen, *The Voices of Mechthild of Magdeburg* (Oxford: Peter
Lang, 2000), 80.

38 Frank J. Tobin, *Mechthild von Magdeburg: A Medieval Mystic in Modern Eyes*
(Columbia, S.C.: Camden House, 1995), 2.

39 Frank J. Tobin, introduction to *The Flowing Light of the Godhead* (New York:
Paulist Press, 1998), 7. By contrast, Lalleśwarī's reception history exhib-
its *increasing* emphasis on erotic imagery as a way to slot her more firmly
with the women poets of India's *bhakti* (devotional) movement. See Voss
Roberts, "Power."

40 For a meticulous examination of the textual transmission of Mechthild's
book, see Sara S. Poor, *Mechthild of Magdeburg and Her Book: Gender and
the Making of Textual Authority* (Philadelphia: University of Pennsylvania
Press, 2004). On the gendered construction and evolution of the category of mysticism, see Grace Jantzen, *Power, Gender and Christian Mysticism*
(Cambridge: Cambridge University Press, 1995).

41 Herbert Grundmann, *Religious Movements in the Middle Ages: The Historical
Links between Heresy, the Mendicant Orders, and the Women's Religious Movement
in the Twelfth and Thirteenth Centuries, with the Historical Foundations of German
Mysticism*, trans. Steven Rowan (Notre Dame: University of Notre Dame
Press, 1995), 11. Here, Grundmann analyzes early twelfth-century apostolic groups around Cologne and in southern France, but these trends
apply to groups like the Waldensians and the beghards and beguines as
well.

42 See Tobin, introduction to *Flowing Light*, 3.

43 Delores S. Williams, *Sisters in the Wilderness: The Challenge of Womanist God-
Talk* (Maryknoll, N.Y.: Orbis Books, 1993), 167.

44 Levinas, "Freedom and Command," 16.

45 Japinga, "Fear," 8–9.

46 For the term "dangerous memories," see Johann Baptist Metz,
"Communicating a Dangerous Memory," in *Love's Strategy: The Political*

Theology of Johann Baptist Metz, ed. John K. Downey (Harrisburg, Penn.: Trinity Press, 1999).

47 Neela Banerjee, "Clergywomen Find Hard Path to Bigger Pulpit," *The New York Times,* August 26, 2006.

48 Levinas, "Freedom and Command," 17.

Chapter 3

1 L. Serene Jones, "Hope Deferred: Theological Reflections on Reproductive Loss," *Modern Theology* 17, no. 2 (2001): 227–45.

2 The question that sparked much of this debate was an 1836 meeting at Oberlin College at which a student asked President Asa Mahan a troubling question: "When we look to Christ for sanctification, what degree of sanctification may we expect from him? May we look to him to be sanctified wholly, or not?" Donald W. Dayton, *Theological Roots of Pentecostalism* (Peabody, Mass.: Hendrickson Publishers, 1991), 66 n. 15.

3 In Christianity, the Bible is often referred to as the Word of God; Jesus is also referred to as the Logos, the Word, as referenced in the Gospel of John. Phoebe Palmer did not distinguish between word and Word; for her, referring to the Bible as Word was an invocation of Jesus, the Word made flesh. Throughout her writings, she often capitalized all of the letters—WORD. When referencing her work, I will use the capitalized "Word" in order to retain the spirit of her writings.

4 "I Have Decided to Follow Jesus," attributed to S. Sundar Singh, folk melody from India.

5 Thomas Oden writes, "She was the most influential woman in the largest, fastest growing religious group in mid-nineteenth century America— Methodism." Thomas Oden, ed., *Phoebe Palmer: Selected Writings* (New York: Paulist Press, 1988), 6.

6 Phoebe Palmer, "Early Married Years: Diary and Poetry, 1828–1836," in *Phoebe Palmer: Selected Writings,* 100.

7 The practice of calling people to the altar (the altar call) preceded Palmer's theology of the altar. "The centrality of the altar as physical object and as spiritual symbol could hardly have been lost on the vast majority of American Methodist hearers. Stress on the altar of the heart sprang quite naturally from the material culture of the revivalistic spirituality in which they, like she [Palmer], had been nurtured. The practice of kneeling for prayer and for communion, an inheritance from Anglicanism, was an integral part of Methodist worship." Charles Edwin Jones, "The Inverted Shadow of Phoebe Palmer," *Wesleyan Theological Journal* 31, no. 2 (1996): 120–31, 123.

8 Palmer, "Entire Devotion to God," in *Phoebe Palmer: Selected Writings,* 199.

9 Jeanne Halgren Kilde, "Church Architecture and the Second Great

Awakening," in *Embodying the Spirit: New Perspectives on North American Revivalism*, ed. Michael J. McClymond (Baltimore: The Johns Hopkins University Press, 2004), 84–108. Describing revivalist Charles Finney's purchase of the Chatham Street Theater in New York, she writes, "Thus, the new, unorthodox space helped to transform the worship experience for audience members. The sloped floor and proscenium arch helped to focus the audience's attention on the stage, that is, on the preacher's performance and message of spiritual regeneration. . . . Standing on the stage, he could look into the eyes of everyone present, seemingly directing his words to each individual and creating an intimate, personal relationship. This was precisely the goal of the several worship practices called the 'new measures' that Finney and other New School revivalists employed. The passionate preaching in the vernacular, the use of individual names and personal situations, the testimony of witnesses from the floor, the altar call and use of the anxious bench for those wrestling with their own sin—each of these 'new measures' personalized the revival experience, encouraging an affective or emotional response within audience members that would lead to the internalizing of the preacher's message. Audiences, revival ministers hoped, would apply the message to themselves and search their souls for true conviction" (89).

10 Sanctification is the term in Christian vocabulary that refers to the process of "becoming holy." It is often coupled with justification, the term that refers to the moment in which a person is "made right"—declared righteous—by God.

11 Phoebe Palmer, *The Way of Holiness with Notes by the Way* (New York: Piercy and Reed, Printers, 1843), 1.

12 "The altar sanctifieth the gift" became a mantra for Palmer's biblical justification of instantaneous sanctification. Her critics worried that Palmer was peddling the promise of sanctification without emphasizing that it was God's work, taking place in God's time. There was a perceived presumptuousness to her view of holiness; believers could claim too much too quickly. In response, Palmer believed that the biblical promise of holiness removed the emotionalism and anxiety that plagued those who wanted to live out the life of faith. The question of sanctification was not whether or not God does that work but, in fact, whether believers dare to lay hold on this claim.

13 Palmer, "The Altar Covenant (1837)," in *Phoebe Palmer: Selected Writings*, 121.

14 Palmer, "Entire Devotion to God," in *Phoebe Palmer: Selected Writings*, 202. Emphasis in original.

15 Richard Wheatley, *The Life and Letters of Mrs. Phoebe Palmer* (New York: Garland Publishing, 1984), 537. Emphasis in original.

16 However, Palmer's emphasis is not so much on the work of the Spirit as it is on the work of Christ. She has what theologians might identify as a highly Christocentric interpretation of the process of sanctification. The work of the Spirit is heavily tied to Jesus.

17 Palmer, "Entire Devotion to God," in *Phoebe Palmer: Selected Writings*, 198.

18 Palmer writes, "No longer think of holiness as a doctrine peculiar to a sect, but rather as a doctrine peculiar to the *Bible*, as the only fitness for admission to the society of the bloodwashed in Heaven. If you are not a holy Christian, you are not a Bible Christian." Phoebe Palmer, "Entire Devotion to God," in *Phoebe Palmer: Selected Writings*, 186. Emphasis in original.

19 Palmer, *The Way of Holiness*, 199.

20 The lyrics convey the emphasis on decision that became so central to Palmer's theology.

21 Rev. George Hughes, *Fragrant Memories of The Tuesday Meeting and The Guide to Holiness, and Their Fifty Years' Work for Jesus* (New York: Palmer and Hughes, 1886), 40.

22 Hughes, *Fragrant Memories*, 40. These are not Hughes' words but in fact are taken from a report from a congregational paper; the author is not named.

23 Hughes, *Fragrant Memories*, 61.

24 An example of this is Nancy Hardesty, *Women Called to Witness: Evangelical Feminism in the Nineteenth Century* (Knoxville: University of Tennessee Press, 1999).

25 Historian David Hempton notes that the "disruptive piety opened up a small but expandable crack in the wall of male power and control." Yet Hempton readily admits that this relationship is not a clear-cut one: "The relationship between the rise of popular evangelicalism during the second Great Awakening and the development of American feminism in the early nineteenth century is a hotly debated topic." Many of the women leaders influenced by evangelical religion did not remain within it: "As a result very few of the major leaders of nineteenth-century American feminism, especially those of a more radical kind, were empowered, sustained, and supported by any of the major evangelical traditions." David Hempton, *Evangelical Disenchantment: Nine Portraits of Faith and Doubt* (New Haven: Yale University Press, 2008), 92–93.

26 Mrs. Hannah H. Pickard, *Guide to Christian Perfection*, T. Merritt and D. S. King, eds., October 18, 1845 (Boston: G. C. Rand, 1845), 47.

27 The language of being owned by God is common. Pickard writes, "My fears and all was gone, save the delightful thought of being His alone. 'Quietness and assurance' filled my heart. It *is* being 'alive unto God.'" September 16, 1840, in *Guide to Christian Perfection*, 12. Emphasis in original.

28   Abiah Root was a close friend of Emily's and was known to be the person with whom Emily most openly shared her sentiments about religion. A great deal of what we know about Dickinson's youth is gleaned from the correspondence between them, spanning from 1845 to 1854.

29   Dickinson would not necessarily have been aware of Palmer, and I am not attempting to argue any kind of literal relationship between the two. The theology of the altar and the practices of altar conversion became normative within the American holiness tradition, and Emily Dickinson would have witnessed an altar experience very much like the one that Palmer prescribed. Without conflating historical periods or mapping contemporary experiences onto history, I am probing the theological inheritance of traditions and their persisting impact and the normative shaping power they bear in the present.

30   Dickinson to Abiah Root, 28 March 1846, in *The Letters of Emily Dickinson*, vol. 1, ed. Thomas H. Johnson and Theodora Ward (Cambridge, Mass.: The Belknap Press of Harvard University Press, 1965), 30–31. See also W. S. Tyler, *History of Amherst College during its First Half Century: 1821–1871* (Springfield, Mass.: Clark W. Bryan, 1873), 352–53. Tyler writes, "In the winter and spring of 1850, there was another general revival. . . . Including seven from the families of the Faculty, there were thirty-three persons who, together, presented themselves at the altar, almost filling the broad aisle, all in the bloom of youth, and who now, for the first time, dedicated themselves by their own voluntary consecration, to the service of their Maker, Redeemer, and Sanctifier" (350).

31   The opening to the Gospel of John reads, "In the beginning was the Logos and the Logos was with God and the Logos was God."

32   Biographer Cynthia Griffin Wolff places the appeal of the religious conversions in Amherst within the context of the pervasiveness of death in mid-nineteenth-century New England. The promise of new life in Christ was compelling amidst the realities of death. Dickinson writes in January 1846 that she feels the importance of attending to the subject of religion: "I feel that life is short and time fleeting—and that I ought now to make my peace with my maker—I hope the golden opportunity is not far hence when my heart will willingly yield itself to Christ." Cynthia Griffin Wolff, *Emily Dickinson* (Reading, Mass.: Addison-Wesley Publishing, 1988), 87.

33   One major example of this was the separation of women at Mount Holyoke Female Seminary into three social groups. Mary Lyon, the head of the seminary, sought to bring all of her students to faith in Christ. Roger Lundin writes, "Lyon divided them each year into three groups: the 'No-Hopers,' the 'Hopers,' and the 'Christians.' The latter group was the largest of the three and was made up of women who could testify to the certainty of their salvation; at the beginning of Emily's year at the

seminary, 150 of the 230 Mount Holyoke students were counted among the 'Christians.' About fifty of the remaining students were 'Hopers'— that is, young women who believed themselves on the verge of conversion. That left a group of about thirty students, including Dickinson, who were 'without hope' and could not attest to faith in Christ. The members of this final group were the subjects of Lyon's most fervent attention." Roger Lundin, *Emily Dickinson and the Art of Belief*, 2nd ed. (Grand Rapids: Eerdmans, 2004), 40–41.

34   Dickinson to Jane Humphrey, 3 April 1850, in *The Letters of Emily Dickinson*, 94.

35   Alfred Habegger, *My Wars are Laid Away in Books: The Life of Emily Dickinson* (New York: Random, 2001), as referenced in Lundin's *Emily Dickinson and the Art of Belief*, 43.

36   Lundin, *Emily Dickinson and the Art of Belief*, 43.

37   Dickinson to Abiah Root, 7 May 1850, in *The Letters of Emily Dickinson*, 98.

38   Dickinson to Jane Humphrey, 3 April 1850, in *The Letters of Emily Dickinson*, 94. Emphasis in original.

39   Dickinson to Abiah Root, 7 and 17 May 1850, in *The Letters of Emily Dickinson*, 99. Emphasis in original.

40   Dickinson to Jane Humphrey, 3 April 1850, in *The Letters of Emily Dickinson*, 95.

41   Jay Leyda, *The Years and Hours of Emily Dickinson* (New Haven: Yale University Press, 1960), 148. Emphasis in original.

42   This is a curious reference, because the biblical story in Luke 10 does not spell out what this one necessary thing is. Dickinson draws on this story to speak about conversion. The one thing necessary is devotion and service to Jesus; Mary gives her full attention to Jesus, while Martha is occupied with other tasks. Martha is often depicted as the busybody in the story, doing lots of things but somehow distracted from the main task of sitting at Jesus' feet, listening to him.

43   The full manuscript of this letter is missing. It was included with letters to Abiah Root and is presumed to be dated around May 16, 1848. *The Letters of Emily Dickinson*, 67. Emphasis in original.

44   Often the language of "sides" is used to describe conversion, suggesting that a person is either on the side of the world or the side of God. A good example of this is the letter written from Emily's sister, Lavinia, to Austin, their brother. Lavinia, known as Vinnie, is a recent convert to Christianity. She writes, "Oh! Austin, I do so long to hear that you have come over to the Lord's side! Oh, if you have *not yet* given yourself to Christ wholly & entirely, I entreat you in the name of the blessed Jesus, to delay no longer, to deprive yourself of that happiness, that Joy, no longer but my Dear Brother, *now*, while pardon is offered you & while

the precious Savior is waiting to receive you, come, yes, now while the Holy Spirit is in your midst & when the attention of all is called to that subject. Do not give up religion as not worth seeking." (Leyda, *Years and Hours*, 96–97). Emphasis in original.

45 Wolff, *Emily Dickinson*, 87. I am highly influenced by Wolff's assessment of Dickinson's experience of revival faith. See chapter 3, "School," 66–104.

46 Wolff, *Emily Dickinson*, 87.

47 Wolff, *Emily Dickinson*, 98.

48 She is reflecting, in a letter to Abiah Root, on the response of people to the "still small voice" of God; people are listening, believing, and obeying. Emily is asking Abiah to explain this to her. Dickinson to Abiah Root, 17 May 1850, in *The Letters of Emily Dickinson*, 99. Emphasis in original.

49 Wolff, *Emily Dickinson*, 92.

50 Dickinson owned a copy of the 1847 *American Webster's Dictionary*.

51 Wolff, *Emily Dickinson*, 91.

52 This biblical story is located in the Hebrew Scriptures, Gen 32:24-32.

53 Dickinson to Abiah Root, late 1850, in *The Letters of Emily Dickinson*, 104.

54 In a letter to Abiah Root on January 31, 1846, Emily admits to her friends that she was "almost persuaded to be a christian." She hears Christianity's call to give up the fleeting pleasures of the world in exchange for the "treasures of heaven." She does appear honestly persuaded by this, but the "almost" separating her from Christianity seems to lie in her insistence on feeling—on being affected by—the world. She writes, "When I am most happy there is a *sting* in every enjoyment. I find no rose without a thorn. There is an *aching void* in my heart which I am convinced the world can never fill." And yet, despite convincing logic, Dickinson chooses the sting and the aching void (*The Letters of Emily Dickinson*, 27, emphasis added). By contrast, Miss A. Mills writes an entry in *Guide to Holiness*, using Dickinson's precise words: "I knew that Jesus must reign there [in my heart] without a rival; but since he has taken possession of that mean above, I feel no 'aching void' within." *The Guide to and Beauty of Holiness*, ed. Mrs. Phoebe Palmer and Rev. E. Foster (New York: Foster and Palmer Jr., 1866), 138.

55 This is rather ironic, given what we know about Emily Dickinson and her subsequent withdrawal from the world. But there are hints that Dickinson, despite her retreat from the world, exercised a certain internal abandon. Interestingly, she was remembered by one of her nieces as the "indulgent" aunt.

56 Death and its corresponding vocabulary—self-emptying, sacrifice, denial, leaving behind, laying it down—always entail loss and separation.

57 See Rita Nakashima Brock and Rebecca Parker, *Proverbs of Ashes: Violence, Redemptive Suffering and the Search for What Saves Us* (Boston: Beacon Press,

2002); Delores Williams, *Sisters in the Wilderness: The Challenge of Womanist God-Talk* (Maryknoll, N.Y.: Orbis, 1993).

58   Mrs. Upsham writes, "He who looks for any other basis of the divine life than self-abandonment, or willingness to sacrifice self for the good of others, is building on a false foundation. It is only in the death of self, torn, bleeding, dying on the cross, after the example of Christ, that the work is finished, and eternal life springs up in the soul." Mrs. Upsham, "Spiritual Way-Marks," in *Guide to and Beauty of Holiness*, 76.

59   Charles E. White, *The Beauty of Holiness: Phoebe Palmer as Theologian, Revivalist, Feminist, and Humanitarian* (Eugene, Ore.: Wipf & Stock, 2008), 27.

60   Rebecca D. Davenport, "Correspondence," in *Guide to and Beauty of Holiness*, 158.

61   Palmer, "Correspondence," in *Guide to and Beauty of Holiness*, 158–59.

62   "Enough and to Spare," in *The Guide to Holiness*, vol. 31, ed. Rev. H. V. Degen and Rev. B. W. Gorham (Boston: Henry V. Degen Publishers, 1857), 159. Emphasis in original.

63   "The Experience of a Baptist Lady," *Guide to Holiness*, 126.

64   Athanasius is an authoritative voice in Christian history and tradition. In his early work, *On the Incarnation*, he provides one of the earliest articulations of the meaning of God's incarnation. It is clear that Athanasius believes that salvation is located in the assumption of flesh (the incarnation) rather than in the event of death. His is, however, not a pure legacy, given the fact that he also presents a "divine dilemma" between God's desire to save humanity and the rule of divine punishment for human disobedience.

65   See n17. Palmer writes, "I resolve that I will search the Scriptures daily on my knees (unless circumstances of health altogether prevent) as in the more immediate presence of God; and that my faith and my duties shall be regulated by the unadulterated WORD OF GOD, rather than by the opinions of men in regard to that Word; and that no impressions in relation to doctrines or duties shall be regarded as coming from God, unless the said doctrine or duty be plainly taught in the Holy Scriptures."

66   A term invoked by Elizabeth A. Johnson in her classic work *She Who Is: The Mystery of God in Feminist Theological Discourse*, 2nd ed. (New York: Crossroad Publishing, 2001), 13. Johnson writes, "Scotosis results when the intellectual censorship function, which usually operates in a good and constructive manner to select elements to give us insight, goes awry. In aberrant fashion this censorship function works to repress new questions in order to prevent the emergence of unwanted insight" (13–14).

67   "Emily Dickinson (1830–1886)," Poetry Foundation, accessed July 12, 2009, http://www.poetryfoundation.org/archive/poet.html?id=1775.

Chapter 4

1   Thomas Aquinas, *Summa Theologiae*, pt. 3 supp., q. 39, art. 1. But see also Gary Macy, *The Hidden History of Women's Ordination: Female Clergy in the Medieval West* (New York: Oxford University Press, 2007).

2   Hildegard of Bingen, "Letter to Bernard of Clairvaux," in *Hildegard of Bingen: Selected Writings*, trans. and ed. Mark Atherton (New York: Penguin, 2001), 3–5.

3   Hadewijch's poems, visions, and letters were written for her community of beguine women. See *Hadewijch: The Complete Works*, trans. Mother Columba Hart (Mahwah, N.J.: Paulist Press, 1980).

4   In "'Who Does She Think She Is?' Christian Women's Mysticism," *Theology Today* 60 (2003): 5–15, Amy Hollywood writes, "Their authority depends on their sanctity, crucially marked by humility. Yet at the same time, the very act of writing and asserting an authoritative voice within thirteenth-century Christian culture was, particularly for women, an audacious act." Medieval women writers "resolve this dilemma by portraying their writing as demanded by God." See also Bernard McGinn, "The Four Female Evangelists of the Thirteenth Century: The Invention of Authority," in *Deutsche Mystik im abendländischen Zusammenhang*, ed. Walter Haug and Wolfram Schneider-Lastin (Tübingen: Niemeyer, 2000), 175–94; and Michelle Voss Roberts, "Retrieving Humility: Rhetoric, Authority, and Divinization in Mechthild of Magdeburg," *Feminist Theology* 18, no. 1 (2009): 55–80.

5   This is the response Amy Hollywood most often receives from her students when encountering Christian women mystical writers for the first time.

6   Hélène Cixous, "Coming to Writing," 9.

7   Cixous has published over seventy works, including twenty-three volumes of poems, six books of essays, and five plays.

8   Hélène Cixous, "Le Rire de la Méduse," *L'Arc* 61 (1975): 39–54; English translation published as "The Laugh of the Medusa" in *New French Feminisms*, ed. Elaine Marks and Isabelle de Courtivron, trans. Keith Cohen and Paula Cohen (New York: Schocken Books, 1980).

9   Cixous, "Le Rire," 39–40 ("Laugh," 246).

10 Cixous draws heavily on psychoanalysis and the concept of the return of the repressed. See especially her essay cowritten with Catherine Clément, *La jeune née* (Paris: Union générale d'Éditions, 1975), 127–44. English translation by Betsy Wing, *The Newly Born Woman* (Minneapolis: University of Minnesota Press, 1986).

11 The Third Order was a lay status midway between a life in the world and the religious lives of the Friars Minor (First Order) and Poor Clares (Second Order).

12 Angela's scribe is identified in the text only as a "trustworthy Friar Minor." The name "Arnaldo" came from a later tradition but has generally been adopted by most Angela scholars. See also Catherine M. Mooney, "The Authorial Role of Brother A. in the Composition of Angela of Foligno's Revelations," in *Creative Women in Medieval and Modern Italy*, ed. E. Ann Matter and John Coakley (Philadelphia: University of Pennsylvania Press, 1994), 34–63.

13 Angela's *Memoriale* and *Instructiones* are published in the critical edition edited by Ludger Their, OFM, and Abele Calufetti, OFM, *Il Libro della Beata Angela da Foligno* (Grottaferrata, Rome: Editiones Collegii S. Bonaventurae ad Claras Aquas, 1985), hereafter cited as *Il Libro*. English quotations are from *Angela of Foligno: Complete Works*, trans. Paul Lachance, OFM (New York: Paulist Press, 1993), hereafter cited as *Complete Works*, with modifications of the translation where noted.

14 Due to the complex evolution of these texts, the role of Brother Arnaldo as scribe, and the subsequent redactions of the material, discerning Angela's voice or experience is a difficult endeavor, especially in comparison to other women writing theology examined in this collection. It is not, however, impossible. Her own interpretation of her experience is evident especially in those moments in which Brother Arnaldo himself seems puzzled by her words and in her short and memorable episodes (such as screaming in the Church of Saint Francis) that seem to have taken everyone by surprise. See Lachance's introduction to *Complete Works*, 81–84.

15 *Il Libro*, 148 (*Complete Works*, 130).

16 See Lachance's introduction to *Complete Works*, 16–17.

17 *Il Libro*, 154 (*Complete Works*, 132).

18 *Il Libro*, 156 (*Complete Works*, 133).

19 At least Brother Arnaldo represents it as a major turning point, in part, no doubt, because that is where he entered her story. Mooney ("Authorial Role of Brother A.," 57) notes, "it seems a strange coincidence that Angela's spiritual life should take such a dramatic swing toward the sublime, begin again as it were, at just the moment when he happened to ask her about it. My point, in short, is that the entire structure of the *Memorial* is built from the perspective of Brother A. He inadvertently casts the day he intruded into her thoughts as a central turning point in her experience and he correlates the beginning of their writing relationship with what he represents as the genesis of her most significant religious experience." From the perspective of the production of her book, however, it is indeed crucial, precisely because it is where he intervened.

20 *Il Libro*, 168 (*Complete Works*, 136).

21 *Il Libro*, 168–70 (*Complete Works*, 136).

22 *Il Libro*, 170 (*Complete Works*, 136–37).

23   *Il Libro*, 170 (*Complete Works*, 137).

24   *Il Libro*, 180 (*Complete Works*, 139–40).

25   *Il Libro*, 184 (*Complete Works*, 142).

26   *Il Libro*, 186 (*Complete Works*, 142).

27   "Deus est praesens in omnibus istis quae scribitis et stat ibi vobiscum. Et comprehendebat anima quod Deus inde delectabatur, et anima istud sentiebat." *Il Libro*, 218 (*Complete Works*, 154).

28   See n19 above.

29   *Il Libro*, 166–68 (*Complete Works*, 136).

30   During one session, Arnaldo wrote, "Then she added that today she had also been told: 'Have these words inserted at the end of what you say, namely, that thanks should be given to God for all the things which you have written'" (*Complete Works*, 156).

31   *Complete Works*, 217–18.

32   Bynum, *Holy Feast and Holy Fast*; and Bynum, *Fragmentation and Redemption: Essays on Gender and the Human Body in Medieval Religion* (New York: Zone Books, 1991). For a more theoretical reflection on the same primary historical material, see Martha J. Reineke, "'This is my Body': Reflections on Abjection, Anorexia, and Medieval Women Mystics," *Journal of the American Academy of Religion* 58, no. 2 (1990): 245–65.

33   Amy Hollywood, *The Soul as Virgin Wife: Mechthild of Magdeburg, Marguerite Porete, and Meister Eckhart* (Notre Dame: University of Notre Dame, 1995); and Hollywood, "Inside Out: Beatrice of Nazareth and Her Hagiographer," in *Gendered Voices: Medieval Saints and Their Interpreters*, ed. Catherine M. Mooney (Philadelphia: University of Pennsylvania Press, 1999).

34   See Cristina Mazzoni's critique of this comparison in *Saint Hysteria: Neurosis, Mysticism, and Gender in European Culture* (Ithaca, N.Y.: Cornell University Press, 1996).

35   This view of Jesus Christ is most evident in the Gospel of John and the Letters of Paul. The theology of the incarnation was developed through the Trinitarian controversies of the fourth century and the Christological controversies of the fifth century. For a classic theological account, see Athanasius, *On the Incarnation*.

36   *Il Libro*, 714 (*Complete Works*, 308), translation modified and emphasis added. The editors of the critical edition of *Il Libro* date this letter to the middle of 1308; it appears to be authentic.

37   Angela here participates in a long tradition that is more prominent in Eastern theology, such as in Athanasius' *On the Incarnation*, sec. 54: "He, indeed, assumed humanity that we might become God."

38   *Il Libro*, 734 (*Complete Works*, 315). One might also translate "amplexatus est me" as "copulated with me," indicating, as the previous words attest, a much more intimate union than an embrace.

39   *Instruction* XXXVI was likely composed by a scribe after Angela's death and based on her remembered words, but Paul Lachance thinks her deathbed visions and teachings are authentic. See his introduction to the complicated history of the *Instructions'* redaction in *Complete Works*, 81–84.

40   Cixous, "Coming to Writing," 12.

41   According to Paul Lachance, "There are three narrators: God speaks and reveals himself to Angela, and she in turn speaks to Arnaldo, who, as the prologue to the Memorial affirms, then narrates what he hears. At the end both claim that it is God who signed the book." *Complete Works*, 47. The text itself, however, is not related in such a sequential fashion. The multiplicity of voices in Angela's *Book* presents a form of "heteroglossia," the term coined for this literary feature by Mikhail Bakhtin in *The Dialogic Imagination*, ed. Michael Holquist, trans. Caryl Emerson and Michael Holquist (Austin: University of Texas Press, 1981). For a reading of medieval women's texts using the literary theories of Bakhtin, see Finke, *Feminist Theory*.

42   Jacques Derrida describes how writing is always productive of other writings, rewritings, and interpretations, so that every written text is, in a sense, unfinished, deferring final meaning. See Derrida, *Of Grammatology*; and *Writing and Difference*.

Chapter 5

1   Sisoes, saying 3 in *The Sayings of the Desert Fathers: The Alphabetical Collection*, trans. Benedicta Ward (Kalamazoo, Mich.: Cistercian Publications, 1975), 213.

2   Derwas Chitty, *The Desert a City* (Oxford: Basil Blackwell, 1966).

3   An anchorite is a monk who lives a solitary life, as opposed to a cenobite, who lives in community. Sarah, sayings 4 and 9 in *Sayings of the Desert Fathers*, 230.

4   See, e.g., Stephanie Y. Mitchem, *Introducing Womanist Theology* (Maryknoll, N.Y.: Orbis Books, 2005), 19–22.

5   See, e.g., Joan M. Martin, *More Than Chains and Toil: A Christian Work Ethic of Enslaved Women* (Louisville, Ky.: Westminster John Knox, 2000).

6   James Cone uses a similar method. See, especially, "Speaking the Truth" in his *God of the Oppressed* (Maryknoll, N.Y.: Orbis Books, 1997), 15–35.

7   Mitchem, *Introducing Womanist Theology*, 79.

8   Delores Williams, "Womanist Theology: Black Women's Voices," in *Weaving the Visions: New Patterns in Feminist Spirituality*, ed. Judith Plaskow and Carol P. Christ (San Francisco: Harper Collins, 1989), 183.

9   Delores Williams, "A Womanist Perspective on Sin," in *A Troubling in my Soul: Womanist Perspectives on Evil and Suffering*, ed. Emilie M. Townes (Maryknoll, N.Y.: Orbis Books, 1993), 130–49.

10   Dwight N. Hopkins, *Shoes that Fit Our Feet: Sources for a Constructive Black Theology* (Maryknoll, N.Y.: Orbis Books, 1999), 51.

11   Williams, "A Womanist Perspective on Sin," 143.

12   Hopkins, *Shoes that Fit Our Feet*, 60.

13   It is possible that Amma Sarah did not internalize the androcentric assumptions of her day and only intended her riposte to turn the tables on her harrassers. Nevertheless, her insult would not have been effective if her opponents themselves had not internalized those assumptions. She chose to speak in the language of self-negation in order to be heard at all. Other women we meet in this study deployed different strageies of resistance.

14   Womanism emphasizes the ways in which race, class, and gender are inseparably linked in the marginalization of poor black women. In late antiquity, we see how two of these dimensions, class and gender, work together to confine women's choices. The understanding of race in late antiquity, however, differs too dramatically from its function in a contemporary North American context to include it in the analysis offered here.

15   See, e.g., Elizabeth A. Clark, "Holy Women, Holy Words: Early Christian Women, Social History, and the 'Linguistic Turn,'" *Journal of Early Christian Studies* 6, no. 3 (1998): 413–30; and "Ascetic Renunciation and Feminine Advancement: A Paradox of Late Ancient Christianity" and "Authority and Humility: A Conflict of Values in Fourth-Century Female Monasticism," in *Ascetic Piety and Women's Faith: Essays on Late Ancient Christianity* (Lewiston, N.Y.: Mellen Press, 1986), 175–208 and 209–28.

16   Clark, "Holy Women, Holy Words," 414.

17   Gillian Clark, *Women in Late Antiquity: Pagan and Christian Lifestyles* (New York: Oxford University Press, 1993), 15.

18   This generalization may not hold for Christians not of the homoousian, the emerging orthodox, variety. Susanna Elm points out the great variety of expressions of Christian asceticism in late antiquity in her work *"Virgins of God": The Making of Asceticism in Late Antiquity* (Oxford: Clarendon, 1994).

19   Jantzen, *Power*, 214. Bynum and Jantzen present their arguments with reference to medieval women, but the point may also be valid for women ascetics in late antiquity.

20   Pseudo-Athanasius, *The Life of Blessed Syncletica*, trans. Elizabeth Bryson Bongie (Toronto: Peregrina Publishing, 1996), 31.

21   Pseudo-Athanasius, *Life of Blessed Syncletica*, 25.

22   Pseudo-Athanasius, *Life of Blessed Syncletica*, 31.

23   Pseudo-Athanasius, *Life of Blessed Syncletica*, 50.

24   Pseudo-Athanasius, *Life of Blessed Syncletica*, 51.

25   Pseudo-Athanasius, *Life of Blessed Syncletica*, 58.

26   Pseudo-Athanasius, *Life of Blessed Syncletica*, 40.

27   Roberta Bondi discusses this view of humility in her work *To Love as God Loves: Conversations with the Early Church* (Minneapolis: Fortress, 1987).

28   Pseudo-Athanasius, *Life of Blessed Syncletica*, 32.

29   Athanasius, "On the Incarnation of the Word," trans. A. Robertson, in *Athanasius: Select Works and Letters*. Nicene and Post-Nicene Fathers, ed. Philip Schaff and Henry Wace (Peabody, Mass.: Hendrickson, 1994), 36–67. For those far advanced in the disciplines of virtue, for those farthest along in their struggle against the passions, even the body will show the signs of incorruptibility as a proleptic participation in the deathlessness of the life to come. For his own depiction of an ascetic whose body becomes virtually incorruptible, see Athanasius, *Life of Antony and the Letter to Marcellinus* (Mahwah, N.J.: Paulist Press, 1980).

30   Pseudo-Athanasius, *Life of Blessed Syncletica*, 68.

31   Pseudo-Athanasius, *Life of Blessed Syncletica*, 70.

32   Gregory of Nyssa, *The Life of Saint Macrina*, trans. Kevin Corrigan (Toronto: Peregrina Publishing, 1997), 25.

33   Gregory of Nyssa, *Life of Saint Macrina*, 19

34   Gregory of Nyssa, "On the Making of Man," trans. H. A. Wilson, in *Gregory of Nyssa: Dogmatic Treatises, Etc.*, Nicene and Post-Nicene Fathers, 406.

35   Gregory of Nyssa, "On Not Three Gods," trans. H. A. Wilson, in *Gregory of Nyssa: Dogmatic Treatises, Etc.*, Nicene and Post-Nicene Fathers, 331–39.

36   Gregory does not explain this odd assertion. He simply claims that originally God intended humankind to procreate through "that mode by which the angels were increased and multiplied," but that this cannot be done after sin. See "On the Making of Man," 407.

37   Gregory especially endorsed virginity as a path to redemption, though he noted that it was a path unavailable to him. See Gregory of Nyssa, "On Virginity," in *Gregory of Nyssa: Dogmatic Treatieses, Etc.*, Nicene and Post-Nicene Fathers, 343–71.

38   Gregory of Nyssa, *Life of Saint Macrina*, 23.

39   Peter Brown, *The Body and Society: Men, Women, and Sexual Renunciation in Early Christianity* (New York: Columbia University Press, 1988), 263.

40   Clark, "Holy Women, Holy Words," 417; Elm, *"Virgins of God,"* 39–47.

41   Gregory of Nyssa, *Life of Saint Macrina*, 28.

42   Gregory of Nyssa, *Life of Saint Macrina*, 30.

43   Gregory of Nyssa, *Life of Saint Macrina*, 25.

44   Elm notes that this gift could have taken the form of a temporary trust, in which case the wealth would have reverted to the family estate after Macrina's death. Elm, *"Virgins of God,"* 89.

45   Gregory of Nyssa, *Life of Saint Macrina*, 25.

46   Elm, *"Virgins of God,"* 94.

47 Gregory of Nyssa, *Life of Saint Macrina*, 38.

48 Gregory advocated the view that the Father and the Son shared the same essence or substance. The Greek term for "same essence" is *homoousias*.

49 Clark notes that though it was rare for a woman to do so, some did engage in public teaching and disputation. See Clark, "Ascetic Renunciation and Feminine Advancement," 187.

50 Gregory of Nyssa, "On the Soul and the Resurrection," in *Gregory of Nyssa: Dogmatic Treatises, Etc.*, Nicene and Post-Nicene Fathers, 430–68.

51 Kevin Corrigan, introduction to *Life of Saint Macrina*, 14.

52 Gregory of Nyssa, *Life of Saint Macrina*, 39.

53 Georgia Frank suggests that the narrative of the discovery of this scar may serve as an allusion to Homer's *Odyssey* where a disguised Odysseus is revealed as the returning hero when a servant recognizes his scar. See Georgia Frank, "Macrina's Scar: Homeric Allusion and Heroic Identity in Gregory of Nyssa's *Life of Macrina*," *Journal of Early Christian Studies* 8, no. 4 (2000): 511–30.

Chapter 6

1 Sara Maitland, *A Book of Silence* (Berkeley: Counterpoint, 2008), 28.

2 Maitland, *Book of Silence*, 260. Emphasis in original.

3 Sara Maitland, *A Big-Enough God: A Feminist's Search for a Joyful Theology* (New York: Henry Holt, 1995).

4 Maitland, *Book of Silence*, 13. Emphasis in original.

5 Maitland, *Book of Silence*, 14.

6 Maitland, *Book of Silence*, 31.

7 Maitland, *Book of Silence*, 36.

8 Maitland, *Book of Silence*, 31–33.

9 Maitland, *Book of Silence*, 28.

10 Maitland, *Book of Silence*, 29.

11 See also page 221 of *A Book of Silence* for a description of the connection between landscape, silence, and freedom. Writing about her pilgrimage to the Sinai desert, Maitland says, "In the desert I learned that silence is more for me than a context for prayer. . . . It is, in itself, a form of freedom; it generates freedom, free choices, inner clarity, and strength. A freedom from one's self and a freedom to be oneself."

12 Maitland, *Book of Silence*, 190.

13 Maitland, *Book of Silence*, 192.

14 Maitland recognizes and discusses other practices and models of silence besides these two, for example, the silence of the Buddhist meditation practitioner and the silence of a Jacques Cousteau explorer. But she devotes more analysis to these two types of silence—the contemplative prayer of the desert hermits versus the "bliss of solitude" sought by the

Romantic poets—to illustrate the two competing paradigms that most captivate her.

15 Maitland, *Book of Silence*, 12.

16 Maitland, *Book of Silence*, 192. Emphasis in original.

17 Maitland, *Book of Silence*, 244.

18 Maitland, *Book of Silence*, 245–46.

19 Maitland, *Book of Silence*, 216.

20 Maitland, *Book of Silence*, 216.

21 Beverly J. Lanzetta, *Radical Wisdom: A Feminist Mystical Theology* (Minneapolis: Fortress, 2005), 99–100. Lanzetta urges readers to appreciate "the intense focus the women mystics placed on achieving the highest spiritual potential and on developing a sophisticated mystical vocabulary to explain the structures of consciousness, contemplative processes, and spiritual techniques in the journey of faith. . . . Personal religious experience was never for its own sake, but was a window into a complex world of learning in which theology—study of God—and mysticism—how to become one with God—were intertwined."

22 Maitland, *Book of Silence*, 285.

23 Maitland, *Book of Silence*, 119. Emphasis in original.

24 Maitland, *Book of Silence*, 121.

25 Maitland, *Book of Silence*, 125.

26 Maitland, *Book of Silence*, 221–22. Emphasis in original.

27 Maitland, *Book of Silence*, 193. Emphasis in original.

28 Maitland, *Book of Silence*, 285.

29 Virginia Woolf, *A Room of One's Own* (New York: Harcourt, Brace & World, 1929), 113.

30 Luce Irigaray, *The Way of Love* (London: Continuum, 2002), 15.

31 Luce Irigaray, *Sharing the World* (London: Continuum, 2008).

32 Irigaray explains to an interviewer, "I talked about silence [in *I Love To You* and *To Be Two*] the way one conceives of the child . . . . I tried to show how in order to keep loving each other man and woman have to beget silence, a condition of their own becoming, each on one's own and together." For Irigaray, silence is a necessary precondition of love and respect. Luce Irigaray, "Man and Woman in Search of Harmony," in *Why Different? A Culture of Two Subjects: Interviews with Luce Irigaray* (New York: Columbia University Press, 2002), 107.

33 Luce Irigaray, "The Spirit of Women Blows," in *Why Different?*, 175. See also Luce Irigaray, *I Love To You: Sketch of a Possible Felicity in History*, trans. Alison Martin (London: Routledge, 1996), 123–24.

34 Maitland, *Book of Silence*, 248. "The psychoanalytic silence does depend on an article of faith: that naming, speaking oneself, is essential to freedom and integrity. . . . Now I would question whether psychoanalysis is appro-

priate or even possible for anyone who is seriously given to contemplative prayer, partly because of Freud's determination that all faith in God was necessarily neurotic, and partly because so much of the encounter with God in prayer is not merely silent but is ineffable. It cannot be spoken or described and yet it is experienced as completely real."

35   Lanzetta, *Radical Wisdom*, 20.
36   Lanzetta, *Radical Wisdom*, 169.
37   Lanzetta, *Radical Wisdom*, 82. Emphasis in original.
38   Woolf, 113–14. Emphasis added.
39   Maitland, *Book of Silence*, 287.

Chapter 7

1   E. J. Dabney, *What It Means to Pray Through* (Memphis, Tenn.: Church of God in Christ Publishing House, 1945), 58–59. This poem is a tribute to Miss Leta Ashley, a beloved co-laborer.
2   The exact date of birth is not known, but this date is estimated from census data and her narrative.
3   Belinda Robnett, *How Long? How Long? African American Women in the Civil Rights Movement* (New York: Oxford University Press, 1997). Robnett posits that African-American women in social movements who were equipped to be formal leaders at various levels were often denied positions. As such, they occupied the "free spaces" of the movement, where they became the foundation upon which the movement was built. My use of this concept also refers to the forums women made for themselves as a result of gender configurations but also as a deliberate and purposeful place for self-expression and fulfillment. Free spaces then also constitute the outgrowth of women's culture and community.
4   Dabney, *What It Means*, 21.
5   Katie McBurrows, September entry in *The Living Heritage Calendar 1981* (Memphis, Tenn.: Church of God in Christ Publishing House, 1981).
6   McBurrows, *Living Heritage Calendar*.
7   This altar is not a tangible thing, a particular space or object constructed of either wood or stone. Instead, it is a "treaty, promise or covenant between God and an individual to meet at a definite place at a definite time." Dabney, *What It Means*, 7.
8   Dabney, *What It Means*, 7.
9   Dabney, *What It Means*, 7.
10 Dabney, *What It Means*, 7.
11 It was not possible to ascertain from her writing the full nature or types of suffering endured by the ministers and their families. However, it was undoubtedly related to the repressions, exigencies, and strictures of the time period, as well as to the general view of Holiness Pentecostalism.
12 Besides Mo. Dabney's goal of being a public speaker, she and Benjamin

Dabney had plans to buy a home and operate a store. She also states that her husband's musical talents would complement her speaking career. Such goals would, she thought, preclude a life of ministry.

13   This vow was an agreement with God to be committed to a rigorous three-year schedule of prayer. This will be discussed in detail later in the essay.

14   Lucille Cornelius, *The Pioneer: History of the Church of God in Christ* (Memphis, Tenn.: Church of God in Christ Publishing House, 1975), 17.

15   This is the supposition and premise of Anthea Butler's research on women in the Church of God in Christ, entitled *Women in the Church of God in Christ: Making a Sanctified World* (Chapel Hill: University of North Carolina Press, 2007).

16   Lizzie Roberson (referred to as both Roberson and Robinson) was the first appointed head and organizer of the Women's Department. She served in this position from 1911 to her death in 1945. Her initial title was Overseer (the same as male counterparts). Eventually her title changed to National Mother, while male counterparts are titled Bishop.

17   The work of Cheryl Townsend Gilkes, Anthea Butler, and others explores the role of the Church Mother in the African-American church. It is an honorific title and an official position given by the church to a morally and spiritually exemplary person. Generally an elder woman, she is a person of high authority and exercises power in the affairs of the church. Often cast in traditional images of caretaker and nurturer, these women utilized their authority in "nontraditional and traditional" ways. The title Mother grows out of this position and is extended to a variety of women in the church beyond the role of Church Mother.

18   Mo. Coffey assumed leadership after Mo. Roberson's death. She was the second in command under Mo. Roberson. During her leadership, she changed the title of the position to General Supervisor of Women. She served until 1964.

19   This may also have been part of the influence on her son pursuing and receiving a degree in English.

20   Bishop O. T. Jones (1891–1972) is an important figure in the life and formative years of the denomination. He was a minister, pastor, and eventually a Bishop, who was elected to the General Board of the denomination. The hallmark of his work was authoring and publishing (in 1916) the first series of Bible study materials for youth. He was said to promote women's rights, to engage the topics of the day, and to advocate for youth in the life of the church. His son follows in his footsteps, continuing work with youth and advocating for women.

21   Dabney, *What It Means*, 11–12.

22   Dabney, *What It Means*, 13.

23 Dabney, *What It Means*, 15.

24 Leonard Lovett, "Black Holiness Pentecostalism: Implications for Ethics and Social Transformation" (Ph.D. diss., Emory University, 1979), 70–75. Lovett identifies the dialectic of authority operative in Black Holiness Pentecostalism. This dialectic holds in tension the authority vested in the preacher, the Scripture, and experience. In varying circumstances, each holds normative authority and acts to limit the influence of the others. Each is part of a pivotal theocultural paradigm that shapes and directs personal authority and empowerment in the Church of God in Christ.

25 Dabney, *What It Means*, 68. This account is written by Miss Jeanette Jones, a co-laborer from Los Angeles, California, who chronicles part of Mo. Dabney's prayer ministry.

26 The Black Women's Club Movement emerged in the mid 1890s, with the greatest thrust of their work culminating in the 1940s. In 1895 in Boston, Massachusetts, the National Association of Colored Women began and continues today typifying the work of the Black Women's Club Movement.

27 Ann Allen Shockley, *Afro-American Women Writers, 1746–1933: An Anthology and Critical Guide* (Boston: G. K. Hall, 1988), 280.

28 The New Negro Movement or Harlem Renaissance (1917–1930s) announced the emergence of a New Negro—intellectual, independent, defiant, and unafraid to be so. Though the revolutionary quality of its perspectives is debated in African-American circles, it is one of the richest periods of authorship for African-Americans.

29 Bishop Mason, cofounder of the denomination, was known as a man of prayer, dedicating two to three hours of every morning in prayer and making it a central feature of his fifty-plus years of administration. It is the hallmark of his ministry. Prominent are stories of healings performed and of conflicts addressed, etc., through the work of prayer. Beginning in 1897, from the initiation of the Holiness Association, Bishop Mason served as coleader with Rev. Charles Price Jones, and as the head of its organization as a Pentecostal body in 1907 until his death in 1961.

30 A prayer warrior is one who is dedicated to the ministry of prayer. Prayer warriors are intercessors who bolster the ministry of the pastoral leadership, the congregants, and the body of believers through their prayers. A great part of that work is fighting Satan on behalf of the church so that believers will work out their salvation and achieve divine victory by being empowered witnesses in the world.

31 Dabney, *What It Means*, 74. In a chapter entitled "His Prayer Life Influenced Me," her introductory words are insightful. "Bishop Mason lives in Memphis, Tennessee. His work and humble devotion to Christ is noted throughout Christendom. I have told you how his conversation

with God attracted my attention and stirred my enthusiasm to covet the spirit of prayer like unto his. He is a little man in stature, but his heart is big, and it is full of love and compassion for everybody everywhere."

32 Butler, *Women in the Church of God in Christ*, 36–37.

33 Ms. Duncan was the founder of the Saints Industrial Academy. She established the elementary level, and eventually it was renamed Saints Academy. Initially directed by Professor James Courts, Dr. Arenia C. Mallory became the head of Saints Academy in 1926. For 50 years Dr. Mallory led the school to denominational and national acclaim. Dr. Mallory, with Mo. Coffey, was active in work with Mary McLeod Bethune.

34 Not much information is available on Faye Bress. I surmise that she was a European-American Christian woman laboring in the gospel and with connections to various Christian ministries and publications that promote mission work.

35 The Azusa Street Revival, 1906–1909, took place in Los Angeles, California, and for three years attracted millions from around the United States and the world. Out of its ecumenical, interracial, and gender-open atmosphere and practices, Pentecostal denominations formed all over the world. William J. Seymour is known as the Father of the Twentieth-Century Movement, and Emma Cotton, Jennie Moore, Lucy Farrow, and others are key figures. See Vinson Synan, *The Holiness-Pentecostal Movement in the United States* (Grand Rapids, Mich.: Eerdmans, 1997); Rufus G. W. Sanders, *William Joseph Seymour, 1870–1922: Black Father of the 20th-Century Pentecostal/Charismatic Movement* (Longwood, Fla.: Xulon Press, 2009); Estrelda Alexander, *The Women of Azusa Street* (Cleveland: Pilgrim Press, 2005); Cecil Robeck, *The Azusa Street Mission and Revival: The Birth of the Global Pentecostal Movement* (Nashville: Thomas Nelson, 2006).

36 These are Misses Stover, Davis, and Serby, Bible school teachers who were co-laborers with her.

37 The exact date of her return to Los Angeles is not given. Mo. Dabney's initiation of national prayer revivals occurred from 1934 to 1939, after her vow was completed. It is likely that this trip took place in the latter period, around 1937–1939.

38 Dabney, *What It Means*, 38–39.

39 For Mo. Dabney, prayer is the first work as it readies the heart for the Word and is the foundation of all work. "It opens the ground for 'His Gospel plow' the Word. It will send the Word piercing through stony hearts; it will sail across the ocean faster than a plane can go; it will take the hand of a lost soul and unite it with our Lovely Saviour." Dabney, *What It Means*, 37–38.

40 Dabney, *What It Means*, 56.

41 Joanne Braxton, *Black Women Writing Autobiography: A Tradition Within a Tradition* (Philadelphia: Temple University Press, 1989), 39–80.

42 Cheryl Sanders, *Saints in Exile: The Holiness-Pentecostal Experience in African American Religion and Culture* (New York: Oxford University Press, 1996), 3–4. Sanders says that the Sanctified Church "emerged within the black community to distinguish congregations of 'the saints' from those of other black Christians, especially the black Baptists and Methodists," who were seen as culturally and organizationally modeling European-American patriarchy. These churches arose out of the Holiness Movement and were seen as reformist, calling churches to a life of biblical holiness.

43 Braxton, *Black Women Writing Autobiography*, 49–50.

44 Dabney, *What It Means*, 49.

45 Shawn Copeland, "Wading Through Many Sorrows: Towards a Theology of Suffering in Womanist Perspective," in *A Troubling in My Soul: Womanist Perspectives on Evil and Suffering*, ed. Emilie M. Townes (Maryknoll, N.Y.: Orbis Books, 1993), 109–29.

46 Williams, *Sisters in the Wilderness*, 60–83.

47 Lovett, "Black Holiness Pentecostalism," 69.

48 C. F. Range Jr., ed., *Church of God in Christ Official Manual* (Memphis, Tenn.: Church of God in Christ Publishing House, 1973), 144–46. It states that "the Church of God in Christ recognizes the scriptural importance of women in the Christian Ministry . . . . but nowhere can we find a mandate to ordain women . . . . Paul styled the women who labored with him as servants or helpers, not Elders, Bishops or Pastors" (146).

49 Dabney, *What It Means*, 19–20.

50 Dabney, *What It Means*, 38.

51 The outpouring of the Spirit at the Azusa Street Revival is often compared to that in Acts. It is posited by many scholars that Pentecost as it is recorded in Acts 2 and the Pentecost at Azusa Street evoke similar characteristics. Egalitarianism and inclusivity are evidenced in that women are present at both events and are an integral part of this new birthing of and in the church. This was particularly true at Azusa Street, as women held key leadership positions and worked daily with the worship services as well as in the administration of the church. Social relations crossed cultural, class, denominational, and language barriers. Acts evidences bringing together varying languages and cultures. The Azusa Street Revival for a period of three years brought together persons of varying races and nationalities such that the event was said to eliminate the color line.

52 Range, *Official Manual*, 79–93. The *Official Manual* gives a sense of what this means. It stresses the importance of a common dogma and provides profiles of particular faiths not approved of.

53 Butler, *Women in the Church of God in Christ*, 119.

54   Dabney, *What It Means*, 26.
55   Dabney, *What It Means*, 44.
56   Dabney, *What It Means*, 54.
57   Dabney, *What It Means*, 51.
58   It was often the practice that women missionaries would "dig out" (or plant) churches in the field. They would evangelize, organize the new converts, teach Bible study, and preach, but then an ordained Elder (only males) would be sent by a Bishop to pastor the new congregation.
59   Dabney, *What It Means*, 63.
60   Dabney, *What It Means*, 71.
61   Dabney, *What It Means*, 71.
62   Dabney, *What It Means*, 10. This is said when she decides to accept her husband's call and answer to the gospel ministry.
63   Dabney, *What It Means*, 39.
64   Quote from Patrice Dickerson in Patricia Collins, *Black Feminist Thought: Knowledge, Consciousness and the Politics of Empowerment* (New York: Routledge, 1990), 35.
65   Jacquelyn Grant, "The Sin of Servanthood and the Deliverance of Discipleship," in *A Troubling in My Soul*, 199–218.
66   Dabney, *What It Means*, 27.

Chapter 8

✳   I am grateful to Emily Holmes, the volume's editor, not only for initiating and seeing this volume through its many stages of development, but also for her insight, adept editorial skill, gentle persistence, and friendship concerning this particular essay.
1   Hagiographic stories are shaped and told for particular pedagogical reasons. In their formative capacity, they reveal the values and hopes of the teller. Thus, hagiographic tellings can be instances of power that are deployed and influential on individuals, especially children and young people. For example, a less controversial hagiographic telling might be of Joseph, the father of Jesus. Although every social and religious convention during his time would have supported his desisting his betrothal to Mary, nevertheless Joseph trusted both the angel of God, who revealed himself in a dream telling Joseph to stay with Mary, and the dream itself as a form of legitimate communication by God. A much more controversial figure is Maria Goretti, who was killed at age 11 during an attempted rape in which she refused to submit to her attacker. She was canonized by Pope Pius XII in 1950 for her purity as a model for youth. Although Goretti is revered by many, a hagiographic upshot is that apparently sexual purity for girls is more important than life itself, thus equating and reducing the life of girls and women to their sexed bodies, a hagiographic

telling that reifies certain misogynistic and patriarchal threads within the development of institutional Christianity.

2   Thomas Head, introduction to *Medieval Hagiography: An Anthology*, by Thomas Head (New York: Routledge, 2001), xvii–xviii, referencing nn. 14, 15, xxxiv.

3   Stein was arrested by the Nazis shortly after the Dutch Roman Catholic bishops spoke out against the Nazi occupation of Holland, where Stein had fled from Germany. As retaliation, Stein and other "Jewish Catholics" were arrested and eventually murdered. Rome argues that she was martyred for her faith (and indeed she was canonized in the category of martyr). Critics argue that she was murdered precisely because of her Jewish background and that canonizing an apostate from Judaism not only does *not* strengthen Jewish-Catholic relations (as some have argued that Rome wanted to do), but it also tries to appropriate the Jewish *shoah* as a fundamental betrayal of and assault on Christianity, specifically Roman Catholicism. The various ways in which Stein is read are themselves fascinating and significantly cultivate interest in her personhood.

4   Sister Teresia de Spiritu Sancto, *Edith Stein*, trans. Cecily Hastings and Donald Nicholl (New York: Sheed & Ward, 1952), 64. Confirmed in Edith Stein, *Wie Ich in den Kölner Karmel Kam*, ed. Maria Amata Neyer (Würzburg, Germany: Echter, 1994). Confirmed also in Edith Stein, *Self-Portrait in Letters*, trans. Josephine Koeppel (Washington, D.C.: ICS Publications, 1993), letter 158a.

5   Today the discalced or "barefoot" Carmelites that Teresa founded (they usually wear brown open-toed sandals) continue in existence both within Roman Catholic and other Catholic churches in communion with the Roman Church, as well as in the Anglican Communion.

6   Edith Stein, *On the Problem of Empathy*, trans. Waltraut Stein (Washington, D.C.: ICS Publications, 1989), 6.

7   Edith Stein, *Philosophy of Psychology and the Humanities (Individual and Community)*, ed. Marianne Sawicki, trans. Mary Catherine Baseheart and Marianne Sawicki (Washington, D.C.: ICS Publications, 2000), 148.

8   Stein, *On the Problem of Empathy*, 6.

9   Stein, *On the Problem of Empathy*, 11.

10   This kind of empathetic understanding is also the basis for intersubjectivity.

11   See my dissertation, "A Performance of Being and the Enacting Texts of Edith Stein" (Ph.D. diss., Emory University, 2006).

12   I am open to other interpretations of what "the truth" might be or mean.

13   Edith Stein, *The Hidden Life*, ed. Lucy Gelber and Michael Linssen, trans. Waltraut Stein (Washington, D.C.: ICS Publications, 1992). This book is a collection of hagiographic essays that Stein wrote, many for the purpose of educating her religious communities.

14   Lucy Gelber, introduction to *The Hidden Life*, xix–xx.

15 Stein, "A Chosen Vessel of Divine Wisdom: Sr. Marie-Aimée de Jésus of the Carmel of the Avenue de Saxe in Paris, 1839–1874," *The Hidden Life*, 81.

16 Stein, "A Chosen Vessel of Divine Wisdom," *The Hidden Life*, 81.

17 Stein, "A Chosen Vessel of Divine Wisdom," *The Hidden Life*, 81.

18 Stein, "A Chosen Vessel of Divine Wisdom," *The Hidden Life*, 82.

19 Stein, "I Am Always in Your Midst," *The Hidden Life*, 117.

20 Stein, "I Am Always in Your Midst," *The Hidden Life*, 119.

21 Stein, "I Am Always in Your Midst," *The Hidden Life*, 120.

22 Stein, "I Am Always in Your Midst," *The Hidden Life*, 120.

23 Stein, "I Am Always in Your Midst," *The Hidden Life*, 120.

24 Stein, "I Am Always in Your Midst," *The Hidden Life*, 120.

25 Stein's letter to Pius XI is available online at http://www.baltimorecarmel .org/saints/Stein/letter%20to%20pope.htm.

26 The theatrical masks worn by actors in ancient Greece were called *personae*. Dramatic characters were recognized not only by their actions, but also through the sounds (*per-sonare*) that were made, resonated, and projected through masks. Although "person" derives its existence from "persona," and thus personhood (being) is achieved through speaking and doing, nevertheless as Western theological thought developed an emphasis on the importance of a fixed or static "I," *person* came to mean real and *persona* came to mean fake. Thus, masks and persona have negative connotations (although increasingly people seem to be mindful of the various *roles* that we play). An individual can only be what she or he already has the capacity toward, but the development and living into of such being capacity depends on doing.

27 Stein, *The Hidden Life*, 129.

28 Lucy Gelber, introduction to *The Hidden Life*, xxiii.

29 Stein, *The Hidden Life*, 132.

30 Emphasis added. At the third ecumenical Council of Ephesus in 431 C.E., Mary is declared to be the "Theotokos," or God-bearer. While this title certainly grants to Mary an elevated status, the doctrinal definition is less about her and more about Jesus. For if Mary were not Theotokos, the divine-human status of Jesus could be questioned.

31 Stein, *The Hidden Life*, 129.

32 Stein, *The Hidden Life*, 130.

33 Stein, *The Hidden Life*, 131.

34 Stein, *Self-Portrait in Letters*, 291, letter 281. The bracketed text here is original to the editor/translator of the Stein letter. The double brackets are added along with the emphasis.

35 Save the Jews from what, I'm not sure, but I suspect Stein meant an eternity without Christ, a statement by her that reflects not only an exclusive soteriology that she came to embrace, but also her full awareness of

the dire situation in Europe. By this point in time, in addition to being a refugee herself, many of her family members had fled Germany.

36 Despite the importance of masking for Stein, her explicit attitude toward masking and masks is typical of a Western attitude (the history of masking is complex, and masking has not always been considered as an attempt to deceive or be fake). She writes, "These typical manners of behavior aren't 'masks' that the individual takes up and under which the individual conceals his 'true face' (although that can be the case, too). Rather, the individual renders himself in the 'social perspective' which is required by the 'social slant' of the moment and which at each moment corresponds to one or another of his essential traits. For in every single case, the typical behavior and the type itself receive their individual imprint from the persons who enter into them" (Stein, *Philosophy of Psychology and the Humanities*, 293). For Stein, masking carries a negative connotation. This is the case, I think, because of how important for Stein is unmediated relationship between the human and God.

37 "Secrets" is a common and multivalent theme in Teresa of Avila's *Book of Her Life*. For Teresa, "secret" can mean God's hidden revelations to Teresa (e.g., chaps. 21:15; 22:9; 27:11, 13, 18; 38:3), the intimacy of prayer (e.g., chap. 8:7), not disclosing to others what is occurring in her prayer life (e.g., chaps. 23:14; 26:5). Angela of Foligno, the thirteenth-century Italian mystic, also said frequently "my secret is mine"; Teresa was probably influenced by her. In the *Vulgate*, which Stein would have been familiar with, Isaiah 24:16 is rendered "secretum meum mihi." Perhaps Stein's use of this phrase is an incorporation of all of these dimensions.

38 See n. 3 above.

39 Plato, *Republic*, trans. G. M. A. Grube (Indianapolis: Hackett, 1974), 376e–383c.

40 Stein asserts that there is no *dogmatic* reason to withhold priestly ordination from women, although her own understanding of the maleness of Jesus, ecclesial tradition, and sexual ontology does not permit it in her own thinking. However, Stein perceives no dogmatic or traditional bar to women's ordination to the diaconate (Edith Stein, *Woman*, trans. Freda Mary Oben [Washington, D.C.: ICS Publications, 1996], 83–84). A difficulty in understanding the consistency of Stein's philosophical thought is that although she refuses to essentialize an individual's race or religion, she *is* willing to essentialize that person's sex and gender.

41 I am grateful to Wendy Farley, who helped me to focus my thinking and language around the significance of Stein's discipleship.

Chapter 9

1 Simone Weil, *Gravity and Grace*, trans. Emma Craufurd (London: Routledge, 1995), 35–36.

2 See my "The Body of Christ, Broken: Child Sexual Abuse Trauma and the Communion of Compassion" (Ph.D. diss., Emory University, 2004); and "The Yearning that is Joy: Hunger for God and Compassionate Care for Survivors of Child Sexual Abuse Trauma," paper presented to Feminist Theory and Religious Reflection Group, American Academy of Religion Annual Meeting, Chicago, November 3, 2008.

3 Paul Celan, *Collected Prose*, trans. Rosmarie Waldrop (Riverdale-on-Hudson, N.Y.: The Sheep Meadow Press, 1986), 35.

4 Simone de Beauvoir, *Memoirs of a Dutiful Daughter*, trans. James Kirkup (New York: Harper & Row, 1974), quoted in Simone Pétrement, *Simone Weil: A Life*, trans. Raymond Rosenthal (New York: Schocken Books, 1976), 51.

5 George Herbert, *The Complete English Poems*, ed. John Tobin (London: Penguin Books, 2004), 178.

6 Simone Weil, "Spiritual Autobiography," in *Waiting for God*, trans. Emma Craufurd (New York: Perennial Classics, 2001), 27.

7 Weil, "Hesitations Concerning Baptism," in *Waiting for God*, 6–7.

8 Judith Van Herik, "Simone Weil's Religious Imagery: How Looking Becomes Eating," in *Immaculate and Powerful: The Female in Sacred Image and Social Reality*, ed. Clarissa W. Atkinson, Constance H. Buchanan, and Margaret R. Miles (Boston: Beacon Press, 1985), 267.

9 Pétrement, *Simone Weil: A Life*, 11.

10 Pétrement, *Simone Weil: A Life*, 81.

11 Pétrement, *Simone Weil: A Life*, 82.

12 Pétrement, *Simone Weil: A Life*, 227.

13 Pétrement, *Simone Weil: A Life*, 377.

14 Pétrement, *Simone Weil: A Life*, 490.

15 Pétrement, *Simone Weil: A Life*, 420.

16 Pétrement, *Simone Weil: A Life*, 537.

17 Pétrement, *Simone Weil: A Life*, 538.

18 Simone Weil, appendix to *Gateway to God*, ed. David Raper (New York: Crossroad, 1982), 149.

19 Simone Weil, *First and Last Notebooks*, trans. Richard Rees (London: Oxford University Press, 1970), 284.

20 Simone Weil, "Draft for a Statement of Human Obligations," in *Simone Weil Reader*, ed. George A. Panichas (Wakefield, R.I.: Moyer Bell, 1999), 219.

21 Weil, "Draft for a Statement of Human Obligations," in *Simone Weil Reader*, 222.

22 Weil, "The Love of God and Affliction," in *Waiting for God*, 71.

23 Weil, "Human Personality," in *Simone Weil Reader*, 332.

24 Weil, "Forms of the Implicit Love of God," in *Waiting for God*, 105.

25 Weil, *First and Last Notebooks*, 284–85.

26 Weil, *First and Last Notebooks*, 110.

27 Weil, *First and Last Notebooks*, 286.

28 Weil, "Forms of the Implicit Love of God," in *Waiting for God*, 106.

29 Weil, "Reflections on the Right Use of School Studies with a View to the Love of God," in *Waiting for God*, 65.

30 Weil, *First and Last Notebooks*, 129.

31 Weil, *First and Last Notebooks*, 297.

32 Weil, *First and Last Notebooks*, 213.

33 Weil, *First and Last Notebooks*, 72.

34 Weil, *First and Last Notebooks*, 72. The rending of God at creation and in the crucifixion are, indeed, the movement of the same love: "This tearing apart [at the crucifixion], over which supreme love places the bond of supreme union, echoes perpetually across the universe in the midst of the silence, like two notes, separate yet melting into one, like pure and heart-rending harmony. This is the Word of God. The whole creation is nothing but its vibration."

35 Weil, "The Love of God and Affliction," in *Waiting for God*, 68.

36 Weil, "The *Iliad*, Poem of Might," in *Simone Weil Reader*, 155.

37 Weil, "The Love of God and Affliction," in *Waiting for God*, 69.

38 Weil, "The Love of God and Affliction," in *Waiting for God*, 73.

39 Weil, "The Love of God and Affliction," in *Waiting for God*, 74.

40 Pétrement, *Simone Weil: A Life*, 420.

41 Pétrement, *Simone Weil: A Life*, 524.

42 Weil, "Theory of the Sacraments," in *Gateway to God*, 56.

43 Weil, "Theory of the Sacraments," in *Gateway to God*, 57.

44 Weil, "Theory of the Sacraments," in *Gateway to God*, 60. In linking hunger and compassionate practice and in conceiving of Eucharist as a purifying fire, Weil's thought resonates profoundly with that of the fifteenth-century mystic Catherine of Genoa. Indeed, Caroline Walker Bynum sees Weil as standing within a tradition of medieval women mystics whose food refusal fueled their devotion to God and their care for afflicted persons. Catherine of Genoa and Battistina Vernazza, *The Life and Doctrine of Saint Catherine of Genoa*, trans. unknown (New York: Christian Press Association Publishing, 1907), 10–11, http://www.ccel.org/ccel/catherine_g/life.html; Bynum, *Holy Feast and Holy Fast*, 297.

45 Weil, "Theory of the Sacraments," in *Gateway to God*, 61.

46 Weil also considers Eucharist in "Forms of the Implicit Love of God," in *Waiting for God*. For an excellent discussion of Weil's argument there, see Ann W. Astell, *Eating Beauty: The Eucharist and the Spiritual Arts of the Middle Ages* (Ithaca, N.Y.: Cornell University Press, 2006), chap. 7.

47 Weil, "Forms of the Implicit Love of God," in *Waiting for God*, 103.

48   Weil, "Forms of the Implicit Love of God," in *Waiting for God*, 103.

49   Weil, *First and Last Notebooks*, 244.

50   Weil, *First and Last Notebooks*, 96.

51   Alec Irwin, "Devoured by God: Cannibalism, Mysticism, and Ethics in Simone Weil," *Cross Currents* 51, no. 2 (2001): 257–72, 263. It should be noted that Irwin is making a very different argument from mine here, that both the inescapability of human violence and images of a violent God are realities with which we need to reckon.

52   Valerie Saiving, "The Human Situation: A Feminine View," in *Womanspirit Rising: A Feminist Reader in Religion*, ed. Carol P. Christ and Judith Plaskow (New York: Harper & Row, 1979), 25–42; Rita Nakashima Brock and Rebecca Parker, *Proverbs of Ashes: Violence, Redemptive Suffering, and the Search for What Saves Us* (Boston: Beacon Press, 2002).

53   Weil, *First and Last Notebooks*, 96.

54   Weil, "Spiritual Autobiography," in *Waiting for God*, 25.

55   Weil, "Spiritual Autobiography," in *Waiting for God*, 25.

56   Weil, *Gravity and Grace*, 30. Emphasis in original.

57   Weil, *Gravity and Grace*, 36.

58   Weil, *Gravity and Grace*, 35–36. Here Weil resonates again with medieval mystics like Catherine of Genoa: fasting, for Catherine, is a process of the soul becoming the "pure operation of a love which looks for no good that we can do, [which] must needs love him purely, without regard to any particular grace which she receives from him, but looking to him alone, for himself alone, who is worthy of being loved without measure, and with no reference either to soul or body." Catherine and Vernazza, *Life and Doctrine*, 11.

59   Weil, *Gravity and Grace*, 28.

60   Weil, "School Studies," in *Waiting for God*, 64–65.

61   Cathy Caruth, *Unclaimed Experience: Trauma, Narrative, and History* (Baltimore: The Johns Hopkins University Press, 1996), 4.

62   Judith Herman, *Trauma and Recovery* (New York: Basic Books, 1997), 53, Emphasis in original.

63   Dori Laub, "Truth and Testimony: The Process and the Struggle," in *Trauma: Explorations in Memory*, ed. Cathy Caruth (Baltimore: The Johns Hopkins University Press, 1995), 63. Emphasis in original.

64   Susan J. Brison, *Aftermath: Violence and the Remaking of the Self* (Princeton: Princeton University Press, 2002), 16.

65   I am clearly very much indebted to Wendy Farley for this notion of compassion as a power. See her *Tragic Vision and Divine Compassion: A Contemporary Theodicy* (Louisville, Ky.: Westminster John Knox, 1990); and "Evil, Violence, and the Practice of Theodicy," in *Telling the Truth: Preaching about Sexual and Domestic Violence*, ed. John S. McClure and Nancy J. Ramsay (Cleveland: United Church Press, 1998), 11–20.

66 Julian of Norwich, *Showings*, trans. Edmund Colledge, OSA, and James Walsh, SJ (New York: Paulist Press, 1978), 220. For Julian, "all that will be saved" is all of humankind, owing to the love by which all human beings are irrevocably united with God: "For in mankind which will be saved is comprehended all, that is to say all that is made and the maker of all. For God is in man and God is all" (192).

67 Sue Monk Kidd, "Birthing Compassion," in *Communion, Community, Commonweal: Readings for a Spiritual Leadership*, ed. John S. Mogabgab (Nashville, Tenn.: Upper Room Books, 1995), 155.

68 Cathy Caruth characterizes trauma as "always the story of a wound that cries out." Caruth, *Unclaimed Experience*, 4.

69 Weil, *First and Last Notebooks*, 286.

Chapter 10

1 According to the Internal Revenue Service, a non-resident alien is a person who is not a citizen or national of the United States and who is in this country on a visa or temporary basis and does not have the right to remain indefinitely. "Topic 851 — Resident and Non-Resident Aliens," IRS. http://www.irs.gov/taxtopics/tc851.html (accessed March 4, 2010).

2 See my dissertation, "*Corpus Christi*, To Be Eaten and To Be Written — Questioning the Act of Writing in Hadewijch of Antwerp and Theresa Hak Kyung Cha" (Ph.D. diss., Emory University, 2011), 1.

3 The term "the third space" was coined by Homi Bhabha. He argues that "[t]he intervention of the *Third Space of enunciation*, which makes the structure of meaning and reference an ambivalent process, destroys this mirror of representation in which cultural knowledge is customarily revealed as *integrated, open, expanding code.* Such an intervention quite properly challenges our sense of the historical identity of culture as homogenizing, unifying force, authenticated by an originary Past, kept alive in the national tradition of the People." Homi Bhabha, *The Location of Culture* (New York: Routledge, 1994), 543. Emphasis added.

4 Michel de Certeau, *The Practice of Everyday Life* (Berkeley: University of California Press, 1988), 134.

5 See Henri de Lubac, *Corpus Mysticum: The Eucharist and the Church in the Middle Ages* (London: SCM Press, 2006); Paul McPartlan, *The Eucharist Makes the Church: Henri de Lubac and John Zizioulas in Dialogue* (Edinburgh: T&T Clark, 1993), 368; Rudolf Voderholzer, *Meet Henri de Lubac: His Life and Work* (San Francisco: Ignatius Press), 54–55.

6 By "institution," I adapt Jonathan Turner's definition: "a complex of positions, roles, norms and values lodged in particular types of social structures and organizing relatively stable patterns of human activity with respect to fundamental problems in producing life-sustaining resources,

in reproducing individuals, and in sustaining viable societal structures within a given environment." In other words, institution can be multiple social forms that reproduce themselves, such as government, family, legal systems, human languages, universities, etc. Jonathan Turner, *The Institutional Order* (New York: Longman, 1997), 6. By the "institutional church," I mean "a visible and social structure of the Church." I adapt the definition of the church given in *Gaudium et Spes* (Pastoral Constitution on the Church in the Modern World): "But [the Church] is already present in this world, and is composed of men, that is, of members of the earthly city who have a call to form the family of God's children during the present history of the human race, and to keep increasing it until the Lord returns. United on behalf of heavenly values and enriched by them, this family has been 'constituted and structured as a society in this world' by Christ, and is equipped 'by appropriate means for visible and social union.' Thus the Church, at once 'a visible association and a spiritual community,' goes forward together with humanity and experiences the same earthly lot which the world does." http://www.vatican.va/archive/hist_councils/ii_vatican_council/documents/vat-ii_cons_19651207_gaudium-et-spes_en.html (accessed February 23, 2011).

7   I resonate with what Trin T. Minh Ha described about the diasporic identities of women in her book, *When the Moon Waxes Red: Representations, Gender and Cultural Politics* (New York: Routledge, 1991), 4.

8   Theresa Hak Kyung Cha, *Dictee* (Berkeley: University of California Press, 1982).

9   The Words of Institution spoken by Christ at the Last Supper: the three synoptic Gospels (Matt 26:27; Mark 14:23; Luke 22:19), as well as 1 Cor (11:24), contain versions of the words spoken by Jesus at the Last Supper. John 6 is also interpreted in connection with the Eucharist: "For my flesh is real food and my blood is real drink. Whoever eats my flesh and drinks my blood remains in me, and I in him" (John 6:55-56, NRSV).

10   This belief is more evident in Catholic tradition. As Jesuit theologian Hans Urs von Balthasar states, "there exist two means to effect incorporation [into Christ's body], two means which bring about the transition from the first to the second bodily form: the eucharist and scripture. They mediate the one, incarnate Logos to the faithful, and make him who of himself is both origin and end the way (*via*); the eucharist does so inasmuch as he is the divine life (*vita*), and scripture inasmuch as he is the divine Word and the divine truth (*veritas*)." Hans Urs von Balthasar, *Explorations in Theology IV: Spirit and Institution* (San Francisco: Ignatius Press, 1995), 16.

11   *Lumen Gentium* (The Dogmatic Constitution on the Church), n. 1.

12   Richard D. McCall, *Do This: Liturgy as Performance* (Notre Dame: University of Notre Dame Press, 2007), 136.

13   The Roman Catholic tradition adopts the Doctrine of Transubstantiation, which means that the change of the substance of bread and wine into the body and blood of Christ occurs in the Eucharist while the appearances and sense of the elements remain as they were before.

14   Thomas Aquinas, *Summa Theologiae* III.76.1.

15   See Caroline Walker Bynum, *Holy Feast and Holy Fast.*

16   Among many, see Susan Ross, *Extravagant Affections: A Feminist Sacramental Theology* (New York: Continuum, 2001); Nathan Mitchell, *Meeting Mystery: Liturgy, Worship, Sacrament* (New York: Orbis Books, 2007); Bernard Cooke, *Sacraments and Sacramentality* (New London, Conn.: Twenty-Third Publications, 1997); and Richard D. McCall, *Do This: Liturgy as Performance.*

17   Regina Schwartz' *Sacramental Poetics at the Dawn of Secularism: When God Left the World* demonstrates a similar perspective (San Francisco: Stanford University, 2008).

18   David N. Power, "The Language of Sacramental Memorial: Rupture, Excess, and Abundance," in *Sacramental Presence in a Postmodern Context*, ed. L. Boeve and L. Leijssen (Leuven, Belgium: Peeters Publishers), 149.

19   Power, "The Language of Sacramental Memorial," 150.

20   Werner G. Jeanrond responds to David N. Power's essay, stating, "Although any interpretation of sacramental action necessarily involves language and acts of signification, the sacraments' very potential of rupture owes itself to an activity deeper or, if one prefers, larger than language." In *Sacramental Presence in a Postmodern Context*, 164.

21   Rebecca S. Chopp, *The Power to Speak: Feminism, Language, God* (New York: Crossroad, 1991), 31.

22   "Pidgon" is intentionally misspelled by the author. Quote from Cha, *Dictee*, 161.

23   Heinz Insu Frenkl, "The Future of Korean American Literature" (presented at the 10th Annual Hahn Moo-Sook Colloquium in the Korean Humanities: One Hundred Years of Korean American Literature, George Washington University, Washington, D.C., October 25, 2003).

24   Cha's biographical information found in Constance Lewallen, Lawrence Rinder, and Trinh T. Minh-Ha, *The Dream of the Audience: Theresa Hak Kyung Cha (1951–1982)* (Berkeley: University of California Press, 2001).

25   It includes the stories of the Korean resistance fighter Yu Guan Soon, Joan of Arc, Cha's mother Hyung Soon Huo, Saint Thérèse of Lisieux, Demeter and Persephone, and Cha herself.

26   Gayatri Spivak, "Explanation and Culture: Marginalia," in *The Spivak Reader* (New York: Routledge, 1995), 33.

27   Cha, *Dictee*, 56.

28   Cha, *Dictee*, 1.

29   Cha, *Dictee*, 1.

30   Cha, *Dictee*, 1.

31   Cha, *Dictee*, 1.
32   Cha, *Dictee*, 3.
33   Cha, *Dictee*, 32.
34   Cha, *Dictee*, 46.
35   Cha, *Dictee*, 56–57.
36   Cha, *Dictee*, 57.
37   Cha, *Dictee*, 85.
38   Cha, *Dictee*, 56.
39   Cha, *Dictee*, 20.
40   For outstanding examples of feminists' contributions to our understanding of Cha's work, see Hyun Yi Kang, Norma Alarcóon, and Elaine H. Kim, eds., *Writing Self, Writing Nation: A Collection of Essays on Dictee by Theresa Hak Kyung Cha* (Berkeley: Third Woman Press, 1994); and Anne Anlin Cheng, *The Melancholy of Race: Psychoanalysis, Assimilation, and Hidden Grief* (New York: Oxford University Press, 2001), 150.
41   My presentation of *Dictee* as a "theological text" should not be understood as an attempt to portray it as a "Christian text" written with the intention of spreading Christian messages in the "public square." I agree with William Storrar's and Andries van Aarde's distinction between "voice" and "identity." Storrar and van Aarde argue that while "identity" is a terminology to categorize believers who constitute institutional Christianity, "voices" are fluid reflections on the divine in everyday life. While "identity" is set up by professional theologians and the ecclesial office, voices flow out of "neighborhood saints," "strangers," and "fellow citizens." The voices of individual Christians in public "does not necessarily imply the identification of the 'Christian's own identity'" defined by the ecclesia and academy. Voices can overlap with Christian messages, but they are not to proclaim particularly Christian messages. Voices, however, can lead Christians to meditate on theological matters and develop either institutional or secular forms of believing. See van Aarde's essay, "What is 'Theology' in 'Public Theology' and What is 'Public' about 'Public Theology'?," *Hervormde Teologiese Studies* 64, no. 3 (2008): 1213–1234, 1215.
42   Paul D. L. Avis, *A Church Drawing Near: Spirituality and Mission in a Post-Christian Culture* (London: T&T Clark, 2003), 108.
43   For insightful readings of Cha's use of the Catholic rites, see Lisa Lowe's "Unfaithful to the Original: The Subject of *Dictee*" in *Writing Self, Writing Nation*, 35–72, and Shelly Sunn Wong's essay, "Unnaming the Same: Theresa Hak Kyung Cha's *Dictee*" in *Writing Self, Writing Nation*, 103–40.
44   Cha, *Dictee*, 13.
45   Lowe, "Unfaithful to the Original: The Subject of *Dictee*," in *Writing Self, Writing Nation*, 59.

46   Wong, "Unnaming the Same: Theresa Hak Kyung Cha's *Dictee*," in *Writing Self, Writing Nation*, 122–23.

47   Cha, *Dictee*, 17–18.

48   Lowe, "Unfaithful to the Original: The Subject of *Dictee*," in *Writing Self, Writing Nation*, 58–61.

49   Lowe, "Unfaithful to the Original: The Subject of *Dictee*," in *Writing Self, Writing Nation*, 59.

50   L. Hyun Yi Kang also presents a similar perspective in her essay, "The 'Liberatory Voice' of Theresa Hak Kyung Cha's *Dictee*," in *Writing Self, Writing Nation*, 87.

51   Lowe, "Unfaithful to the Original: The Subject of *Dictee*," in *Writing Self, Writing Nation*, 59.

52   Bhabha, *The Location of Culture*, 122. Emphasis in original.

53   Bhabha, *The Location of Culture*, 126.

54   Bhabha, *The Location of Culture*, 126.

55   Homi Bhabha addresses the difficulty of defining postcolonial subjectivity in his essay "Unpacking my Library . . . Again," in *The Post-Colonial Question: Common Skies, Divided Horizons*, ed. Iain Chambers and Lidia Curtis (New York: Routledge, 1996), 210.

56   Bhabha, "Unpacking my Library," 130.

57   Bhabha, "Unpacking my Library," 128.

58   Michel de Certeau, *The Practice of Everyday Life* (Berkeley: University of California Press, 1988), 131–48.

59   Cha, *Dictee*, 87.

60   Walter Benjamin, *Illuminations* (New York: Schocken Books, 1969), 81.

61   I allude to Hélène Cixous' famous phrase, "woman must write herself," in her "The Laugh of the Medusa." Cixous writes, "Woman must write herself: must write about women and bring women to writing. . . ." See Hélène Cixous, "The Laugh of the Medusa," in *The Women and Language Debate: A Sourcebook*, ed. Camille Roman, Suzanne Juhasz, and Cristanne Miller (New Brunswick, N.J.: Rutgers University Press, 1994), 78.

62   Cha, *Dictee*, 140.

63   Cha, *Dictee*, 163.

Chapter 11

1   Edward W. Said, *Culture and Imperialism* (New York: Vintage Books, Random House, 1994), 336. Emphasis in original.

2   Stuart Hall, "When Was 'the Post-Colonial'? Thinking at the Limit," in *The Post-Colonial Question*, 252.

3   Hall, "When Was 'the Post-Colonial'? Thinking at the Limit," 252.

4   Nikos Papastergiadis, *The Turbulence of Migration: Globalization, Deterritorialization and Hybridity* (Cambridge: Polity Press, 2000), 1.

5   See, e.g., N. C. Aizenman's article "U.S. to Grow Grayer, More Diverse, Minorities Will Be Majority by 2042, Census Bureau Says," *Washington Post*, August 14, 2008, http://www.washingtonpost.com/wp-dyn/content/article/2008/08/13/AR2008081303524.html. The shift will be more noticeable among children. By 2023 more than half are expected to be representatives of a racial or ethnic minority.

6   Avtar Brah, *Cartographies of Diaspora: Contesting Identities* (London: Routledge, 1996), 180–81, 208–9.

7   Brah, *Cartographies of Diaspora*, 209.

8   I am using the idea put forth by Stephen Bouman and Ralston Deffenbaugh in their recent book *They Are Us: Lutherans and Immigration* (Minneapolis: Augsburg Fortress, 2009).

9   LELCA is the global umbrella organization of the Latvian Lutherans in diaspora. It was initially formed after World War II by the thousands of war refugees who became "displaced persons," or DPs, as they fled to the West from the second incoming Soviet occupation of the Baltic states and its totalitarian terror in 1944–1945.

10 Wonhee Anne Joh, *Heart of the Cross: A Postcolonial Christology* (Louisville, Ky.: Westminster John Knox, 2006), xviii–xix.

11 Peter C. Phan, "Betwixt and Between: Doing Theology with Memory and Imagination," in *Journeys at the Margin: Toward an Autobiographical Theology in American-Asian Perspective*, ed. Peter C. Phan and Jung Young Lee (Collegeville, Minn.: Liturgical Press, 1999), 113.

12 Rita Nakashima Brock, "Interstitial Integrity: Reflections toward an Asian American Woman's Theology," in *Introduction to Christian Theology: Contemporary North American Perspectives*, ed. Roger A. Badham (Louisville, Ky.: Westminster John Knox, 1998), 187.

13 Brock, "Interstitial Integrity," in *Introduction to Christian Theology*, 190.

14 Kwok Pui-lan, "A Theology of Border Passage," in *Border Crossings: Cross-Cultural Hermeneutics*, ed. D. N. Premnath (Maryknoll, N.Y.: Orbis, 2007), 113.

15 Avtar Brah makes an important point distinguishing the "homing desire" from a "desire for a 'homeland'" and an ideology of return which some diasporas and some diasporic subjects sustain, but some do not. There are situations when "home" is more a place of terror than an object of nostalgic longing. *Cartographies of Diaspora*, 16, 192–93.

16 See Marcia Mount Shoop's essay "Embodying Theology: Motherhood as Metaphor/Method" in the present book.

17 Kwok Pui-lan, *Postcolonial Imagination and Feminist Theology* (Louisville, Ky.: Westminster John Knox, 2005), 46. Emphasis added.

18 Ludwig Wittgenstein, *Tractatus Logico-Philosophicus*, trans. C. K. Ogden (London: Routledge, 1981), section 5.6, 148–49.

19   To my knowledge the only published collection of Latvian women's theological output consisting of sermons, reflections, interviews, and poetry, alongside informative historical overviews about Latvian women in theology in a "nonboutique" language, is the recent *Marijas—Lettische Theologinnen melden sich zu Wort* (Uebersetzung von Vija Funknere und Inta Funknere; Leipzig: Gustav-Adolf-Werk, 2008). The volume is an enlarged edition and translation of the earlier collection published in Latvian as *Marijas dziesmas un stāsti*: Latviešu garīdznieču raksti (redaktores: Zilgme Eglīte, Ieva Graufelde, Inese Radziņa, Indra Skuja-Grīslis, Maruta Strautmale; Rīga: Klints, 2005).

20   Edouard Glissant, *Caribbean Discourse: Selected Essays*, trans. J. Michael Dash (Charlottesville: University of Virginia Press, 1999), 64–65. Glissant remarks that "History is a highly functional fantasy of the West, originating at precisely the time when it alone 'made' the history of the World" (64).

21   On Baltic crusades, see William L. Urban, *The Baltic Crusade*, 2nd ed. (Chicago: Lithuanian Research and Studies Center, 1994). In 1202 Livonia was named Terra Mariana and declared a property of the papal curia, even though the status of this formation changed numerous times before various segments were conquered or acquired by later modern Western European empires.

22   Introduction to *Postcolonial Theologies: Divinity and Empire*, ed. Catherine Keller, Michael Nausner, and Mayra Rivera (Saint Louis: Chalice Press, 2004), 14.

23   Nils Blomkvist, *The Discovery of the Baltic: The Reception of a Catholic World-System in the European North (AD 1075–1225)* (Leiden: Brill, 2005), 9.

24   Blomkvist, *The Discovery of the Baltic*, 704.

25   Blomkvist, *The Discovery of the Baltic*, 668. Blomkvist argues that "the invention of apartheid is perhaps thought to be one of the many cruelties of the 20th century. It is not. The South African contribution was to formulate a robust term for a long-standing Christian practice . . . —to keep various ethnic categories apart" (671). "Apartheid is of course normality in all forms of colonial rule. One of the earliest clear cases is Livonia . . ." (671).

26   Among the otherwise rather conspicuous indifference of postcolonial studies toward the colonial histories of Eastern and Central Europe, see the collection of essays on the implications of colonial legacies in the region, *Baltic Postcolonialism*, ed. Violeta Kelertas (Amsterdam: Rodopi, 2006).

27   Maruta Lietiņa Ray, "Recovering the Voice of the Oppressed: Master, Slave, and Serf in the Baltic Provinces," *Journal of Baltic Studies* 34, no. 1 (2003): 3. Lietiņa Ray argues that "in the interests of democratizing history, validating the enserfed and enslaved experience of the Baltic

peoples, and ending the hegemony of history written by the colonizers, this voice should be added to the historical record of the Baltics" (19).

28   Karlis Racevskis in *Modernity's Pretenses: Making Reality Fit Reason from Candide to the Gulag* (Albany: State University of New York Press, 1998) has described the *dainas* as the "value system of the ancient Latvians" which "stands in complete contrast with the obsession to dominate nature and others, to dominate the Other—that could be considered a central tenet of the modern Western ethos since the time of Bacon and Descartes," 120–21.

29   Racevskis, *Modernity's Pretenses*, 121.

30   I do not intend to say that margins and other ostracized spaces in the Christian lifeworld would be triumphantly emptied of women's presence there—alas, far from it, despite the exponentially growing representation of women in congregational leadership, clergy, and theological scholarship in the Latvian diaspora.

31   Women have been prominent in the Latvian poetical scene from the genius of Aspazija (1865–1943) during the emergence of the professional Latvian literary milieu in the late nineteenth century until World War II, to name just the most accomplished poets such as Elza Stērste, Anna Brigadere, Paulīna Bārda, Austra Skujiņa, and Biruta Skujeniece, among others. In the tragic postwar decades in Latvian history, no history of Latvian literature can be written without the magisterial figures of Mirdza Ķempe, Ārija Elksne, Veronika Strēlerte, Vizma Belševica, Velta Toma, Elza Ķezbere, and, arguably the most distinguished living Latvian woman poet, Māra Zālīte (b. 1952). Among the women poets who write with an explicitly theological orientation today are Anda Līce, Broņislava Martuževa, Anna Rancāne, Milda Klampe, and Māra Zviedre.

32   *The Hymnal of the Evangelical Lutheran Church of Latvia and Exile* (Raamattutalo Pieksämäki, Finland: The Lutheran Church of Latvia, The Evangelical Lutheran Church of Latvia in Exile, Latvian Evangelical Lutheran Church in America, 1992).

33   Jānis Vanags, "Arhibīskaps: Par baznīcu, Jāņiem un grāmatām" [Archbishop: On Church, the Midsummer and Books], Latvijas Evaņģēliski Luteriskā Baznīca, accessed June 21, 2010, http://www.lelb .lv/lv/?p=news2arch&fu=sh&id=776&month=7&year=2009.

34   Geoffrey Wainwright, *Doxology: The Praise of God in Worship, Doctrine, and Life: A Systematic Theology* (New York: Oxford University Press, 1984), 7.

35   Wainwright, *Doxology*, 183.

36   Wainwright, *Doxology*, 200.

37   Zygmunt Bauman, *Does Ethics Have a Chance In a World of Consumers?* (Cambridge, Mass.: Harvard University Press, 2008), 11.

38   I am grateful to Wendy Farley for invoking this term.

39   Teresa Berger, *Women's Ways of Worship: Gender Analysis and Liturgical History* (Collegeville, Minn.: Liturgical Press, 2000), 151.

40   Marcella Maria Althaus-Reid, "Gustavo Gutierrez Goes to Disneyland: Theme Park Theologies and the Diaspora of the Discourse of the Popular Theologian in Liberation Theology," in *The Bible and Postcolonialism 3*, ed. Fernando F. Segovia (Sheffield: Sheffield Academic Press, 2000), 36–58.

41   Mark Jordan, *Telling Truths in Church: Scandal, Flesh, and Christian Speech* (Boston: Beacon Press, 2003), 27.

42   Derek Walcott, "The Caribbean: Culture or Mimicry?" in *Postcolonialisms: An Anthology of Cultural Theory and Criticism*, ed. Gaurav Desai and Supriya Nair (New Brunswick, N.J.: Rutgers University Press, 2005), 261.

43   For a particularly insightful explication of the predicament of creativity in the colonial shadows of the modern Western superpowers, see R. Radhakrishnan, "Derivative Discourses and the Problem of Signification," *The European Legacy 7*, no. 6 (2002): 783–95.

44   Stephanie Newell, "Redefining Mimicry: Quoting Techniques and Role of Readers in Locally Published Ghanaian Fiction," *Research in African Literatures 31*, no. 1 (2000): 35–36. Emphasis in original.

45   Even though there is no univocal definition of code-switching among various scholarly fields that widely employ this term, linguistic code-switching generally describes a process of alternation between languages and dialects that happens in the thought process and increments of speech as short as a single sentence or phrase by persons who have grown up using more than one language or have acquired proficiency in several languages. When code-switching, a bilingual or multilingual person can shift back and forth among languages during a conversation thus and develop particular cognitive linguistic abilities. The use of various codes—or languages—usually depends on who the conversation partners are, what the social setting of a conversation is, and what the goals of a particular communication are.

46   Kwok, *Postcolonial Imagination and Feminist Theology*, 50.

47   Margaret R. Miles, *Reading for Life: Beauty, Pluralism, and Responsibility* (New York: Continuum, 1999).

48   Miles, *Reading for Life*, 201. Emphasis in original.

49   R. S. Sugirtharajah, *Postcolonial Reconfigurations: An Alternative Way of Reading the Bible and Doing Theology* (London: SCM Press, 2003), 84.

50   Sugirtharajah, *Postcolonial Reconfigurations*, 84.

51   Sugirtharajah, *Postcolonial Reconfigurations*, 22.

52   Wainwright, *Doxology*, 215.

53   *Grove Dictionary of Music, Oxford Music Online, The Oxford Companion of Music*, accessed November 19, 2008, http://www.oxfordmusiconline.com:80/subscriber/article/oprt114/e1670.

54 Edward W. Said, *Reflections on Exile and Other Essays* (Cambridge, Mass.: Harvard University Press, 2000), 172.

55 Said, *Culture and Imperialism*, 32.

Chapter 12

1 This shift toward intuitive intention invites a different way of being at home in our bodies that brings with it multiple questions and challenges. For a full explication of this invitation, see my book *Let the Bones Dance: Embodiment and the Body of Christ* (Louisville, Ky.: Westminster John Knox, 2010).

2 This intuition should not be equated with some internal/personal phenomenon. I am suggesting a particular mode of awareness that has collective capacity. I use intuition to invite (as indicated in the previous note) us to embrace a theological awareness that is a multilayered embodied mode, not simply cerebral.

3 This essay is closely related to my chapter on motherhood in *Let the Bones Dance* (chap. 3).

4 A quote from a sermon on Mother's Day preached at a Presbyterian church.

5 Carol Gilligan's ethic of care provides important insights. Her work has been expanded on in many helpful ways by Nel Noddings, Alison Jagger, and other feminist social theorists. I am suggesting that we expand our exploration beyond these suggested characteristics of femininity, which have tended to be an accepted part of the theological conversation.

6 In Patrice DiQuinzio's helpful book, *The Impossibility of Motherhood: Feminism, Individualism, and the Problem of Mothering* (New York: Routledge, 1999), she chooses to use "mothering" rather than "motherhood" because she sees "mothering" as a reference to the actual "birthing and rearing of children" and "motherhood" as an "ideological construct of essential motherhood" which she determines is an impossibility for real women (xv). I agree that mothering may point more directly to the activity of being a mother than does motherhood, and I agree with her critique of "essential motherhood" as a problematic construction of being a mother. But while DiQuinzio's critique of essential motherhood is important, I do not wish to abandon "motherhood" as a concept with which we should be concerned. The importance of "motherhood" rests precisely in the fact that it includes ideological construction but is not limited to or apart from the work of mothering itself. I cannot somehow strictly separate the ideological aspects of being a mother and the actual activity of being a mother. My use of the term "motherhood" is not to suggest that these experiences, institutions, and practices cannot be analyzed with some precision as to how and why they develop and function as they do. The use of the term

"motherhood" suggests that there is no way to point to activities of mothering that stand apart from the multilayered nature of motherhood (I do not believe, incidentally, that DiQuinzio assumes the possibility of this strict kind of separation either).

7   Bonnie Miller-McLemore argues for a closer look at "generativity" as a way to address theologically the imbalance created by a strong cultural focus on productivity. Bonnie Miller-McLemore, *Also a Mother: Work and Family as Theological Dilemma* (Nashville, Tenn.: Abingdon, 1994).

8   Chris Weedon uses the language of "conflicting discourses" to describe how subjectivity is formed. The subject is nothing but that particular location of the conflicting discourses themselves. Seyla Benhabib fills out Weedon's poststructuralism with an "interactive universalism"— Benhabib does not reduce the self only to conflicting discourses, but leaves more space for some perspectival coherence. Ideally this perspective is malleable enough to exercise the "reversability" of perspectives that she holds necessary for a sound moral life. Judith Butler also describes the subject as the location of shifting discourses. Benhabib holds on, albeit critically, to a stronger concept of agency than Butler does. Weedon is between them although closer to Butler in her understanding of the thoroughgoing nature of social construction. My use of this idea of "conflicting discourses" here is somewhere between Weedon's and Benhabib's. See Chris Weedon, *Feminist Practice and Poststructuralist Theory* (Oxford: Blackwell Press, 1987); Seyla Benhabib, *Situating the Self: Gender, Community, and Postmodernism in Contemporary Ethics* (New York: Routledge, 1992); and Judith Butler, *The Psychic Life of Power* (Stanford: Stanford University Press, 1997).

9   Shulamith Firestone, *The Dialectic of Sex* (New York: Bantam, 1972). Some examples of texts in which these ideas are explored are Sara Ruddick, "Maternal Thinking," in *Feminist Social Thought: A Reader*, ed. Diana Tietjans Meyers (New York: Routledge, 1997), 588; Luce Irigaray, *This Sex Which is Not One*, trans. Catherine Porter (Ithaca, N.Y.: Cornell University Press, 1985); and Julia Kristeva, "Stabat Mater," in *Feminist Social Thought*, 303–4 (Kristeva's words here were originally published in 1986).

10   See Marilou Awiatka, *Selu: Seeking the Corn-Mother's Wisdom* (Golden, Colo.: Fulcrum Publishing, 1993); Patricia Hill Collins, *Black Feminist Thought: Knowledge, Consciousness, and the Politics of Empowerment* (New York: Routledge, 1990); and Williams, *Sisters in the Wilderness*. These women (and others) have challenged the presiding assumptions and deconstruction of motherhood as stemming largely from the white, middle-class, heterosexual context.

11   For an explanation on how theology might be "in-formed," see *Let the Bones Dance*, 143.

12   One of my favorite children's books growing up was *The Way Mothers Are*, by Miriam Schlein. The story is about a little cat who keeps asking his mother why she loves him. Finally, it is not because of what he does (good and bad) or how he does things, but because he simply is her little boy. Miriam Schlein, *The Way Mothers Are*, ill. Joe Lasker (Morton Grove, Ill.: Albert Whitman, 1963).

13   This invitation for theology from motherhood points toward a generalized experience of humanity that is perhaps further obscured when motherhood is not the "work" one does. Motherhood does not have a corner on the market for idiosyncrasy, ambiguity, and interdependence. It simply embodies these things with an intensity that makes them especially recognizable.

14   Cited in bell hooks, *Yearning: Race, Gender, and Cultural Politics* (Boston: South End Press, 1990), 44.

15   Edward Casey works in the trajectory of Maurice Merleau-Ponty, who has been deliberate about his consideration of the body and ambiguity. Edward Casey, "The Ghost of Embodiment: On Bodily Habitudes and Schemata," in *Body and Flesh: A Philosophical Reader*, ed. Donn Welton (Oxford: Blackwell, 1998).

16   Casey coaxes the body back from the exile of Cartesian dualism, not as a transparent, static object of examination, but as a "lived body." Casey uses schema and habitudes to trace the body as it operates as the "matrix of nature and culture." Casey, "The Ghost of Embodiment," in *Body and Flesh*, 214.

17   Casey, "The Ghost of Embodiment," 217.

18   Casey, "The Ghost of Embodiment," 217. Emphasis in original.

19   Casey, "The Ghost of Embodiment," 217.

20   Casey, "The Ghost of Embodiment," 218.

21   Casey, "The Ghost of Embodiment," 218.

22   Ann Crittenden offers a clearly argued case for how the economic system operative in the United States devalues mothers. Sharon Hays, a sociologist, tracks how the ideals of "intensive mothering" are in direct contradiction to the rewarded behaviors of Western individualism. See Ann Crittenden, *The Price of Motherhood: Why the Most Important Job in the World is Still the Least Valued* (New York: Metropolitan Books, 2001); and Sharon Hays, *The Cultural Contradictions of Motherhood* (New Haven: Yale University Press, 1996).

23   The hysteric's body takes an idea or social standard which is "incompatible" (Freud's language) and "converts" it into something "somatic." Casey describes how some trauma, in order to be survived, takes up residence (what Casey calls a "home-place") in some body part rather than in dreams or conscious memory. Hysteria is a form of bodily memory.

Freud referred to this kind of embodied expression of trauma as "somatic compliance." Casey, "The Ghost of Embodiment," 218.

24   I am suggesting something here that is a shade different from my understanding of how the symbolic power of the unconscious is described in the traditional pyschoanalytical tradition (most notably in the work of Freud and Jung). I am suggesting that the body is not simply creating a symbolic where the consciousness is unable to express feelings or emotion. The body is immediate to the experience on a cellular level—"beneath" or prior to some modification of the unconscious or subconscious. See my chapter on feeling in *Let the Bones Dance*.

25   Freud used the language of "conversation" in reference to how hysterical symptoms seek an audience in the society which helped give birth to them and which was the cause of the body's own estrangement from social parlance. Casey, "The Ghost of Embodiment," 218.

26   Freud's classic case of hysteria was a young woman, called Dora in his writings, whom Freud believed inhabited her sexual confusion through somatic "conversions" like chronic coughing and fatigue.

27   Adrienne Rich, *Of Woman Born: Motherhood as Experience and Institution* (New York: W. W. Norton, 1976), 21. Emphasis in original.

28   See Miller-McLemore, *Also a Mother*; and Cynthia Rigby, "Exploring Our Hesitation: Feminist Theologies and Nurture of Children," *Theology Today* 56, no. 4 (2000): 540–54.

29   For example, a "mother's intuition" functions strongly in some women, with results like "knowing" a child is in distress or sick, being able to do the work of mothering with no prior experience, negotiating how to breastfeed, etc.

30   I use the word "feeling" here not as emotion or intuition, but as a primal mode of existence that is not limited to consciousness. Feeling in a Whiteheadian and/or Schleiermacherian sense suggests such a primal mode of operation. See Alfred North Whitehead's *Process and Reality (Corrected Edition)*, ed. David Ray Griffin and Donald W. Sherburne (New York: Free Press, 1978); Friedrich Schleiermacher's *The Christian Faith*, 2 vols. (New York: Harper & Row, 1963), first published in 1821, whose English translation is based on the updated version published in 1830; and my chapter on feeling in *Let the Bones Dance*.

31   Michelle Boulous Walker, in her *Philosophy and the Maternal Body: Reading Silence* (London: Routledge, 1998), discusses the ambiguity symbolized in writing between mother and daughter as that which "mirrors the disruption of our sense of space in such a way as to re-figure relations between inside and out" (176). She describes such writing as "elastic" and as resistant to spatial organization. In Walker's work the ambiguity of maternal bodies is translated into the context of philosophical writing. She plays

with ambiguity and the disruption of oppositions and the falsity of the perceived inside/outside dichotomy that composes the self in Western philosophical individualism.

32   bell hooks, *Yearning*, 41–42.

33   La Leche League International, *The Womanly Art of Breastfeeding*, 6th ed. (New York: Plume Books, 1997), 363.

34   La Leche League International, *The Womanly Art of Breastfeeding*, 364.

35   Many of these kinds of occurrences are documented in literature about breastfeeding; some are anecdotal from La Leche League meetings and/ or from conversations with others who have and have not breastfed.

36   Marvin S. Eiger, M.D., and Sally Wendkos Olds, *The Complete Book of Breastfeeding*, 3rd ed. (New York: Workman Publishing, 1999), 27.

37   Patricia Hill Collins describes "othermothers" in *Black Feminist Thought*.

38   Ann Belford Ulanov describes this dynamic psychoanalytically with the help of Christopher Bollas when she describes how the ego models the self most closely in line with the parent who was most active in "transform[ing] our environment to adapt to us when we were infants." Ann Belford Ulanov, *Attacked by Poison Ivy: A Psychological Understanding* (York Beach, Maine: Nicolas-Hays, 2001), 11.

39   Collins explains that much of the work of womanists and black feminists on motherhood reflects less on motherhood as symbolic and more on the "historical experience of nurturing." See Collins, *Black Feminist Thought*.

40   Collins describes mothers (in the context of black mothers) as those who can mediate the identities of children who are oppressed over and against mainstream cultural norms. Collins, *Black Feminist Thought*, 57. Also, Williams describes black mothers as those who resist and defy, those who give their children "survival and quality of life skills." Williams, *Sisters in the Wilderness*, 16–22, 57.

41   Collins quotes Darlene Clark Hine's apt description of this illustration of complex subjectivity: "Because of the interplay of racial animosity, class tensions, gender role differentiation, and regional economic variation, Black women, as a rule, developed and adhered to a cult of secrecy, a culture of dissemblance, to protect the sanctity of inner aspects of their lives. The dynamics of dissemblance involved creating the appearance of disclosure, an openness about themselves and their feelings, while actually remaining an enigma. Only with secrecy, thus achieving a self-imposed invisibility, could ordinary Black women accrue the psychic space and harness the resources needed to hold their own." Collins, *Black Feminist Thought*, 96.

42   Collins, *Black Feminist Thought*, 118.

Chapter 13: Postscript

1   See Mari Kim, "Eros in Eden: a Praxis of Beauty in Genesis 3" (Ph.D. diss., Emory University, 2010).

2   Melissa Johnston is developing a criticism of the myth of punishment at the heart of mainstream theology by exploring narratives of bipolar disorder.

3   Wesley Barker is working on a dissertation describing the difficulties of women's writing as well as the importance of community to open a path for writing women.

4   Marguerite Porete, *The Mirror of Simple Souls*, trans. and intro. Ellen L. Babinksy (New York: Paulist Press, 1993), 79.

INDEX

311